Governing the Present

Governing the Present

Administering Economic, Social and Personal Life

Peter Miller

and

Nikolas Rose

polity

First published in 2008 by Polity Press
Reprinted 2008 (twice), 2009 (six times), 2010, 2011, 2012 (twice), 2014

Polity Press
65 Bridge Street
Cambridge CB2 1UR, UK.

Polity Press
350 Main Street
Malden, MA 02148, USA

ISBN-13: 978-07456-4100-3
ISBN-13: 978-07456-4101-0 (pb)

A catalogue record for this book is available from the British Library.

Typeset in 10.5 on 12 pt Times
by SNP Best-set Typesetter Ltd., Hong Kong
Printed and bound in Great Britain by Clays Ltd, St Ives plc

The publisher has used its best endeavours to ensure that the URLs for external websites referred to in this book are correct and active at the time of going to press. However, the publisher has no responsibility for the websites and can make no guarantee that a site will remain live or that the content is or will remain appropriate.

Every effort has been made to trace all copyright holders, but if any have been inadvertently overlooked the publishers will be pleased to include any necessary credits in any subsequent reprint or edition.

For further information on Polity, visit our website: www.polity.co.uk

Contents

Acknowledgements

This volume brings together arguments that we have been making, individually and jointly, over the last fifteen years, and which have been published in a number of specialist journals. In bringing them together in this way, editing and updating them, and introducing them with a specially written essay, our aim is to demonstrate the empirical basis, scope and enduring contribution of this approach to the analysis of the present.

The chapters in this volume are based on papers originally published in the following sources:

Chapter 2: P. Miller and N. Rose, 'Governing economic life', *Economy and Society* 19 (1) (February 1990): 1–31.

Chapter 3: N. Rose and P. Miller, 'Political power beyond the state: problematics of government', *British Journal of Sociology* 43 (2) (June 1992): 173–205.

Chapter 4: N. Rose, 'The death of the social? Refiguring the territory of government', *Economy and Society* 25 (3) (August 1996): 327–56.

Chapter 5: P. Miller and N. Rose, 'Mobilizing the consumer: assembling the subject of consumption', *Theory, Culture and Society* 14 (February 1997): 1–36.

Chapter 6: P. Miller and N. Rose, 'On therapeutic authority', *History of the Human Sciences* 7 (3) (August 1994): 29–64.

Chapter 7: P. Miller and N. Rose, 'Production, identity and democracy', *Theory and Society* (USA) 24 (3) (June 1995): 427–67.

Chapter 8: N. Rose, 'Governing "advanced" liberal democracies', in A. Barry, T. Osborne and N. Rose, eds, *Foucault and Political Reason: Liberalism, Neo-Liberalism and Rationalities of Government* (London: UCL Press, 1996).

1

Introduction
Governing Economic and Social Life

Why study 'governmentality'? Our own path to governmentality began with a series of diverse, but loosely connected questions. How, and to what ends, did so many socially legitimated authorities seek to interfere in the lives of individuals in sites as diverse as the school, the home, the workplace, the courtroom and the dole queue? How were such wishes articulated, whether in relatively local settings such as individual organizations and firms, in the form of more systematized and articulated policy proposals or political programmes, or in the more abstract realms of political theory? What sort of knowledge base and knowledge claims underpinned such schemes for intervention, and were they drawn from the realms of psychological, sociological or economic theory, from other knowledge claims, or from 'common sense'? What sorts of devices made such interventions possible, to what extent did they deploy existing instruments, and to what extent were they invented? What understandings of the people to be acted upon – whether explicit or implicit – underpinned these endeavours, and how did they shape or reshape the ways in which these individuals understood and acted on themselves? What has it meant to intervene in the lives of individuals in 'liberal' societies, that is to say, societies that proclaimed the limits of the state and respect for the privacy of the individual? And how, in particular, could one analyse the programmes, strategies and techniques emerging in the context in which we were writing – Northern Europe and the United States in the last decades of the twentieth century? This was a time when the state was seeking to withdraw from so many spheres, and when notions of choice, the customer and the ideal of the entrepreneurial self were gaining such ascendancy. Finally, what kinds of empirical inquiries, and what kinds of conceptual tools, would enable us to understand these issues in a way that enhanced our capacity to evaluate their consequences, and perhaps even to intervene into them? We did not start from governmentality, but this was the term under which our own attempts to address these questions, empirically and conceptually, came to be grouped. In this Introduction to some of our key papers, and at the risk of over-emphasizing our own work to the exclusion of others, we try to trace this path, and to cast some light from our own perspective on the field of research that has now, for good or ill, come to be termed 'governmentality'.

From Ideology and Consciousness to Government and Ethics

A politics and a political conjuncture had contributed to the way in which we framed these questions. The politics was formulated initially in terms of ideology. Radical thought at that time – we are talking about the 1970s – was in the grip of Marxism, but it was a Marxism trying to free itself from economic determinism. Along with others, we felt that the organization of economic life was important, perhaps crucial, in the forms of social power that had taken shape in capitalist societies over the last 150 years. But, again with others, we felt that contemporary forms of financial, multinational shareholder capitalism could hardly be understood through the formulae of Marx's *Capital* (Cutler et al. 1977, 1978). In any event, economic power could only maintain itself, could only reproduce itself, on the basis of a particular legal system, a set of ideas about the organization of work and the definition of profit, a set of institutional arrangements for shaping and moulding the hopes, aspirations and capacities of individuals and collectivities, and much more. At the very least, the accumulation and distribution of capital was intrinsically linked to the accumulation and distribution of persons and their capacities. We needed to find some more sophisticated ways to understand the operation of these complicated apparatuses – of law and the criminal justice system, of social security, of social work, of education, of medicine, of the family, of economic life itself. They could not, we felt, be seen as simple – or even complex – effects of economic relations of ownership or the form of the commodity, and hence bound to them, and bound to change with them. If these apparatuses and practices were to be the site of political intervention and transformation, we needed to understand what made them tick.

Marxism here had taken a particular form under the influence of a variety of structuralisms – the structural Marxism of Louis Althusser, Étienne Balibar and Nicos Poulantzas, the structuralist semiotics of

Ferdinand de Saussure and all those who followed him from Bakhtin to Barthes, and even to some extent the structuralist psychoanalysis of Jacques Lacan. Structuralism was significant, as a style of thought, because it redirected our attention towards the sets of relations, not available to common sense and direct observation, which underpinned and made possible what one could see, think, understand and even feel. This reshaped the field of ideology – which for so long, in Marxism, had been the way to approach the questions that concerned us. Despite its many and varied forms, and whatever its level of sophistication, Marxist notions of ideology designated a domain of false ideas that served the social function of masking and legitimating the dominance of a ruling class. But, from the perspective of these structuralisms, ideology could no longer be regarded as a matter of ideas, no longer critiqued as a field of falsity or disguise, and no longer explained in terms of its social function. It consisted of apparatuses that were complex assemblages with their own conditions of possibility and their own regularities. Their operation was inextricably bound up with a particular vocabulary or language that circumscribed what could be said and what could be done in ways that were meaningful. And the apparatuses were populated with human beings whose individuality or subjectivity was itself shaped to fit the expectations and demands of others. In that setting, the new task of critical analysis became to understand the formation and functioning of ideological apparatuses, and those who were constituted in and through them.[1]

Some elements from this configuration remained relatively constant in the detours that led to the analytics of governmentality. Notably the recognition that to understand what was thought, said and done meant trying to identify the tacit premises and assumptions that made these things thinkable, sayable and doable. Some elements were transformed. For example, the idea of structures as closed systems of difference gave way to a looser conception of open regimes of regularities not organized in binary oppositions of presence and absence, nature and culture, and the like. Some elements did not stand the test of analysis. Althusser's conception of ideological state apparatuses was found wanting in many respects. For it assumed in advance that the role of these apparatuses, from religion to schooling, was ultimately – and possibly indirectly – to satisfy economic functions, to reproduce the relations of production. It tied these apparatuses rhetorically to an idea of the state, without adequately specifying what that enigmatic term signified. It failed to unpack in any usable manner the relations between the different 'orders' into which it divided reality – 'the economic', 'the political', 'the ideological' – while the notion of 'relative autonomy' proved to be no more than gestural. Its deployment of the notion of ideology already assumed that the objects of study were falsehoods that had a function, whereas we rapidly become more interested in the question of truth, along with the means of production of truth, and the consequences of the production of truth effects in specific domains. And its gesture towards subjectivity, framed in terms of Lacanian metaphysics, was far too general, despite its initial appeal as a way of countering the *a priori* humanisms of those such as George Lukács and the Frankfurt School, which could only view power as falsifying and suppressing the essence of human subjects (Miller 1987). The notion of the subject as the bearer or support of relations of production, and reducible to the places and functions created by them, did not enable one to analyse the multiplicity and variability of modes of subject formation, and the relations to the self engendered and enjoined in specific practices.

It was in this conjuncture, in the 1970s, that Michel Foucault's work entered British debates. Of course, his book on madness had been translated into English in an abridged form in the mid-1960s (Foucault 1967), and we had each worked with ideas from that and other similar analyses in our different engagement with the radical politics of psychiatry (Adlam and Rose 1981; Miller 1981; Miller and Rose 1986; Rose 1986). But the impact of that book was, at least initially, largely confined to those working in and around the psychiatric and medical fields. The same also held for Foucault's analysis of the birth of clinical medicine, even though both books made clear the interrelations between a knowledge and expertise of the individual and the administration of populations. *The Birth of the Clinic* (Foucault 1973) showed – in a precise and direct manner – how novel ways of thinking, doing and relating to oneself emerged at a particular historical moment, linked up in all sorts of constitutive ways with the emergence of a new politics and valorization of health, which was in turn linked with new forms of production in factories, new ways of life in towns and new ways of managing populations and epidemics. It showed how a way of seeing disease and of practising medicine – the kind of clinical medicine that was beginning to mutate at the very moment he wrote – was assembled at the intersection of heterogeneous developments. These ranged from changes in the laws of assistance to a new philosophy of disease, and brought into existence new forms of subjectivity both for those who suffered and for those who treated, embodied in a set of practices from which they were inseparable. The cherished distinction between ideas and practices was not so much 'deconstructed' as by-passed in the form taken by these historical and empirical analyses. There were no gestures here to relative autonomy, the materiality of ideology or dialectics, but rather there was a precise, meticulous and scholarly tracing of the small and dispersed events that brought something new into existence, and in doing so, irreversibly reshaped human ontology and ethics.

The more or less immediate translation into English of *Discipline and Punish* (1977) – no doubt helped by its explicit concern with issues of discipline and surveillance – helped bring about a more widespread shift in ways of thinking about power. The analysis of the birth of the prison extended Foucault's prior analyses of the administration of the self, and showed vividly how individualization was a way of exercising power. Despite its focus on the prison, discipline was no longer to be viewed as only carceral. Or, to put it differently, the engineering of conduct and the normalizing of behaviour that emerged within a carceral institution such as the prison provided a more generalized technology of social power. Such a perspective demonstrated the important normalizing role played by a vast array of petty managers of social and subjective existence, whether this occurred in the factory or the schoolroom. The concepts that Foucault used for his analysis were important, of course, but more important was the mode of analytics, the ethos of investigation that was opened up, and the focus – the who and what one should study in the critical investigation of the relations of knowledge, authority and subjectivity in our present (Miller 1987).

Our own analyses over the course of the 1980s were of this form, if more modest in scope. We followed the birth and the activities of many of these little engineers of the human soul, and their mundane knowledges, techniques and procedures – psychologists, psychiatrists, medics, accountants, social workers, factory managers, town planners and others (Miller 1980, 1981, 1986a; Miller and O'Leary 1987; Rose 1985, 1986, 1989a, 1989b). As we did so, it became clear to us that these were more than regional histories, of importance only to those interested in these specific local domains. There seemed no obvious discipline, theory or approach that addressed the range of linked questions and sites that seemed important to us. Political scientists seemed to know at the outset what was of importance – the State or the political apparatus. Political historians focused on the great figures and affairs of state. And historians of philosophy focused on the great names of the philosophical canon, even when their ideas were placed 'in context'. But, for us at least, it became clear that the political history of our present needed to be written in terms of the activities of the minor figures that we studied, yet who were largely below the threshold of visibility for these other approaches. For it was only through their activities that states, as they were termed by those who seemed untroubled by the meaning of this term, could govern at all.

Our own work, individually and jointly, had focused on the histories of these varied and often lowly forms of expertise: the history of accounting, of management, of psychology and psychiatry, and of social work and education. And yet it seemed that these apparently diverse areas had something in common. It seemed unlikely that techniques as apparently diverse as standard costing and mental measurement shared much, but they did. They had in common a concern with the norm and deviations from it, a concern with ways in which the norm might be made operable, and a concern with all those devices that made it possible to act on the actions of individuals so as to generalize the norm yet without telling people daily how to live their lives and what decisions to take. We were working at the margins of our disciplines, apparently concerned with small, mundane problems, with the grey literature, with minor figures in history a long way away from the grand theories of world systems, modernization, globalization, and so forth. And yet, we believed increasingly, it was only because of the work of our small figures, with their own aspirations as well as those foisted on them, together with their little instruments, that rule could actually occur. It was only through these means that the 'cold monster' of the state could actually seek to shape the ways in which people conducted their daily lives, their interactions with themselves and others, and their relations with the various manifestations of social authority. It was these authorities, whether questioned, contested, admired or aspired to, that made it possible for states to govern. In trying to anatomize this activity of governing, we came to focus increasingly on the three axes that had interested us from the outset – systems for the production of truth, regimes of authority and practices of subjectification.

Perhaps the first key move was 'from why to how'. Theorists of the state addressed 'why'-type questions. Why did something appear a problem to certain people at a particular time – a question often answered by appeal to pre-given notions of class or professional 'interests'. Why did a new institution appear, or why did an existing one change – a question often answered by gesturing to global processes such as modernization or individualization. We asked a different question, not 'why' but 'how', thereby lightening the weight of causality, or at least multiplying it, and enabling us to abstain from the problems of 'explaining' such indigestible phenomena as state, class, and so on – indeed we argued that these typically went unexplained despite the claims of those theorists who wrote in these terms. Instead, why not be content to trace small histories and their intersecting trajectories? Why not study events and practices in terms of their singularity, the interrelations that define them and the conditions that make them possible (Veyne 1997)? Why not focus on the encounters, the plays of force, the obstructions, the ambitions and strategies, the devices, and the multiple surfaces on which they emerge? Why not, as Foucault put it, focus on events, on the conditions that constitute an event – 'eventalization': 'making visible a *singularity* at places where there is a temptation to invoke a historical constant, an immediate anthropological trait or an obviousness that imposes itself uniformly on all. To show that things weren't as "necessary as all that" . . . uncovering the procedure of causal multiplication: analysing an event according to the multiple processes that constitute it' (Foucault 1996: 277)?[2] For, in this way, one can begin to discern the web of relations and practices that result in particular ways of governing, particular ways of seeking to shape the conduct of individuals and groups.

A further shift was required. We were interested in subjectivity. But while others tried to write the history of subjectivity, to identify the effects of certain practices on the subjectivity of mothers, workers, children, and so forth, we found this unhelpful. For unless one posited a universal form to the human subject, unless one privileged subjectivity as moral autonomy, unless one adopted some position, psychoanalysis for example, within the contested field of the psy disciplines, that question – of the effects of certain types of experience on the mental life of the human beings caught up within them – could not be answered. That question could only be answered on the basis of some explicit or implicit assumptions about human mental processes. Yet for us, the historical forms taken by those presuppositions were exactly what we were studying. We were interested in what conceptions of the human being – whether as citizen, schoolchild, customer, worker, manager or whatever – were held at certain times and places and by whom, how such conceptions were problematized, and how interventions were devised that were appropriate to the object that was simultaneously a subject.

How, then, to proceed? Once more, it required only a slight shift in perspective. Instead of writing the history of the self or of subjectivity, we would study the history of individuals' *relations* with themselves and with others, the practices which both were their correlate and condition of possibility, and enabled these relations to be acted upon. Not who they were, but who they thought they were, what they wanted to be, the languages and norms according to which they judged themselves and were judged by others, the actions they took upon themselves and that others might take, in the light of those understandings. These were genuinely empirical and historical questions open to study. One could ask these questions without any 'theory of the human subject' – since such theories were precisely the object of genealogical analysis. One could examine, not subjectivities, but technologies of subjectivity, the aims, methods, targets, techniques and criteria in play when individuals judged and evaluated themselves and their lives, sought to master, steer, control, save or improve themselves. This was the field of concerns that Foucault, in his later work, came to term 'ethics'. And, of course, one could ask these questions where such steering was undertaken by others. Once more, Paul Veyne (1997) addresses this point. There are no universal subjects of government: those to be governed can be conceived of as children to be educated, members of a flock to be led, souls to be saved, or, we can now add, social subjects to be accorded their rights and obligations, autonomous individuals to be assisted in realizing their potential through their own free choice, or potential threats to be analysed in logics of risk and security. Not subjects, then, but subjectifications, as a mode of action on actions. Not a critique of discipline for crushing the authentic self-realizing subject of humanism, but an approach that recognizes that our own idea of the human subject as individuated, choosing, with capacities of self-reflection and a striving for autonomy, is a result of practices of subjectification, not the ahistorical basis for a critique of such practices.

It was from this perspective that we adopted some of the terminology and concepts sketched out – no more – by Michel Foucault in his brief writings on 'governmentality'. In the development of our approach, we preferred not to be Foucault scholars. We picked and chose, added ideas and concepts from elsewhere, made up a few of our own, and spent a great deal of time discussing specific cases with those others who came together in the study groups that worked under the banner of the History of the Present, as well as in other locales. While some have come to refer to the 'British School of Governmentality', such a designation is rather misleading. What emerged in Britain, but also in Canada, Australia, and even in the United States, was an informal thought community seeking to craft some tools through which we might come to understand how our present had been assembled, and hence how it might be transformed.

Laboratories of Governmentality

We did not set out to create a general theory of governmentality, but began by working on some specific issues. We were, in fact, fortunate in our objects – the Tavistock Clinic, the history of applied psychology, the genealogy of accounting and management: each of these in its different ways made it impossible, if one was to be a good empiricist, to separate out the social, the personal and the economic dimensions, for they were inextricably intertwined. We began increasingly to realize that this interconnectedness – the fact that the making up of people might be simultaneously a matter of social authorities seeking to promote personal fulfilment, improved productivity and increased social welfare – was much of the point, even if the partitioning of academic life tended to efface the intrinsic links between these domains while publicly pleading the cause of interdisciplinarity.

We were engaged not in a speculative and experimental work of theory building, but in something more limited: to craft concepts that would enable the analysis of these laboratory sites. Our papers were published in the various places where people interested in such matters might look – journals on sociology, on the history of the human sciences, on accounting, on management, and so forth. Even there, and in relation to some of our more book-like publications, many were perplexed while some were hostile – were these histories, sociologies, critiques, some kind of lapsed Marxism or what? And how did they interconnect? But, and this was gratifying, others, usually those at an earlier stage of their academic careers, found the approaches we were developing to be of use to them as well. An early paper on the government of subjectivity and social life, based on our work on the Tavistock Clinic and the Tavistock Institute of Human Relations, was published in the journal *Sociology* (Miller and Rose 1988). This approach slipped beneath the radar of major social theorists, but it was taken up by others working in the newly flourishing minor disciplines of the history of psychology, accounting, medicine and professional power.

Issues of power were a central concern in these localized studies, but it was not our aim to develop a *theory* of power. Or rather, what concerned us were forms of power very different from those typically analysed by political theorists, political commentators and most social scientists. This was power without a centre, or rather with multiple centres, power that was productive of meanings, of interventions, of entities, of processes, of objects, of written traces and of lives. Issues of freedom were central to these forms of power and hence to our analyses, prompted by the political context in which freedom had become a political mantra from all shades within the political spectrum. It was not our aim to critique a sham freedom in the name of a truer freedom, but to point to ways in which contemporary forms of power were built on a premise of freedom, a type of regulated freedom that encouraged or required individuals to compare what they did, what they achieved, and what they were with what they could or should be (Rose 1991).

Here we drew on our own work on the history of the psy sciences and their role in 'making up' people. In this work, we argued that these sciences formed as disciplines around certain 'surfaces of emergence': the line of development did not work from the pure to the applied, the academy to the application, the normal to the abnormal, but the other way round. It was around problems of abnormality, difference and divergence that the psy disciplines took shape. It was because of their perceived or claimed technical capacities to administer persons rationally, in light of a knowledge of what made them tick, that they gained their social credibility. But this was not to say that they had a function of repression or social control, that they were ripe to be critiqued from the point of a humanism, or from the aspiration to liberate a true and authentic subjectivity. The very idea of a true and authentic subjectivity had a history that was intertwined with that of the psy domain. And the powers of the psy domain that had become significant across the twentieth century – in the army, the factory, the school and the family – were actually couched in terms of the identification and management of this real subjectivity, the forging of an alliance between the ambitions of those who would manage persons, and the real wishes, desires and nature of those persons themselves. In this sense, criticisms of the psy domain as individualistic had actually played a part in creating a form of expertise capable of managing persons legitimately, even thera- peutically, individually and collectively, whether in terms of the idea of the group, the democratic management of the workplace, self-fulfilment or whatever.

Thus the forms of power that we were interested in operated across distances and domains. They spoke equally and conjointly to individuals and collectivities. They were as much at home in the most personal domains – such as sexual activity or eating habits – as in the most impersonal domains – such as timetables, work plans and accounting systems. And, possibly most importantly, these forms of power operated 'beyond the state': they did not begin with the state as point of origin, nor did they end with the state as the emblem or locus of power.

Governmentality Takes Shape

Our own attempts to systematize these modes of analysis began with an analysis of the government of economic life, which caused some contro- versy when it appeared in a general social science journal, *Economy and Society* (Miller and Rose 1990 [reproduced as chapter 2 of this volume]). At the same time, in the late 1980s, we began work on a lengthy discussion paper entitled 'Cutting off the King's Head', which we circulated widely for comments, and which was subsequently published in 1992 in the *British Journal of Sociology* (Rose and Miller 1992 [reproduced as chapter 3 of this volume]). We began with Foucault's own scattered comments on governmentality. But our aim was to generate from them a set of concep- tual tools that characterized the sort of work that we had been doing in our empirical analyses, and that would make the link more directly with the problem space of political power and its various forms. To make sense of things, we looked around for help. We borrowed concepts and approaches from many places, which we can roughly group into four.

Firstly, there were those working in the broad area of science studies, whether as sociologists, historians, philosophers or some admixture. Writers such as Michel Callon and Bruno Latour had demonstrated the benefits of focusing on very specific practices and events, while extrapolating from them some more general lessons such as the conditions for intervening at a distance. Ian Hacking similarly linked the analysis of specific practices, such as statistics, with broader theoretical or philosophical reflections which always managed to cut through the impenetrable and often fruitless hand-wringing of those more keen to fret than to analyse. Many others contributed to this still expanding and increasingly influential set of literatures.[3] From our perspective, the most important lesson of this work was the importance of focusing on instruments and interventions, even if we felt the need to supplement this with a broader concern or a more explicit link with modes of power. We took the idea of instruments broadly, to include not only actual instruments – tools, scales, measuring devices, and so forth – but also the ways of thinking, intellectual techniques, ways of analysing oneself, and so forth, to which they were bound. And we took the idea of intervention to require us to undertake detailed analyses of how interventions were actually done, the techniques and technologies that made intervention possible.

A second set of writings addressed the 'economy'. The work of the great historians of economic thought of the mid-twentieth century had made it clear, at least to us, that 'the economy' was not a given domain with its own natural laws, but was brought into existence as a way of thinking and acting in particular historical and intellectual events, and that it was transformed as those ways of thinking and acting were themselves transformed (Polanyi 1944; Schumpeter 1954). This work highlighted the constitutive role of economic calculation, and its interrelations with changing economic forms, changing economic discourses and changing economic policies. These 'made up' the economy, for the economy was itself a zone constituted by certain ways of thinking and acting, and in turn constituting ways of thinking and acting. Economic theories, laws and concepts such as profit and loss, marginal returns, equilibrium, and so forth, together with their associated calculative technologies, did not so much describe economic life as make it possible and manageable. This interplay between ways of calculating and ways of managing was demonstrated in a loosely connected set of writings, by those working at the margins of economics and sociology (Cutler et al. 1978; Thompson 1982; Tomlinson 1981b; Tribe 1978). Those working more specifically on accounting were making a similar point, namely that we should focus on calculative *practices*, and explore how these shape the ways in which we frame the choices open to individuals, businesses and other organizations, which in turn influences the ways in which we administer the lives of others and ourselves (Burchell et al. 1980; Hopwood, 1983). Meanwhile, others offered a broader historical perspective, which helped us understand how and why we have come to place such trust in numbers (Porter 1995; see also Hirschman 1977).[4]

A third set of writings focused on the professions and expertise. While those such as Illich had sought to debunk or discredit expertise, and those such as Freidson depicted the professions as self-serving, others such as Thomas Haskell and Harold Perkin were more concerned with the ways in which deference to experts had come to be woven into even the homeliest routines of everyday life, as well as the very structure and fabric of social life. Our focus on expertise was in large part an attempt to differentiate ourselves from the literature on the sociology of the professions, which we found too constraining empirically and unsatisfying theoretically, since it pre-empted so many of the questions that seemed to us important and narrowed the terrain of analysis. It was not that we saw the more traditional professions as unimportant, but we felt it equally important to attend to the plethora of minor and petty expertises that emerged in the interstices of daily life. We were not primarily interested in how these groups carved out an empire for themselves, pursued their own interests, or made themselves into socio-political forces, although all those issues were significant. Nor were we concerned to critique them for their imperialism or for their professional dominance. Rather, we were interested in the ways in which such expertise had been formed, the historical emergence of the problems which seemed to call for professional 'know-how', the new domains and enclosures that began to form around such issues, and the ways in which that expertise itself made it possible to conduct conduct in new ways. We were interested in particular in those forms of expertise that based their claims to special competence on a knowledge of human beings, individually and collectively. We were interested in how these 'engineers of the human soul' contributed to the dual process of problematizing and acting on individual behaviours, how they were able to shape and manage 'personal' conduct without violating its formally private status.

A fourth set of writings, emerging from those rather more closely associated with Foucault, helped extend the range of substantive studies and also enabled us to reflect on some of the concepts we were beginning to experiment with. Jacques Donzelot addressed the 'policing' of families, Robert Castel explored developments in the 'psy' domain in the nineteenth and twentieth centuries, while Giovanna Procacci examined the government of poverty in the nineteenth century (Deleuze 1988, 1989; Gordon 1991; Procacci 1993; Veyne 1997). In a distinctive mode, dating back over several decades, Georges Canguilhem had produced a remarkable series of studies of the biological sciences that delineated them as 'veridical' discourses, practices animated by the desire to formulate true propositions. Ian Hacking's work on making up persons and the looping effects of human kinds had helped pose the question of what kinds of creatures we human beings have become. Like him, we saw our work as in part a work on historical ontology, studies of the kinds of persons we take ourselves to be, how we have come to understand ourselves under such descriptions, and with what consequences. Indeed, our own work on the history of the discourses and technologies of subjectification, in personal, social and economic life, had shown not only the impossibility of separating them, but the way that subjectivity was a stake in all three, and the very separation of them had to be seen as an historical achievement. And, amongst the welter of critiques of Foucault from a range of social scientists who judged his work and found it guilty, there were a series of astute reflective pieces on Foucault's own writings that helped us begin to make sense of this often bewildering array of concepts, objects and practices.

We had no idea that our writings on governmentality, together with Foucault's own limited comments on this theme, would provide a reference point for the development of 'governmentality studies' over the 1990s, or that many of our formulations and conceptual tools would be retrospectively attributed to Foucault. While we certainly wrote in an interdisciplinary spirit, or at least without regard to disciplinary boundaries, we could not have anticipated the range and scope of studies that subsequently were to appear across so many disciplines under the rubric of governmentality. Responding to a rather odd assessment of our work in the mid-1990s (Curtis 1995; Miller and Rose 1995b), we identified a first phase of such work, which included investigations of the following: the emergence of social insurance (Defert 1991; Donzelot 1991a; Ewald 1986); education (Hunter 1988, 1994); accounting (Hopwood and Miller 1994; Power 1994); crime control (O'Malley 1992; Stenson 1993); the regulation of unemployment (Walters 1994); poverty and insecurity (Dean 1991; Procacci 1991, 1993): strategies of development; medicine, psychiatry and the regulation of health (Castel et al. 1982; Castel 1988; Greco 1993; Miller and Rose 1986; Osborne 1993); child abuse and sexual offences (Bell 1993); and new social strategies of empowerment (Baistow 1995; Barron 1995; Cruikshank 1994). As we said at that point, this literature certainly does not constitute a homogeneous 'school', and different authors have followed different paths and addressed different questions. We pointed to the way that such approaches have proved attractive – though not unproblematic – to researchers in a range of disciplines, including political philosophy (Hindess 1996; Tully 1989) and social history (Joyce 1994), and to the fact that these studies relate to a wider literature that, whilst not drawing explicitly on notions of governmentality, has discernible affiliations with it (Hacking 1990, 1991; Meyer 1986a; Porter 1986, 1992).

In the decade that followed, a host of other studies were published on governing children, refugees, cities, the countryside, China, colonial India and postcolonial Africa, desire, paedophilia, the workplace, shopping malls, security and insecurity, crime, madness and much more. These studies have taken place in disciplines from history to human geography, literary studies to law, economics to political science. Initially taken up in the English-speaking world – notably the UK, USA, Canada, Australia, New Zealand – 'governmentality' studies now flourishes in Germany, Switzerland, the Nordic countries and even, after some years of neglect of Foucault and his legacy, in France itself.

Doing and Theorizing Governmentality

Today, there are many meticulous textual analyses of the lectures of Michel Foucault, attentive to subtle shifts in terminology and usage over short periods of time. The focus on governmentality will increase with the publication of his 1978 lecture course on 'Security, Territory, Population', in which he introduced the notion (Foucault 2007). Others take a different route, and try to formulate a general theory of governmentality. No doubt there is some virtue in such labours, although we find them largely unrewarding. Our own approach is somewhat looser. Working within the broad ethos we have sketched above, we reflected on what it meant to govern, if, by that, one meant to conduct conduct. If the conduct of individuals or collectivities appeared to require conducting, this was because something in it appeared problematic to someone. Thus, it makes sense to start by asking how this rendering of things problematic occurred. The term 'problematizing' was a useful way of designating this as a *process*, for it removed the self-evidence of the term 'problems'. It suggested that 'problems' are not pre-given, lying there waiting to be revealed. They have to be constructed and made visible, and this construction of a field of problems is a complex and often slow process. Issues and concerns have to be made to appear problematic, often in different ways, in different sites, and by different agents. The latter may take the form of accredited experts or professionals, pressure groups, politicians, corporate leaders, the media and others. The sites to which it might refer can be as varied as the home, the school, the workplace, the street or shopping centre, or indeed almost any locale that can be transformed into a zone that is considered to need governing, even if it is not already viewed as such. Differences of opinion have to be addressed, whether fundamental or not, and brought into some kind of alignment with one another. And difficulties identified in one locale have to be linked up with difficulties identified elsewhere, so that they seem to have some common features, which can then be the basis for a way of explaining them, and perhaps also for devising strategies to address them.

Once there was a certain level of agreement that a problem existed that needed to be rectified, such problems usually came to be framed within a common language, or at least one that made dialogue possible between different groups, even if they explained it differently or proposed different solutions. Many problems came, at some point, to be articulated in terms of a more or less formalized knowledge. Sometimes the formalization by experts came at an early stage, sometimes it was this formalization that enabled the problem to become stabilized – for example, as unemployment or maladjustment or dependency – and sometimes the formalization came after the fact, the problem space being seen as a fertile territory for exploration. In any event, we were particularly interested by those moments when a problem became the focus for analysis by those who claim expertise deriving from one or more of the developing social and human sciences. It could then be assessed in terms of the various, and sometime competing, norms of the different bodies of knowledge in question. It was almost certain that some aspect of individual or collective conduct would be held responsible in some way for that problem. It might be that conduct was deemed dangerous, vicious or hurtful in some way or another. It might be viewed as unproductive and inefficient. Or it might simply be viewed as insufficient in terms of some ideal or optimal state of health, happiness or contentment.

Equally importantly, the conduct in question had to be made amenable to intervention. It had to be susceptible to some more or less rationalized set of techniques or instruments that allowed it to be acted upon and potentially transformed. There was little point, or so it seemed from the perspective of government, in identifying a problem unless one simultaneously set out some measures to rectify it. The solidity and separateness of 'problems' and 'solutions' are thus attenuated. Or, to put it differently, the activity of problematizing is intrinsically linked to devising ways to seek to remedy it. So, if a particular diagnosis or tool appears to fit a particular 'problem', this is because they have been made so that they fit each other. For to presume to govern seemed to require one to propose techniques to intervene – or to be dismissed as a mere critic or philosopher. In short, to become governmental, thought had to become technical.

We took up Foucault's rather awkward neologism – governmentality – and began to tease apart two distinct aspects of this art of governing. The first of these we termed 'rationalities' or 'programmes' of government, and the second we designated with the term 'technologies'. Through this distinction, which we did not regard as designating different domains found in reality, we meant to indicate the intrinsic links between a way of representing and knowing a phenomenon, on the one hand, and a way of acting upon it so as to transform it, on the other. For problems did not merely represent themselves in thought – they had to be rendered thinkable in such a way as to be practicable or operable. Rationalities were styles of thinking, ways of rendering reality thinkable in such a way that it was amenable to calculation and programming. We tried to suggest some dimensions along which one might identify these styles – in terms of their intrinsic moralities, the forms of knowledge upon which they base themselves, their idioms and rhetorics, and the division of labour among authorities which they presuppose and enact. We used the term 'rationalities' to indicate that there was not *a* rationality, against which to posit an irrational, but varieties of rationality, forms of reason. There were not 'mentalities' in the sense used by the Annales School, that is, structures of collective beliefs or illusions, collective or individual meaning structures, far less totalized mentalities that characterized an epoch. This was not an analysis that presupposes homogeneity or a Zeitgeist, or some set of enclosed and self-contained systems of ideas or attitudes. But nonetheless, this approach shared something with the work of the Annales School: the rejection of a political history written in terms of wars, states, great men. There was no continuous narrative of history or philosophy of unfolding, or of reading the present through its origins. There was no necessity – fragility, chance, contingency, have made human beings what they have become. There was no single historical time, but multiple times, moving at different speeds and according to their own trajectories, multiple forms of reason, formed in specific locales in relation to particular problems. Our focus, in particular, was on veridical knowledges, knowledges that claimed the status of truth and were oriented around a norm of the elimination of errors. But, like at least some of those working in the Annales tradition, we shared a focus on how experience was made amenable to being thought, and the consequences of ordering things and persons under certain descriptions or labels, whether these be madness, pauperism, criminality or whatever.

Our other dimension was technological. Technologies were assemblages of persons, techniques, institutions, instruments for the conducting of conduct. For, to become operable, rationalities had to find some way of realizing themselves, rendering themselves instrumental, and we termed these 'technologies' – human technologies. This referred to all those devices, tools, techniques, personnel, materials and apparatuses that enabled authorities to imagine and act upon the conduct of persons individually and collectively, and in locales that were often very distant. These were assemblages that enabled what we termed, borrowing loosely from the writings of Bruno Latour, 'government at a distance'.[5] Rationalities and technologies, thought and intervention, were two indissociable dimensions through which one might characterize and analyse governmentalities and begin to open them up to critical judgement.

Families of Governmentality

We argued that while one could identify multiple governmentalities, one could also discern family resemblances in these ways of rendering problems thinkable at certain times and places. These were not temporal epochs succeeding one another, but resemblances in ways of thinking and acting. These resemblances were along a number of axes. There were similarities in conceptions of the objects and objectives of government, the differing roles and responsibilities of different authorities, the nature and limits of politics and intervention, the ways in which problems should be understood, the forms of knowledge and expertise drawn upon, and the conceptions of the subjects of government themselves. And we suggested that governmentalities change by entering into periods of criticism and crisis, where multiple perceptions of failure coalesce, and where alternatives are proposed – for the failures of one mode of governing are opportunities for the formulation of another. As we put it, and in a manner that is often misunderstood as an assessment, governmentalities were eternally optimistic, but government is a congenitally failing operation.

For heuristic purposes, we suggested – in a possibly oversimplified way – that it was possible to identify three 'families' of governmentality.

Classical liberalism, we suggested, needed to be analysed as a mode of government, not merely a philosophy. Here the state limited itself by designating zones exterior to it – private life, the market, civil society, and so forth, that had their own density and autonomy and were not just creatures of 'reason of state' to be known, dominated and administered at will. But the political apparatus depended on the activities of multiple governing agents external to it – the churches, philanthropic organizations, trades unions and friendly societies, and so forth. And yet, as we saw in the second half of the nineteenth century, the capacities of these came under question, and the political apparatus itself began to extend its obligations into new spheres. These were the governmental inventions of actually existing liberalism which were much criticized by liberal philosophers – town planning and sanitation, medical provisions, various types of educational provision, expanded role of state bureaucracy, the so-called 'Victorian revolution in government and administration', and so forth.

Governing 'from the social point of view', as we termed it, was grounded in the argument that began to take shape at the turn of the nineteenth and twentieth centuries that 'government would have to be social or it would cease to exist', that a kind of social government was necessary if one was to be able to combat the twin threats of unbridled market individualism and communist revolution. This was the original third or middle way to save private enterprise, to transform subjects into social citizens with social rights. It was rendered technical through the invention of social insurance, social welfare, indeed of 'the social' itself. It entailed a new conception of the state as the ultimate guarantor of the welfare of the individual, but required strategies to do this without destroying individual morality and responsibility. These depended heavily on the invention of new professionals of the social, and new forms of inculcation of civility into citizens especially via home and domestication.

What we termed 'advanced' liberalism took shape in the last three decades of the twentieth century, although it was prefigured by the neo-liberal thinkers of the immediate post-war period such as Hayek. While at that time these thinkers were marginal, by the 1960s, one saw the criticism of the overblown state from both the left and the right, not just from neo-liberals, but also from classical liberals, from left critics of the welfare state, from proponents of human rights against powers of authorities. These criticisms were formulated both at a general level and in various local practices.

While left critiques of the welfare state had largely failed because of their incapacity to generate technically feasible alternatives, now the inventiveness of governmental thought came from the right, and worked on several fronts. There was an extension of rationalities and technologies of markets to previously exempt zones such as health and education. It entailed the deployment of new technologies of governing from a centre through powerful means of governing at a distance: these appeared to enhance the autonomy of zones, persons, entities, but enwrapped them in new forms of regulation – audits, budgets, standards, risk management, targets, shadow of the law, etc. It entailed a new conception of the subjects to be governed: that these would be autonomous and responsible individuals, freely choosing how to behave and act. We saw the emergence of novel strategies of activation and responsibilization, and novel professionals of activation, in policies for the government of economic life and of social security. We saw the birth of a new ethic of the active, choosing, responsible, autonomous individual obliged to be free, and to live life as if it were an outcome of choice. Clearly, certain psychological conceptions of subjectivity – which emerged over the twentieth century and particularly its last half – were central to imagining ourselves in this way and seeking to act upon ourselves in the name of this idea of freedom.

But these governmentalities, of course, were constantly judged to fail, and new solutions were proposed. The first, perhaps, was in the emergence of the idea of community as a central means of government, so that the relation between identity and community would displace that of individual and society. And now, perhaps, this whole family of liberal governmentalities is coming under strain as a new problematization takes shape, that of insecurity, risk and precaution.

Reflections on Governmentality

Reflecting now, almost two decades later, on these developments, perhaps it is possible to identify some distinctive features that made this way of thinking useful to us in our own work and so attractive to others.

Firstly, there is the encouragement it provides to transgress or ignore the distinction of the domains of personal, economic and social life, and instead to see these as requiring interlinked and overlapping strategies of inquiry. One consequence of the disciplinary partitioning of the social sciences across the twentieth century has been the partitioning of these domains, not only allocating them to different bodies of scholarship, but also treating them as if that distinction was a reflection in thought of some natural division of reality. One benefit of analysing these domains in terms of governmentality is that one is forced to recognize the historical processes that have contributed to the co-production of this differentiation. For the differentiating of disciplines has co-emerged with the invention of differentiated ways of diagnosing and seeking to act on the behaviours of individuals and groups of individuals. To diagnose the ills of the economy in terms of economic performance, or the ills of the individual in terms of maladjustment, requires both the forming of distinct disciplines, and the forming of tools for intervening in the domains in question. This is not a 'sociological' observation, one that allows us to make large claims about the consequences of industrialization, modernization, globalization or whatever. It is rather a genealogical observation, that is to say it can be discerned if one examines the co-emergence of specific programmes, projects, technologies, diagnoses, aspirations, and the like, that address the management of this or that problem.

Secondly, there is the importance of moving beyond the public/private divide in understanding the varied ways in which social authorities seek to shape and fashion the conduct of persons. We should not accept at face value the distinctions that are so valued within political philosophy and everyday life between the public and the private, only to then ask why and to what extent the boundary has been inappropriately transgressed. It is in such terms that others have diagnosed eras and framed critiques of the 'colonization of the private sphere' or the rise of a culture demanding the public display of private attributes. We need instead to examine how the very idea of the private sphere was formed at the same moment as notions of public spaces, public morality, and so forth (Rose 1987). Once again, a genealogy of governmentality draws attention here to the issue of co-production.

Thirdly, we believe it has been useful to insist on the interlinking and interdependence of programmes or rationalities and technologies. For governmentalities, we have always emphasized, are both mentalities and technologies, both ways of thinking and tools for intervening, and it is important to keep in view the irreducibility of each dimension to the other, at the same time as their often intimate and intricate interdependence. Also, it is important to be attentive to the multiplicity of programmes and the variable surfaces on which they have emerged. In the late 1980s and early 1990s, we were certainly not alone in pointing to the importance of the programmatic in attempts to manage or administer lives. But we felt it important to attend not only to what one might call the 'meta-level' programmes implicit in the writings of political economy or political theory.[6] We wanted to emphasize also the somewhat more prosaic and lower-level programmes that emerged in relation to specific domains and specific problematizations, while remaining attentive to the ways in which initially disparate and unconnected aims and ambitions came to achieve some sort of similarity or family resemblance. And yet we wanted to achieve this without resorting to the partitioning of analytical frames that finds solace in notions such as 'laboratory life' or the differentiating of organizations and institutions. While we have drawn much inspiration from such modes of analysis, we felt it was both possible and important to keep in view both the programmatic nature of social life, and its intrinsic links with the panoply of instruments for intervening.[7]

Fourthly, and perhaps most generally, we have found the insistence on analysing power and politics without necessary recourse to the state as locus, origin or outcome to be incredibly fruitful. This is not because states and the political apparatus are unimportant – that would be to misunderstand our argument. Rather, we argue that analyses should start from elsewhere, from the practices of governing themselves. These might be forms of calculation, ways of categorizing persons, rearrangements of factory layouts, treatments for various disorders, the testing of various groups or populations, and so on. In this way, as has now been shown, one might be able to start to map out the multiple centres of calculation and authority that traverse and link up personal, social and economic life. And it might even allow us to understand that 'non-state' modes of exercise of power are one of the defining features of our present.

Fifthly and finally, we have felt it important to keep in view always the linking of the local and the non-local. While we have been particularly mindful of the often highly specific circumstances in which particular problematizations, programmes or technologies emerge, we have not considered this to be an excuse to focus on the arcane, the frivolous or the purely idiosyncratic. For modes of managing, intervening and administering become modes of power to the extent that they are generalized and linked to a centre, or at least linked up with other comparable or similar modes. Of course delineations of micro- and macro-levels, individual and society, or organizations and institutions have been ever present in the social sciences. But we wanted to avoid falling prey to such easy categorizing of phenomena. We wanted to avoid the hierarchical images and explanatory schemata that tended to go hand in hand with such binary frameworks, and we wanted also to avoid a simplistic and sequential style of analysis, notwithstanding the false sense of comfort it can induce. We wanted simply to tease out how traces are left, linkages formed, connections established and some degree of stability is achieved in an assemblage. Or, to put it differently, we were confident that one could find the programmatic in the most mundane and local parts of economic and social life, thereby offering the opportunity to analyse what was said and done from the perspective of historical/genealogical research as well as from the perspective of more anthropological or fieldwork-based endeavours.

Outline of the Book

Our aim in putting together this collection has been to counter some of the abstract forms that some of these ideas have taken, and to demonstrate how our conceptual tools were forged in the analysis of some very specific problem fields.

Chapter 2, 'Governing Economic Life', proposes some new ways of analysing the exercise of political power in advanced liberal democratic societies. These are developed from Michel Foucault's conception of 'governmentality' and address political power in terms of 'political rationalities' and 'technologies of government'. This approach draws attention to the diversity of regulatory mechanisms which seek to give effect to government, and to the particular importance of indirect mechanisms that link the conduct of individuals and organizations to political objectives through 'action at a distance'. The chapter argues for the importance of an analysis of language in understanding the constitution of the objects of politics, not simply in terms of meaning or rhetoric, but as 'intellectual technologies' that render aspects of existence amenable to inscription and calculation. It suggests that governmentality has a characteristically 'programmatic' form, and that it is inextricably bound to the invention and evaluation of technologies that seek to give it effect. It draws attention to the complex processes of negotiation and persuasion involved in the assemblage of loose and mobile networks that can bring persons, organizations and objectives into align-ment. The argument is exemplified through considering various aspects of the regulation of economic life: attempts at national economic planning in post-war France and England; the role ascribed to changing accounting practices in the UK in the 1960s; techniques of managing the internal world of the workplace that have come to lay special emphasis upon the psychological features of the producing subjects. The chapter contends that 'governmentality' has come to depend in crucial respects upon the intel-lectual technologies, practical activities and social authority associated with expertise. It argues that the self-regulating capacities of subjects, shaped and normalized through expertise, are key resources for governing in a liberal democratic way.

Chapter 3, 'Political Power beyond the State: Problematics of Govern-ment', sets out an approach to the analysis of political power. It argues against an overvaluation of the 'problem of the State' in political debate and social theory. A number of conceptual tools are suggested for the analysis of the many and varied alliances between political and other authorities that seek to govern economic activity, social life and individual conduct. Modern political rationalities and governmental technologies are shown to be intrinsically linked to developments in knowledge and to the powers of expertise. The characteristics of liberal problematics of govern-ment are investigated, and it is argued that they are dependent upon tech-nologies for 'governing at a distance', seeking to create locales, entities and persons able to operate a regulated autonomy. The analysis is exempli-fied through an investigation of welfarism as a mode of 'social' govern-ment. The chapter concludes with a brief consideration of neo-liberalism which demonstrates that the analytical language structured by the philo-sophical opposition of state and civil society is unable to comprehend contemporary transformations in modes of exercise of political power.

Chapter 4, 'The Death of the Social? Re-figuring the Territory of Gov-ernment', argues that the social, as a plane of thought and action, has been central to political thought and political programmes since the mid-nineteenth century. This chapter argues that, while themes of society and concerns with social cohesion and social justice are still significant in political argument, the social is no longer a key zone, target and objective of strategies of government. The rise of the language of globalization indicates that economic relations are no longer easily understood as orga-nized across a single bounded national economy. Community has become a new spatialization of government: heterogeneous, plural, linking indi-viduals, families and others into contesting cultural assemblies of identities and allegiances. Divisions among the subjects of government are coded in new ways; neither the included nor the excluded are governed as social citizens. Non-social strategies are deployed for the management of expert authority. Anti-political motifs such as associationism and communitarianism which do not seek to govern through society are on the rise in political thought. The chapter suggests some ways of diagnosing and analysing these novel territorializations of political thought and action.

Chapter 5, 'Mobilizing the Consumer: Assembling the Subject of Consumption', engages with debates about consumption and the creation of consumer society, through a detailed analysis of the involvement of the Tavistock Institute of Human Relations in such matters. By analysing the ways in which the 'Tavi' sought to understand and shape demand for such varied products as ice cream, frozen fish fingers, home perms, soft toilet tissue and petrol, we explore the diverse ways in which different images of the subject of consumption have operated *internal* to one element of the new 'economy of consumption'. Making up the subject of consumption, we suggest, has been a complex technical process. To understand this process, it is necessary to look beyond general shifts in cultural understanding or the imperatives of profit, and examine the ways in which the understandings of human individuality, personality and psychology elaborated by the psychological sciences have played a key role in the construction of consumption technologies. Psychological expertise in advertising provides a site where we explore the extent to which this has been less a matter of dominating or manipulating consumers than of 'mobilizing' them by forming connections between human passions, hopes and anxieties, and very specific features of goods enmeshed in particular consumption practices. Through this case study, we argue that psychological knowledges are not merely tools of manipulation or legitimation, or techniques incidental to global logics of consumption, but are central to the human technologies that should be the focus for analyses of the government of the consuming passions.

Chapter 6, 'On Therapeutic Authority: Psychoanalytical Expertise under Advanced Liberalism', argues that in contemporary European and North American societies, authority has acquired a new therapeutic vocation, and there has been a partial reshaping of the ethical warrant required to exercise authority over the conduct of one's fellow human beings. This entails new ways of thinking and acting upon all those points where an individual's relations with others intersect with their relations with themselves. Crucial here have been the new ways of thinking and acting on human conduct made possible by an expertise of 'the group' which helps at the same time to construct and give solidity to the notion of the group. These novel ways of understanding life in small and large groups, and of orienting ourselves towards the most intimate of personal relations, have constructed a new density for the world we inhabit in the family, the factory, the school, the hospital, the office and all the locales of everyday life. We investigate the formation of this new species of authority through one particular set of events: the ideas and actions associated with the Tavistock Clinic and the Tavistock Institute of Human Relations. But we suggest that the specific events in which the Tavi was involved are elements within something that proliferates more widely through our contemporary experience: a complex of loosely connected expertises, technologies and representations addressed to the management of problems of living, or the problematization of life from the perspective of its potential amenability to therapy.

Chapter 7, 'Production, Identity and Democracy', argues that the workplace is a pre-eminent site for contestations about the nature of human identity, and for attempts to shape and reshape the identity of individuals. Attempts over the course of the twentieth century to transform production relations, in particular those that have been animated by the imperatives of democracy, have depended on specific, and changing, conceptions of the person. These interventions upon work, in which concerns with the identity of the individual have provided ways of linking the sphere of production with the nature of democracy, form the focus of this chapter. Particular conceptions of human identity, subjectivity and personhood have been intrinsic to attempts to govern the world of work in a manner deemed legitimate in democratic societies. Our general claim is that transformations in identity should not be studied at the level of culture, or solely in terms of the history of ideas about the self. A genealogy of identity must address the practices that act upon human beings and human conduct in specific domains of existence, and the systems of thought that underpin these practices and are embodied within them. For at least the last century, ways of thinking about and acting on work have been fully engaged with the philosophical question of what kinds of persons human beings are. And these concerns with the identity of the person at work have intersected with a range of different ways of problematizing the nature of work, democratic ideals and productivity.

Chapter 8, 'Governing Advanced Liberal Democracies', analyses the emergence of what can be termed 'advanced liberal' governmentalities. It suggests that these differ both from classical liberal mentalities and technologies of rule and those which sought to govern in the name of the social. Advanced liberal rule depends upon expertise in a different way, and connects experts differently into the technologies of rule. It seeks to degovernmentalize the state and to de-statize practices of government, to detach the substantive authority of expertise from the apparatuses of political rule, relocating experts within a market governed by the rationalities of competition, accountability and consumer demand. It seeks to govern not through 'society', but through the regulated choices of individual citizens, now construed as subjects of choices and aspirations to self-actualization and self-fulfilment. Individuals are to be governed through their freedom, but neither as isolated atoms of classical political economy, nor as citizens of society, but as members of heterogeneous communities of allegiance, as 'community' emerges as a new way of conceptualizing and administering moral relations amongst persons. The chapter argues that 'advanced' liberal formulae of government ask whether it is possible to govern without governing *society*, that is to say, to govern through the regulated and accountable choices of autonomous agents – citizens, consumers, parents, employees, managers, investors – and to govern through intensifying and acting upon their allegiance to particular 'communities'. As an autonomizing and pluralizing formula of rule, this form of rule is dependent upon the proliferation of little regulatory instances across a territory and their multiplication, at a 'molecular' level, through the interstices of our present experience. It is dependent, too, upon a particular relation between political subjects and expertise, in which the injunctions of the experts merge with our own projects for self-mastery and the enhancement of our lives.

Notes

1. The figure of Gramsci, so much less easy to situate theoretically, reinforced this interest in issues of ideology, and was central for some of our co-workers at the time, but figured less prominently in our own work.
2. In fact this piece, arising from a panel discussion with French historians on 20 May 1978, was first published in French in 1980 (Perrot 1980a), and translated into English by Colin Gordon that same year (Perrot 1980b).
3. Of course there were many influential others, including Mirowski (1989), Pickering (1992), Shapin and Schaffer (1985), Wise (1988).
4. Theodore Porter's *Trust in Numbers*, although not published till 1995, existed in embryonic form several years earlier.
5. Latour had written on 'action at a distance', and this formulation inspired our own.
6. We note here, in particular, the work of Albert Hirschman and Giovanni Procacci.
7. A good example of this is Power (1994), who shows that the humble audit is both a programme and a technology, and almost infinitely variable in terms of the domains it can define as its own.

2

Governing Economic Life

In advanced liberal democracies, political power has come to embrace many facets of economic, social and personal existence. Political power is exercised today through a multitude of agencies and techniques, some of which are only loosely associated with the executives and bureaucracies of the formal organs of state. We suggest that Michel Foucault's concept of 'government' provides a potentially fruitful way of analysing the shifting ambitions and concerns of all those social authorities that have sought to administer the lives of individuals and associations, focusing our attention on the diverse mechanisms through which the actions and judgements of persons and organizations have been linked to political objectives (e.g. Foucault 1979). We argue that an analysis of modern 'government' needs to pay particular attention to the role accorded to 'indirect' mechanisms for aligning economic, social and personal conduct with socio-political objectives. We draw upon some recent work in the sociology of science and technology in analysing these mechanisms, borrowing and adapting Bruno Latour's notion of 'action at a distance' (cf. Latour 1987b). We argue that such action at a distance mechanisms have come to rely in crucial respects upon 'expertise': the social authority ascribed to particular agents and forms of judgement on the basis of their claims to possess specialized truths and rare powers. We contend that the self-regulating capacities of subjects, shaped and normalized in large part through the powers of expertise, have become key resources for modern forms of government and have established some crucial conditions for governing in a liberal democratic way.

We begin with a general discussion which sets out and develops the concept of 'governmentality'. In the remainder of the chapter we seek to exemplify the mechanisms and processes discussed through a consideration of various aspects of the 'government' of economic life. We consider the 'government' of 'the economy', firstly through centralized systems of economic planning, and secondly through attempts to transform the calculative procedures of economic actors. We then turn to the 'government' of the internal world of the enterprise and examine this in relation to the changing techniques of management. We argue that management has come to depend upon expertise not only concerning the technical features of production, but also concerning the psychological features of the producing subjects. Finally, we look at the techniques by which the self-regulating capacities of subjects have become vital resources and allies for the 'government' of economic life, especially insofar as they have come to be understood and regulated in terms of the notions of autonomy and self-fulfilment. We link this to some remarks on contemporary transformations in 'governmentality'.

First, let us consider the notion of government. Michel Foucault argued that a certain mentality, which he termed 'governmentality', had become the common ground of all modern forms of political thought and action. Governmentality, he argued, was an 'ensemble formed by the institutions, procedures, analyses and reflections, the calculations and tactics, that allow the exercise of this very specific albeit complex form of power' (Foucault 1979: 20). And, he claimed, since the eighteenth century population had appeared as the terrain *par excellence* of government. Authorities have addressed themselves to the regulation of the processes proper to the population, the laws that modulate its wealth, health, longevity, its capacity to wage war and to engage in labour and so forth. Thus, he implies, societies like our own are characterized by a particular way of thinking about the kinds of problems that can and should be addressed by various authorities. They operate within a kind of political *a priori* that allows the tasks of such authorities to be seen in terms of the calculated supervision, administration and maximization of the forces of each and all.

This way of investigating the exercise of political rule has a number of advantages. Firstly, it refuses the reduction of political power to the actions of a state, the latter construed as a relatively coherent and calculating political subject. Instead of viewing rule in terms of a state that extends its sway throughout society by means of a ramifying apparatus of control, the notion of government draws attention to the diversity of forces and groups that have, in heterogeneous ways, sought to regulate the lives of individuals and the conditions within particular national territories in pursuit of various goals. Rather than 'the State' giving rise to government, the state becomes a particular form that government has taken, and one that does not exhaust the field of calculations and interventions that constitute it.

It is to the analysis of these aspirations and attempts that the notion of government directs us. This path may appear to lead, in a rather idiosyncratic way, to a familiar and well-trodden field – that of the historical and contemporary analysis of economic and social policy. However, the apparent familiarity of these concerns is likely to mislead. It is true that the earliest forms of governmentality in Europe went under the name of the science of 'police', and that 'police' and 'policy' share a common root. But the analysis of policy suggested by the concept of government implies that the very existence of a field of concerns termed 'policy' should itself be treated as something to be explained. It draws attention to the fundamental role that knowledges play in rendering aspects of existence thinkable and calculable, and amenable to deliberated and planful initiatives: a complex intellectual labour involving not only the invention of new forms of thought, but also the invention of novel procedures of documentation, computation and evaluation. It suggests that we need to consider under what ethical conditions it became possible for different authorities to consider it legitimate, feasible and even necessary to conduct such interventions. It suggests that the concerns that have occasioned and animated policy are not self-evident. The emergence of unemployment, crime, disease and poverty as 'problems' that can be identified and construed as in need of amelioration is itself something to be explained. It points to the diversity of the groupings that have problematized such aspects of existence in relation to social and political concerns, and that have developed and sought to implement policies. These are not just 'political' authorities, in the traditional sense, but also those whose basis is intellectual, spiritual, and so forth. It implies that there is no smooth path of development or evolution of policies, but that lasting inventions have often arisen in surprising and aleatory fashion and in relation to apparently marginal or obscure difficulties in social or economic existence, which for particular reasons have come to assume political salience for a brief period. Hence the notion of government highlights the diversity of powers and knowledges entailed in rendering fields practicable and amenable to intervention. It suggests that the analysis of 'policy' cannot be confined to the study of different administrative agencies, their interests, funding, administrative organization, and the like. A complex and heterogeneous assemblage of conditions thus makes it possible for objects of policy to be problematized, and rendered amenable to administration.

Of course, these dimensions can be studied, and have been studied, without drawing upon the notion of government. But the approach suggested by these writings of Michel Foucault has two further features that we consider important. Policy studies tend to be concerned with evaluating policies, uncovering the factors that led to their success in achieving their objectives or, more usually, deciphering the simplifications, misunderstandings, miscalculations and strategic errors that led to their failure (e.g. Williams et al. 1986). We, on the other hand, are not concerned with evaluations of this type, with making judgements as to whether and why this or that policy succeeded or failed, or with devising remedies for alleged deficiencies (cf. Thompson 1987). Rather, we are struck by the fact that this very form of thinking is a characteristic of 'governmentality': policies always appear to be surrounded by more or less systematized attempts to adjudicate on their vices or virtues, and are confronted with other policies promising to achieve the same ends by improved means, or advocating something completely different. Evaluation, that is to say, is something internal to the phenomena we wish to investigate. For us, this imperative to evaluate needs to be viewed as itself a key component of the forms of political thought under discussion: how authorities and administrators make judgements, the conclusions that they draw from them, the rectifications they propose and the impetus that 'failure' provides for the propagation of new programmes of government.

'Evaluation' of policy, in a whole variety of forms, is thus integral to what we term the programmatic character of governmentality. Governmentality is programmatic not simply in that one can see the proliferation of more or less explicit programmes for reforming reality – government reports, White Papers, Green Papers, papers from business, trade unions, financiers, political parties, charities and academics proposing this or that scheme for dealing with this or that problem. It is also programmatic in that it is characterized by an eternal optimism that a domain or a society could be administered better or more effectively, that reality is, in some way or other, programmable (cf. Gordon 1987; MacIntyre 1981; Miller and O'Leary 1989b; Rose and Miller 1989). Hence the 'failure' of one policy or set of policies is always linked to attempts to devise or propose programmes that would work better, that would deliver economic growth, productivity, low inflation, full employment, or the like. Whilst the identification of failure is thus a central element in governmentality, an analysis of governmentality is not itself a tool for social programmers. To analyse what one might term 'the will to govern' is not to participate enthusiastically in it.

The Discursive Character of Governmentality

Governmentality has a discursive character: to analyse the conceptualizations, explanations and calculations that inhabit the governmental field requires an attention to language. There is nothing novel in the suggestion that language and politics are interrelated, or even in the suggestion that the relation between the two is neither one of simple homology or reflection, nor one of ideological mystification, but is mutually constitutive (e.g. Connelly 1987; Shapiro 1984; Taylor 1987). In relation to economic policy, a number of studies have directly addressed the discursive constitution of the domain and the component parts of the economy. They have demonstrated the conceptual conditions under which it came to be possible to conceive of a specifically economic domain composed of various economic entities with their own laws and processes that were amenable to rational knowledge and calculation, and hence to various forms of regulatory intervention (Burchell et al. 1985; Hopwood 1987; Loft 1986; Thompson 1982; Tomlinson 1981a, 1981b, 1983; Tribe 1978).

Our approach has much in common with this. But we would like to place these concerns within a rather different framework. On the one hand, we suggest that policy should be located within a wider discursive field in which conceptions of the proper ends and means of government are articulated: an analysis of what Michel Foucault terms 'political rationalities'. On the other hand, we argue for a view of 'discourse' as a technology of thought, requiring attention to the particular technical devices of writing, listing, numbering and computing that render a realm into discourse as a knowable, calculable and administrable object. 'Knowing' an object in such a way that it can be governed is more than a purely speculative activity: it requires the invention of procedures of notation, ways of collecting and presenting statistics, the transportation of these to centres where calculations and judgements can be made, and so forth. It is through such procedures of inscription that the diverse domains of 'governmentality' are made up, that 'objects' such as the economy, the enterprise, the social field and the family are rendered in a particular conceptual form and made amenable to intervention and regulation.

Political argument does not have the systematic and coherent character of theoretical discourse. Nonetheless, we suggest, it is possible to specify and differentiate political rationalities in terms of the relatively systematic discursive matrices within which the activity of government is articulated, the particular languages within which its objects and objectives are construed, the grammar of analyses and prescriptions, the vocabularies of programmes, the terms in which the legitimacy of government is established. For it is out of such linguistic elements that rationalities of government such as welfarism or neo-liberalism are elaborated as assemblages of philosophical doctrines, notions of social and human realities, theories of power, conceptions of policy and versions of justice, and much else. And it is from these assemblages that ways of specifying appropriate bases for the organization and mobilization of social life are articulated.

All government, we suggest, depends on a particular mode of 'representation': the elaboration of a language for depicting the domain in question that claims both to grasp the nature of that reality represented, and literally to *re*present it in a form amenable to political deliberation, argument and scheming. This gives us a clue to a further way in which language is significant for government. For it is in language that programmes of government are elaborated, and through which a consonance is established between the broadly specified ethical, epistemological and ontological appeals of political discourse – to the nation, to virtue, to what is or is not possible or desirable – and the plans, schemes and objectives that seek to address specific problematizations within social, economic or personal existence.

The forms of political discourse characteristic of 'governmentality' open a particular space for theoretical arguments and the truth claims that they entail. The government of a population, a national economy, an enterprise, a family, a child or even oneself becomes possible only through discursive mechanisms that represent the domain to be governed as an intelligible field with its own limits and characteristics, and whose component parts are linked together in some more or less systematic manner (Burchell et al. 1985; Hopwood 1984, 1985, 1986; Miller 1989; Miller and O'Leary 1989a; Rose 1989a). Before one can seek to manage a domain such as an economy it is first necessary to conceptualize a set of processes and relations as an economy which is amenable to management. The birth of a language of national economy as a domain with its own characteristics, laws and processes that could be spoken about and about which knowledge could be gained enabled it to become an element in programmes which could seek to evaluate and increase the power of nations by governing and managing 'the economy'. 'Government', that is to say, is always dependent on knowledge, and proponents of diverse programmes seek to ground themselves in a positive knowledge of that which is to be governed, ways of reasoning about it, analysing it and evaluating it, identifying its problems and devising solutions. Theories here do not merely legitimate existing power relations but actually constitute new sectors of reality and make new fields of existence practicable.

In drawing attention to the role of language in government in this way, we do not wish to suggest that the analysis of political power should become a sub-department of the history of ideas, or that our concern should be with the problem of meaning. The features of language that we have described have a more active role than this, one perhaps best captured in the term 'intellectual technology'. Language, that is to say, provides a mechanism for rendering reality amenable to certain kinds of action. And language, in this sense, is more than merely 'contemplative': describing a world such that it is amenable to having certain things done to it involves inscribing reality into the calculations of government through a range of material and rather mundane techniques (Rose 1988; cf. Latour 1987a).

The Technologies of Government

'Government', of course, is not only a matter of representation. It is also a matter of intervention. The specificity of governmentality, as it has taken shape in 'the West' over the last two centuries, lies in this complex inter-weaving of procedures for representing and intervening (cf. Hacking 1983). We suggest that these attempts to instrumentalize government and make it operable also have a kind of 'technological' form (cf. Foucault 1986: 225–6). If political rationalities render reality into the domain of thought, these 'technologies of government' seek to translate thought into the domain of reality, and to establish 'in the world of persons and things' spaces and devices for acting upon those entities of which they dream and scheme.

We use the term 'technologies' to suggest a particular approach to the analysis of the activity of ruling, one which pays great attention to the actual mechanisms through which authorities of various sorts have sought to shape, normalize and instrumentalize the conduct, thought, decisions and aspirations of others in order to achieve the objectives they consider desirable. To understand modern forms of rule, we suggest, requires an investigation not merely of grand political schemata, or economic ambi-tions, or even of general slogans such as 'state control', nationalization, the free market, and the like, but of apparently humble and mundane mecha-nisms which appear to make it possible to govern: techniques of notation, computation and calculation; procedures of examination and assessment; the invention of devices such as surveys and presentational forms such as tables; the standardization of systems for training and the inculcation of habits; the inauguration of professional specialisms and vocabularies; building design and architectural forms – the list is heterogeneous and is, in principle, unlimited.

The classical terminology of political philosophy and political sociology – State v. Civil Society, public v. private, community v. market, and so forth – is of little use here. Such language certainly needs to be investi-gated, to the extent that it functions in important ways within political rationalities and political programmes, providing them with an ethical basis and differentiating the legitimacy of varied types of governmental aspiration. But at the technical level, operationalizing government has entailed the putting into place, both intentionally and unintentionally, of a diversity of indirect relations of regulation and persuasion that do not differentiate according to such boundaries. In particular, the capacities that have been granted to expertise – that complex amalgam of professionals and quasi-professionals, truth claims and technical procedures – provide versatile mechanisms for shaping and normalizing the 'private' enterprise, the 'private' firm, the 'private' decisions of business people and parents and the self-regulating capacities of 'private' selves in ways that are simply not comprehended in these philosophies of politics. Yet it is precisely these indirect means of action and intervention that are central to modern 'mentalities of government' and crucial for the possibility of modern forms of rule (MacIntyre 1981; Miller and O'Leary 1989b; Rose 1987, 1989a). The analysis of such technologies of government requires a 'microphysics of power', an attention to the complex of relays and interdependencies which enable programmes of government to act upon and intervene upon those places, persons and populations which are their concern.

It is through technologies that political rationalities and the programmes of government they articulate become capable of deployment. But this should not be understood simply as a matter of the 'implementation' of ideal schemes in the real, still less as the extension of control from the seat of power into the minutiae of existence. By drawing attention to the technological dimension of government, we do not mean to summon up an image of a 'totally administered society'. It is true that, in certain European countries, the early versions of 'police' were inspired by the utopian dream that all regions of the social body could be penetrated, known and directed by political authorities. But, as Michel Foucault has pointed out, nineteenth-century liberalism marks the point from which this dream was abandoned in those nations that called themselves liberal democracies. The problem became, instead, one of governing a territory and a population that were independent realities with inherent processes and forces. With the emergence of such an idea of 'society', the question became 'How is government possible? That is, what is the principle of limitation that applies to governmental actions such that things will occur for the best, in conformity with the rationality of government, and without intervention' (Foucault 1986: 242).

It is for these reasons that we have suggested the need for the analysis of the 'indirect' mechanisms of rule that are of such importance in liberal democratic societies: those that have enabled, or have sought to enable government at a distance.

In conceptualizing such indirect mechanisms by which rule is brought about, we adapt for our own ends Bruno Latour's notion of 'action at a distance' (Latour 1987b: 219 et seq.). He develops this notion in answering the question 'how is it possible to act on events, places and people that are unfamiliar and a long way away?' Eighteenth-century French navigators could only travel to unfamiliar regions of the East Pacific, colonize, domesticate and dominate the inhabitants from their European metropolitan bases because, in various technical ways, these distant places were 'mobilized', brought home to 'centres of calculation' in the form of maps, drawings, readings of the movements of the tides and the stars. Mobile traces that were stable enough to be moved back and forward without distortion, corruption or decay, and combinable so that they could be accumulated and calculated upon, enabled the ships to be sent out and to return, enabled a 'centre' to be formed that could 'dominate' a realm of persons and processes distant from it. This process, he suggests, is similar whether it is a question of dominating the sky, the earth or the economy: domination involves the exercise of a form of intellectual mastery made possible by those at a centre having information about persons and events distant from them.

Our notion of 'government at a distance' links this idea to a related approach developed in the work of Latour and that of Michel Callon (Callon 1986; Callon and Latour 1981; Latour 1986). In the context of analysing the establishment and generalization of scientific and technical innovations, Callon and Latour have examined the complex mechanisms through which it becomes possible to link calculations at one place with action at another, not through the direct imposition of a form of conduct by force, but through a delicate affiliation of a loose assemblage of agents and agencies into a functioning network. This involves alliances formed not only because one agent is dependent upon another for funds, legitimacy or some other resource which can be used for persuasion or compulsion. It is also because one actor comes to convince another that their problems or goals are intrinsically linked, that their interests are consonant, that each can solve their difficulties or achieve their ends by joining forces or working along the same lines. This is not so much a process of appealing to mutual interests as of what Gallon and Latour term '*intéressement*' – the construction of allied interests through persuasion, intrigue, calculation or rhetoric. In the process occurs what Callon and Latour refer to as 'translation', in which one actor or force is able to require or count upon a particular way of thinking and acting from another, hence assembling them together into a network not because of legal or institutional ties or dependencies, but because they have come to construe their problems in allied ways and their fate as in some way bound up with one another. Hence persons, organizations, entities and locales which remain differentiated by space, time and formal boundaries can be brought into a loose, approximate and always mobile and indeterminate alignment.

Language, again, plays a key role in establishing these loosely aligned networks, and in enabling rule to be brought about in an indirect manner.

It is, in part, through adopting shared vocabularies, theories and explanations that loose and flexible associations may be established between agents across time and space – Departments of State, pressure groups, academics, managers, teachers, employees, parents – whilst each remains, to a greater or lesser extent, constitutionally distinct and formally independent. Each of these diverse forces can be enrolled in a governmental network to the extent that it can translate the objectives and values of others into its own terms, to the extent that the arguments of another become consonant with and provide norms for its own ambitions and actions. The language of expertise plays a key role here, its norms and values seeming compelling because of their claim to a disinterested truth, and the promise they offer of achieving desired results. Hence expertise can appeal, in one direction, to the ambitions of politicians, administrators, educators and others seeking to achieve particular objectives in the most efficacious manner, and, on the other, to those who have come to feel the need for expert guidance for their conduct in the firm, the office, the airline, the hospital or the home.

Such networks, of course, are not the simple aggregate of rationally planned technologies for shaping decisions and conduct in calculated ways. And whilst 'governmentality' is eternally optimistic, 'government' is a congenitally failing operation. The world of programmes is heterogeneous and rivalrous, and the solutions for one programme tend to be the problems for another. 'Reality' always escapes the theories that inform programmes and the ambitions that underpin them. Technologies produce unexpected problems, are utilized for their own ends by those who are supposed merely to operate them, are hampered by underfunding, professional rivalries and the impossibility of producing the technical conditions that would make them work – reliable statistics, efficient communication systems, clear lines of command, properly designed buildings, well-framed regulations, or whatever. Unplanned outcomes emerge from the intersection of one technology with another, or from the unexpected consequences of putting a particular technique to work. Contrariwise, techniques invented for one purpose may find their governmental role for another, and the unplanned conjunction of techniques and conditions arising from very different aspirations may allow something to work without or despite its explicit rationale. The 'will to govern' needs to be understood less in terms of its success than in terms of the difficulties and the variability of operationalizing it.

Governing the National Economy

In the remainder of this chapter, we wish to illustrate some of the mechanisms to which we have drawn attention by means of a number of examples. None of these is intended as an exhaustive historical account of policy development and implementation, let alone an evaluation of policies or the politics behind them. Our concern is with 'governmentality' in the sense in which we have discussed it above, with the mentalities that have constituted the changing attempts to modulate economic activity, the varying vocabularies through which economic activity has been rendered thinkable, the different problems that have concerned these mentalities, the role of intellectual technologies of theorization and inscription within them, the diversity of regulatory technologies that have been invented together with the difficulties of implanting them, and the key role that has been taken by and accorded to expertise. It is in the assemblage formed by this heterogeneity, and in particular in the part accorded to the self-regulating activities of 'private' social actors under the guidance of expertise, that the possibility has emerged for governing the economic life of the nation in ways consonant with liberal democratic ideals.

We begin with an investigation of one attempt to 'govern' the economy through a centralized system of economic planning. Even in consideration of such 'centralized' mechanisms, it is necessary to recognize that programmes for the government of economic life do not emanate from a central point – the State. The notion of government directs attention instead to the diversity of the elements out of which particular rationalities are formed, and to the mechanisms and techniques through which they are rendered operable. Whilst the rationalities and technologies do not stand in a one-to-one relationship, the relays and linkages between them are decisive conditions for the elaboration of each. The emergence of a particular political vocabulary requires as one of its conditions of possibility the implanting of a number of mechanisms of inscription, recording and calculation. Political rationalities, even those which profess to limit the scope of government and promote autonomy and freedom of choice, require for their functioning a complex array of technologies if they are to operate.

We can illustrate the complexity of these relays and linkages between a particular political vocabulary and a range of devices for producing, tabulating and calculating information through a discussion of the development of national accounting and planning in post-war France (Fourquet 1980; Miller 1986a). National accounting is not a simple matter of mirroring the dispersed activities of individual enterprises and producers at the macro-level of the nation. Rather it is the opening up of a new domain of knowledge, involving not merely the installation of a new set of concepts by which to think of 'the economy' as an economy, but also the construction of a vast statistical apparatus through which this domain can be inscribed, tabulated, calculated and acted upon. It entails the formation of a novel relationship between government and society which makes possible distinctive forms of calculation and management of economic and social life. The process by which the national economy becomes an object of possible knowledge, calculation and possible intervention is not an unproblematic linear unfolding. The language through which the economy comes to be understood does not emerge effortlessly in the realm of an autonomous theoretical debate. And once formulated it is not a simple matter of its 'application'.

At stake in the complex process of articulating the national economy as an object to be known, recorded, calculated and operated upon is a decisive shift in the principles of government. The shift is from a notion that the ruler need do no more than extract from his or her subjects whatever wealth they may produce, to a notion that a ruler should seek to renew and even augment such wealth. This shift places the calculation of national economic resources at the heart of the objectives of government. It entails the integration of the different activities of production, consumption and investment into a table, the calculation of the proportion and movement of each of these elements, and an indication of the activities to be encouraged, the fiscal system deemed appropriate, and the correct allocation of public expenditure.

In the case of France, the development of national accounting is inseparable from the project of national planning as developed under Jean Monnet. National accounting is implicated in the attempt to undertake post-war economic reconstruction, itself part of a project of political modernization designed to eliminate elements of 'backwardness' from French society. The political vocabulary through which the project to modernize French society was formulated had as its central terms the notions of 'growth', 'progress' and 'solidarity'. It was through this political language that a variety of concrete and micro-level issues were to be thought about and acted upon. And it was by reference to this language that the categories of national accounting were articulated.

The category of production was central to this process of translating a political vocabulary into a set of techniques of recording and calculation. By means of the category of production it was possible to introduce a fundamental distinction between activities regarded as productive and those regarded as unproductive. What is production? Who is productive? Both questions lead us to the citizens, for it is through them that wealth is created and it is to them that government must look if it is to enhance its resources. Whilst one can trace certain elements of such a tradition to the late seventeenth century through the writings of Petty, King and Davenant, it is in the early post-war years that such an objective was provided with a language in terms of which it could be thought, an institutional apparatus through which it could be enacted, and a set of statistical and economic-calculative techniques through which it could be rendered operable. And it was during World War II that the process of elaborating a conceptual architecture for national accounting and establishing its statistical basis commenced in France. The role of the Vichy regime in installing a statistical infrastructure which would provide an 'avalanche of numbers' was crucial in this process. After the war these developments provided a basis for the 'programming of hope' that was national planning, the attempt to deploy the language of growth and modernization in turning France 'into a truly developed country'.

To construct a set of national accounts which would enable the requirements of planning, modernization and growth to be achieved is not a simple matter of implementing a given political vocabulary. In trying to render activities and processes in a certain manner, technologies encounter various difficulties. One important component of a system of national accounts is the input–output table. Between 1952 and 1960 the French attempted to construct a table divided according to sectors (a group of enterprises defined by their principal activity; a sector can produce various products) rather than branches (the ensemble of divisions of enterprises producing one product only) of industry. It was thought that a table organized according to sectors could be immediately integrated into the accounting system since it was based on the actual loci of decisions. But despite the massive commitment of personnel and resources, and the conceptual acrobatics of those who tried to translate accounts of enterprises organized according to sectors into accounts organized according to branches, the attempt to devise a table organized around sectors ended in failure. Statistically, the notion of a table organized according to sectors made good sense. But to work with the planning commission, a table organized around branches was required (Fourquet 1980; Miller 1986a).

A degree of congruence or translatability is thus necessary between calculative technologies and the programmes they are designed to instrumentalize. Different modes of aggregating the economic activities of the nation bring different results. Programmes of government are idealized schemata for the ordering of social and economic life. As such they are not simply 'applied' through techniques such as national planning and accounting. Programmes constitute a space within which the objectives of government are elaborated, and where plans to implement them are dreamed up. But the technologies which seek to operate on activities and processes produce their own difficulties, fail to function as intended, and sometimes intersect poorly with the rationalities in terms of which their role is conceived. The example of attempts at economic planning in post-war France not only illustrates the importance of the 'technological' side of intellectual labour in rendering a domain amenable to government – in particular the key role of inscription of technologies – but also shows that governing is not the 'realization' of a programmer's dream. 'The real' always insists in the form of resistance to programming; and the programmer's world is one of constant experiment, invention, failure, critique and adjustment.

In the theoretico-practical matrix of government, political programmes are inescapably associated with operational devices and critical judgements. Whilst a particular political programme sets out specific objectives for government, and proposes mechanisms to realize them, the operationalization of a programme is achieved through a complex and difficult process: formulating the categories and techniques to make it realizable; assembling and sometimes devising technologies to give effect to its objectives in the lives of individuals, enterprises and organizations; and evaluating, debating and contesting the consequences of such programmes and the conditions of their failure and success.

Governing the Economy at a Distance

Contemporary 'governmentality', we have argued, accords a crucial role to 'action at a distance', to mechanisms that promise to shape the conduct of diverse actors without shattering their formally autonomous character. And, we have argued, it relies, in significant ways, upon the powers and the ways of thinking and acting of expertise. In the government of the economy, one important mechanism through which this has operated is the transformation of the calculative capacities of economic actors. We can illustrate this through a discussion of economic regulation in the UK in the 1960s.

The politics of the UK from about 1962 to 1975 is conventionally seen as the high point of the interventionist state. Political arguments, from both the Conservative and Labour parties, diagnosed a failure in 'hands-off' techniques of economic regulation, in which government did not intervene directly in economic decisions, and in which the Treasury pulled various levers in order to set the overall framework within which a range of economic actors would make their calculations and decisions. This assessment of failure was itself dependent in part upon the political vocabularies and techniques of inscription that we have discussed in the previous section. At the level of what we have termed 'political rationalities', 'growth' had emerged as a key indicator of the economic health of the nation, and one by which the success or failure of economic policy was to be judged (cf. Leruez 1975). There were many differences in understanding what growth was and how it was to be achieved. For example, the Federation of British Industry and similar organizations considered it imperative that Britain be able to compete fully with other nations in the international economic order. For Labour, on the other hand, growth was to be the motor of a social dynamic for eliminating poverty and building a fair and just society. And there were various intellectual preconditions for the emergence of a discourse of growth as something that could be made calculable. Systems of national accounting such as those discussed earlier had rendered national economic activity into thought as a calculable and comparable entity. International bodies such as the OECD produced tabular comparisons of the 'rates of growth' of the industrial nations, which could then be utilized in political arguments. But these different ways of thinking about growth and calculating it operated upon a common ground: politicians, business people and academics across a large swathe operated upon the *a priori* that 'growth' was a national goal, and that new policies needed to be set in place to achieve it.

The policy changes of the 1960s are usually seen as a strengthening of the state's powers of planning and regulation of economic life. Certainly, many argued that the way in which economic agents made their decisions had to be transformed if 'growth' was to occur. But applying the notion of government to such a period suggests it is misleading to counterpose an interventionist to a non-interventionist state. One needs to conceptualize the relations differently, to attend to the diversity of mechanisms, both direct and indirect, through which political authorities have sought to act upon the entities and processes that make up a population in order to secure economic objectives, and the loose linkages between political ambitions, expert knowledge and the economic aspirations of individual firms.

Within the political vocabulary of the 1960s in the UK, the objective of economic growth was to be achieved through a number of mechanisms. Central to these were increased industrial output, improved efficiency within the enterprise, and better investment decisions. There were many initiatives through which it was hoped that this objective might be achieved, including the National Plan, the National Economic Development Council (NEDC), the Industrial Reorganization Corporation, Regional Employment Premiums and the legal regulation of industry through the 1965 Monopolies and Mergers Act. But whilst all these projects are indicative of an interventionist political aspiration, they are all equally constrained when it comes to intervening directly within the 'private' enterprise and at the micro-level of individual decisions. This is particularly so for interventions that would bear directly on the question of economic growth: investment decisions. It is here that a new relationship between thinking and doing was called for as a way of operationalizing the vocabulary of

economic growth. It is here that a way of conceptualizing investment decisions and calculating them within the enterprise was called for actually to
deliver the objective of growth through individual investment decisions.
Whilst politicians and their economic advisers could not themselves control
the actual decisions of individual enterprises, whether private or nationalized, persuading managers of the advantages of a particular technique –
Discounted Cash Flow Analysis (DCF) – held out the promise of delivering
economic growth (Miller 1989).

DCF techniques were not invented in the 1960s. But it was during this
period that they were actively promoted through government bodies such
as the NEDC and strongly recommended by the Treasury for the Nationalized Industries (HC 440/VIII 1967; NEDC 1965). In the context of a
government policy committed to some form of intervention and planning,
the regulation of individual investment decisions by means of the calculus
of DCF techniques made it possible to weaken the distinction between a
centre which would direct the economy, and individual enterprises which
would act according to instructions and inducements. DCF techniques
offered the prospect that individual firms and individual managers within
them would willingly transform the manner in which they thought about
and calculated investment opportunities. Intuition and rule of thumb would
be replaced by a new knowledge which allowed management to increase
the 'productivity of capital', in particular through the concept of the time
value of money. Personal judgement was to be replaced by the objectivity
of economic-financial calculation, which allowed management to rank
investment opportunities, compare alternatives and consider the net economic worth of particular options to the company. The widespread failure
of management objectively to calculate the investment value of individual
proposals would be counteracted if these decisions shifted toward the
centre. The language of 'growth' could thus be instrumentalized by a
specific calculative regime within this crucial area of economic life.

Thus, whilst the language of growth was one of the central features of
the political rationality of the mid-1960s, to realize such an objective at
the level of individual enterprises and in the public sector was far from
easy. Even a government disposed towards the regulation and supervision
of industry could not take over day-to-day investment decisions within
private firms or even the Nationalized Industries. The technique of DCF
analysis provided an ideal mechanism for such a situation. DCF techniques
made possible a range of renewed attempts to govern economic life 'at a
distance'. If government could not intervene directly, it could certainly
seek to act upon that group responsible for investment decisions by translating their decisions and judgements into a particular form of calculative
expertise. By promoting DCF techniques for private industry, by insisting

on their use in the Nationalized Industries, and by recommending that they be taught to management within the new business schools, the ideal of economic growth was rendered congruent with other notions such as democratic freedom, social justice and a fair standard of living. Social and private net returns on investment could be reconciled, so it was held, by transforming ways of thinking about and calculating investments. The political rationality of growth and its orientation toward the future could be rendered operable within the enterprise by a technology which made the future calculable. The processes of calculation would take place at the micro-level of the enterprise, but they would henceforth be congruent with national economic growth. 'Growth' as an ideal to be sought, an objective to be realized and a rationality by which to evaluate society was to be delivered in the final analysis not by politicians and planners but by a multitude of local centres of calculation. A political programme, it was hoped, could be rendered operable by installing a technology of incessant calculation.

Governing the Psychological World of the Enterprise

Governing involves not just the ordering of activities and processes. Governing operates through subjects. The individual manager who comes to think of investments in terms of the discounting of future cash flows is a resource for a strategy of government oriented toward economic growth. Government to that extent is a 'personal' matter, and many programmes have sought the key to their effectiveness in enrolling individuals as allies in the pursuit of political, economic and social objectives. To the extent that authoritative norms, calculative technologies and forms of evaluation can be translated into the values, decisions and judgements of citizens in their professional and personal capacities, they can function as part of the 'self-steering' mechanisms of individuals. Hence 'free' individuals and 'private' spaces can be 'ruled' without breaching their formal autonomy. To this end, many and varied programmes have placed a high value upon the capacities of subjects, and a range of technologies have sought to act on the personal capacities of subjects – as producers, consumers, parents and citizens, organizing and orienting them in the decisions and actions that seem most 'personal', and that confront them in the multitude of everyday tasks entailed in managing their own existence.

Experts have played a key role here. They have elaborated the arguments that the personal capacities of individuals can be managed in order to achieve socially desirable goals – health, adjustment, profitability, and the like. They have latched on to existing political concerns, suggesting that they have the capacity to ameliorate problems and achieve benefits. They have allied themselves with other powerful social authorities, in particular business people, translating their 'lay' problems into expert languages and suggesting that rational knowledges and planned techniques hold the key to success. They have problematized new aspects of existence and, in the very same moment, suggested that they can help overcome the problems that they have discovered. And they have acted as powerful translation devices between 'authorities' and individuals, shaping conduct not through compulsion but through the power of truth, the potency of rationality and the alluring promises of effectivity.

Again, we will take our examples from economic life, focusing here upon the internal world of the enterprise and the management of the productive subject. The government of economic life across the twentieth century entailed a range of attempts to shape and modulate the relations that individuals have with society's productive apparatus (Miller 1986b; Rose 1989a). In the process, the activities of individuals as producers have become the object of knowledge and the target of expertise, and a complex web of relays has been formed through which the economic endeavours of politicians and business people have been translated into the personal capacities and aspirations of subjects.

The programmes of 'scientific management' that were devised in the first two decades of the twentieth century – called Taylorism after their leading proponent, F. W. Taylor – are often taken as the paradigm of all 'scientific' attempts to make the worker an object of knowledge and an asset for management. Within Taylorism and associated techniques such as standard costing (Miller and O'Leary 1987), the worker was depicted as a brute, the motivations of the person were viewed as purely economic, and the only tactic available to management was to issue commands derived from the imperatives of the productive process. But Taylorism was not merely a cynical attempt to increase control over the workplace and maximize the rate of exploitation of the worker. Rather, it was one of a set of programmes articulated in the language of 'efficiency', entailing an alliance between macro-political aspirations and the powers of expertise. These programmes sought to increase the national wealth and international competitiveness of states through employing scientific knowledge and rational techniques to make the most productive use of natural, mechanical and human resources. The labouring subject came into view as an object of knowledge and a target of intervention, as an individual to be assessed, evaluated and differentiated from others, to be governed in terms of individual differences.

The productive subject, for Taylorist programmes and the technologies that sought to implement them, was essentially a passive entity to be managed externally through a complex technology of the workplace. This entailed assembling and creating a range of practical and intellectual instruments to produce what Taylor termed the 'mechanism' of scientific management: standard tools, adjustable scaffolds; methods and implements of time study, books and records, desks for planners to work at, experiments leading to the establishment of formulae to replace the individual judgement of workers, a differentiation of work into standard tasks, written instructions and instruction cards, bonus and premium payments, the scientific selection of the 'working man', and many more (Thevenot 1984). This list may be heterogeneous, but, as Thevenot points out, for Taylor its elements were parts of a single mechanism. Taylor here provides a perfect example of what we have termed a technology of government, an attempt to produce a stable, standard and reproducible form of relations amongst persons and things that purports to enable production to be undertaken predictably in the most efficient manner.

But Taylorism does not provide a diagram for all technical interventions to govern the productive subject through expertise. In Britain in the interwar years, a new vocabulary and technology for programming the employment relationship was born, associated in particular with the writings of Charles Myers and the work of the National Institute of Industrial Psychology (cf. Myers 1927). This way of construing the productive subject had intellectual conditions of possibility, in the 'new psychology' of instincts and adjustment that had been formulated in the years following World War I, and in the mental hygiene movement that sought the roots of a plethora of social troubles in the minor and untreated problems of mental life that prevented efficient functioning (Rose 1985). When this intellectual technology was applied to industry, it had three distinctive features. First, it addressed the relationship individuals have with their selves in their work. The worker came to be viewed as having a personal life that continued into his or her productive work, and that influenced the ways in which it was carried out. The worker was to be understood as an individual with a mind, with fears and anxieties. Not just monotony, fatigue and attentiveness, but motivation and morale became a concern for various expertises of the psyche. This way of construing the psychology of the working individual was linked to a range of attempts to produce congruence between the needs of production and the motives, fears and wants of the worker. Second, this new vocabulary brought into view the relationships that individuals have with other workers – colleagues, superiors and subordinates. The informal life of the enterprise emerged as a new terrain to be known through expert investigations and administered by expertise. Third, this language established interdependence between the worker viewed as a productive machine and the worker viewed as a person with a family and home life. Departures from norms in a worker's home and personal life could henceforth be seen to have possibly disruptive effects on his or her work performance. From now on, the mental hygiene of the worker would be a key concern for experts, for managers, for bosses and for politicians (Miller and Rose 1988).

This new attentiveness to the personal dimension of the productive process was more than simply a concern to increase productivity. Doubtless this objective animates the history of the capitalist enterprise. Doubtless too the new promoters of mental hygiene sought to convince the bosses that their expertise would contribute to such an end. But the novel ways of understanding the relationship of the worker to the productive apparatus in the inter-war years contributed more than this. They opened up a new domain of knowledge and possible intervention. This had as its objective to ensure that the bond linking the individual to the enterprise, and also the individual to society, would henceforth not be solely economic. The wage relation and the power of the boss would be supplemented by a personal bond that would attach individuals to the lives they lived in the world of work, to their co-workers and bosses, and to society as a whole (Miller 1986b). It would be possible to conceive of administering the working environment to ensure simultaneously the contentment and health of the worker and the profitability and efficiency of the enterprise. Macro-political programmes, the quest for profit on the part of entrepreneurs and the personal well-being of employees could at least in principle be brought into alignment through a psychological expertise that was allied with none of these parties but only with the values of truth and rationality.

Within this new set of programmes and technologies of the productive subject, the subjectivity of the worker still tended to be viewed in terms of individual capacities, and judged in the negative sense of departures from norms. The worker was still to be administered externally, by a wise and prescient management informed by a rational knowledge and a neutral expertise. Following World War II, a further transformation occurred in conceptions of the worker which entailed the formulation of a concern with positive mental health in the workplace. 'Defective' individuals still had to be identified, but a more important terrain was to be opened up – one that would seek to optimize the mental health of all individuals in their relation to their work. New alliances had been forged between industrialists, psychologists, managers and politicians in the course of managing the human problems of the war: it appeared that the enlightened administration of human relationships in work and elsewhere could maximize contentment at the same time as it maximized productivity, as well as corresponding to the values of democracy with its respect for the citizen (e.g. Brown 1954; Taylor 1950). The responsibility for promoting the health of a society did not reside just in its medical services, but also in its social practitioners – managers, politicians, teachers and others in positions of leadership. These new concerns were articulated in terms of the expert management of human relations in groups. In the new vocabulary of group relations, the intersubjective life of the enterprise could be construed as a vital mechanism upon which government should operate, not only binding the individual psychologically into the production process, but also, through work, linking the worker into the social order as a democratic citizen with rights and responsibilities.

The new technologies of the enterprise promoted by government reports, management organizations and industrial psychologists sought to instrumentalize its relational life for economic ends (Miller and Rose 1988). It appeared that the subjective capacities and intersubjective dynamics of employees could be shaped and utilized in a way that would simultaneously recognize the stake of the employee in the firm and the stake of the firm in the employee. Leadership could be utilized as a resource for management, not only the leadership capacities of the top employees, but also those of crucial intermediaries such as foremen. The key to this technology was that leadership could be re-conceptualized, not as an individual quality to be obtained by careful selection procedures, but as the effectiveness of an individual in a specific role within a specific group united for a particular purpose. Hence leadership could be produced and promoted by a relational technology of the workplace, a calculated reorganization of the relations of persons and tasks.

Similarly, it was argued by industrial psychologists that industrial accidents should not be understood as the result of personal attributes. 'Accident-proneness' rather should be understood as a phenomenon of the group. Accidents were to become social as well as personal events, caused by virtue of the fact that the people concerned are members of some kind of work organization. In this and other ways, the vocabulary of the group provided here a new route for understanding and operating on the personal dimension of productive activity. Productivity and efficiency were now to be understood in terms of the attitudes of workers to their work, their feelings of control over their place of work and environment, their sense of cohesion within their small working group, and their beliefs about the concern and understanding that the bosses had for their individual worth and their personal problems.

It is not just that a new vocabulary emerges for speaking about the tasks of management. It is that a new importance is accorded to regulating the internal psychological world of the worker through a calculated administration of the human relations of the workplace, in order to turn the personal wishes of the employee from an obstacle into an ally of economic efficiency. This aspiration sought to overcome the opposition between work as a sphere of dull compulsion within which selfhood is denied or suppressed, and the home, family and leisure as spheres for the satisfaction of personal wants and the realization of the self. From this time forth, management would seek to recruit the self-regulating capacities of the worker, the desires of the worker for his or her personal goals, for its own ends. A neutral, rational and humane expertise was to assume the task of aligning the ethics of the worker as a psychological individual with needs with the bosses' quest for profitability.

Rendering the intersubjective world of the factory into thought as a calculable entity required more than a new theory, it entailed the invention of new devices to chart and evaluate it. Social psychologists were to enter the workplace, using such instruments as non-directed interviews to get at the thoughts, attitudes and sentiments amongst workers, foremen, supervisors, and so forth, which gave rise to problems, dissatisfactions and conflict (Rose 1989a). Techniques of measurement and scaling could be developed and deployed in order to render intersubjectivity into tables and charts which could give management material upon which to calculate, to diagnose the problems of the factory, to evaluate the consequences of this or that initiative. And the technology of the interview was a regulatory mechanism in its own right, for in speaking and being heard, workers' subjective states were to be transformed, frustrations dispelled, anxieties reduced, contentment increased and solidarity and commitment enhanced.

In the 1950s and 1960s, the social psychological experts of industry, and the management theorists with whom they allied, did not confine their programmatic aspirations within the factory walls. The new vocabulary of the group and its attendant technologies established a series of relays connecting interventions on the interior life of the enterprise and calculations concerning the economic well-being of the nation. The notion of the proper sphere of politics and appropriate modes of intervention by the state was transformed. A variety of programmes argued for a complete reorganization of industry and the economy along social psychological lines (e.g. Brown and Jacques 1965; Emery and Thorsrud 1969; Taylor 1950; Trist et al. 1963). These programmes in their stronger forms may have remained little more than a dream in the United Kingdom, though not in Denmark, Norway, Sweden and elsewhere. In any event, the point of these new ways of thinking about and acting upon the workplace and the worker is less to do with 'implementation' in a particular context, and more to do with the new relations that they make possible. Expertise could henceforth secure its position by linking the values of economic productivity, political democracy and personal contentment into a single theoretico-practical matrix.

Governing the Autonomous Self

The forms of political rationality that took shape in the first half of the twentieth century constituted the citizen as a social being whose powers and obligations were articulated in the language of social responsibilities and collective solidarities. The individual was to be integrated into society in the form of a citizen with social needs, in a contract in which individual and society had mutual claims and obligations. A diversity of programmes for social security, child welfare, physical and mental hygiene, universal education and even the form and content of popular entertainment operated within this rationale and numerous technologies were invented – from social insurance to the child guidance clinic – that sought to give effect to it.

The three decades after the end of World War II may be seen as a high point of these ways of thinking and acting, marked by attempts to weld these diverse programmes and technologies into a coherent and centrally directed system. But, commencing in the mid-1980s, there was an apparently decisive displacement of these political rationalities. Not only within the revived vocabulary of neo-liberalism, but also in political programmes articulated from the centre and the left of the political field and from more radical critics, the language of freedom, autonomy and choice increasingly came to regulate arguments over the legitimate means and ends of political power.

No longer was citizenship construed in terms of solidarity, contentment, welfare and a sense of security established through the bonds of organizational and social life. Citizenship was to be active and individualistic rather than passive and dependent. The political subject was to be an individual whose citizenship was manifested through the free exercise of personal choice amongst a variety of options (cf. Meyer 1986a). Programmes of government were to be evaluated in terms of the extent to which they enhanced that choice. And the language of individual freedom, personal choice and self-fulfilment came to underpin programmes of government articulated from across the political spectrum, from politicians and professionals, pressure groups and civil libertarians alike.

Such a new political language may be seen as an ephemeral phenomenon, as ideology or as merely a reprise on the atomistic individualism characteristic of capitalism. However, the perspective we have sketched out in this chapter suggests a different approach, one that emphasizes the manner in which this new language not only served to articulate and legitimate a diversity of programmes for rectifying problematic areas of economic and social life, but also enabled these programmes to be translated into a range of technologies to administer individuals, groups and sectors in a way that was consonant with prevailing ethical systems and political mentalities (Rose 1989b). We can illustrate this by focusing upon the notions of enterprise and choice that were so central to doctrines of the new right in many countries and regions for more than two decades.

The language of enterprise became so significant, we suggest, because it enabled a translatability between the most general *a priori* of political thought and a range of specific programmes for administering the national economy, the internal world of the firm and a whole host of other organizations from the school to the hospital, reframing them as discrete entities pursing their undertakings as enterprises (cf. Gordon 1987). The notion of choice today plays a similar role, underpinning the reform of virtually all public services and forming new relations between acts of consumption in the market and acts of consumption in domains long viewed as outside the market, such as health care and education.

Within these rationalities, new relations could be formed between the economic health of the nation and the 'private' choices of individuals. The citizen was assigned a vital economic role in his or her activity as a consumer. Consumers were considered as, in a sense, entrepreneurs of themselves, seeking to maximize their 'quality of life' through the artful assembly of a 'lifestyle' put together through the world of goods. The expertise of market research, of promotion and communication, provides the relays through which the aspirations of ministers, the ambitions of business and the dreams of consumers achieve mutual translatability. Design, marketing and image construction play a vital role in the transfiguring of goods into desires and vice versa, imbuing each commodity with a 'personal' meaning, a glow cast back upon those who purchase it, illuminating the kind of person they are, or want to become. Through this loose assemblage of agents, calculations, techniques, images and commodities, consumer choice can be made an ally of economic growth: economic life can be governed through the choices consumers make in their search for personally fulfilling forms of existence.

Similarly, the rationalities of personal autonomy and self-fulfilment could be linked to a transformation in programmes and technologies for regulating the internal world of the enterprise (e.g. Peters and Waterman 1982; see Rose 1989a). The vocabulary of enterprise provided versatile tools for thought: the worker was no longer construed as a social creature seeking satisfaction of his or her need for security, solidarity and welfare, but as an individual actively seeking to shape and manage his or her own life in order to maximize its returns in terms of success and achievement. Organizations were to get the most out of their employees, not by managing group relations to maximize contentment, or by rationalizing management to ensure efficiency, but by releasing the psychological strivings of individuals for autonomy and creativity and channelling them into the search of the firm for excellence and success. Psychological consultants to the organization charted the cultural world of the enterprise in terms of its success in capitalizing upon the motivations and aspirations of its inhabitants and invented a whole range of new technologies in order to give effect to these programmes by reducing dependency, encouraging internal competitiveness and stimulating individual entrepreneurship.

The 'autonomous' subjectivity of the productive individual was a central economic resource in such programmes: autonomy was to be an ally of economic success, not an obstacle to be controlled and disciplined. The self-regulating capacities of individuals were to be aligned with economic objectives through the kinds of loose and indirect mechanisms that we have described earlier: the capacities of language to translate between rationalities, programmes, technologies and self-regulatory techniques, and the particular persuasive role of expertise. These programmes also sought to act upon the selves of managers: as innumerable training courses and seminars argued, to become a better manager was to become a better self. The values of self-realization, the skills of self-presentation, self-direction and self-management were both personally seductive and economically desirable. Expertise played the role of relay, teaching managers the arts of self-realization that would fulfil them as individuals as well as employees. Economic success, career progress and personal development intersect in this new expertise of autonomous subjectivity.

No doubt there is a considerable discrepancy between the images portrayed in the proliferating texts written along these lines, and the reality of the practices of management. And, no doubt, the promises of this new generation of programmers of the enterprise will soon be deemed to have failed: increased productivity, improved flexibility and enhanced competitiveness will still prove elusive goals. But it is more than ideology that can be observed here. As with the previous illustrations, what is at issue here is the establishing of connections and symmetries, at both the conceptual and practical level, between political concerns about the government of the productive life of the nation, the concerns of owners of capital to maximize the economic advantages of their companies, and techniques for the governing of the subject. Expertises of the enterprise play a crucial role in linking up these distinct concerns into a functioning network. Their languages and techniques provide both the necessary distance between political authorities and organizational life, and the translatability to establish an alliance between national economic health, increased organizational effectiveness and progressive and humanistic values.

Conclusion

In this chapter we have suggested that Michel Foucault's concept of 'governmentality' can be usefully developed to analyse the complex and heterogeneous ways in which contemporary social authorities have sought to shape and regulate economic, social and personal activities. We have proposed an analysis of political rationalities that pays particular attention to the role of language, and the language of social science in particular. Vocabularies and theories are important not so much because of the meanings that they produce, but as intellectual technologies, ways of rendering existence thinkable and practicable, amenable to the distinctive influence of various techniques of inscription, notation and calculation.

We have sought to draw attention in particular to the programmatic character of government, and to suggest that an analysis of this programmatic field of government should not be restricted to a judgement of success or failure. We have highlighted the ways in which expert knowledges, and experts as accredited and skilled persons professing neutrality and efficacy, have mobilized, and have been mobilized, within such programmes. We have argued that an analysis of modern 'governmentality' needs to free itself from a focus upon 'the state' and from a restricted conception of the kinds of mechanism through which authorities seek to regulate the activities of a differentiated assembly of social agencies and forces. Further, we have proposed that the analysis of 'governmentality' needs to be accompanied by an investigation of the 'technologies' which seek or claim to give effect to the aspirations of programmers. Our argument has been that in advanced liberal democracies such as our own, these technologies increasingly seek to act upon and instrumentalize the self-regulating propensities of individuals in order to ally them with socio-political objectives.

A range of 'new technologies' have been devised which provide citizens as economic and social actors with numerous techniques through which they can instrumentalize the diverse spheres of social life themselves, in order to avoid what they have come to consider unwelcome and achieve what they have come to believe they want. In this context, the rise to prominence since the 1980s of political rationalities placing emphasis upon the self-government of individuals, and seeking to limit the incidence of 'the state' upon the lives and decisions of individuals, can be seen as one articulation, at the level of a political rationality, of the new possibilities for political rule which these technologies have established. Political authorities no longer seek to govern by instructing individuals in all spheres of their existence, from the most intimate to the most public. Individuals themselves, as workers, managers and members of families, can be mobilized in alliance with political objectives, in order to deliver economic growth, successful enterprise and optimum personal happiness. Programmes of government can utilize and rely upon a complex net of technologies – in management, in marketing, in advertising, in instructional talks on the mass media of communication – for educating citizens in techniques for governing themselves. Modern political power does not take the form of the domination of subjectivity (Miller 1987). Rather, political power has come to depend upon a web of technologies for fabricating and maintaining self-government.

3

Political Power beyond the State
Problematics of Government

The state, wrote Nietzsche, is 'the coldest of all cold monsters . . . [it] lies in all languages of good and evil; and whatever its says, it lies – and whatever it has, it has stolen . . . only there, where the state ceases, does the man who is not superfluous begin' (Nietzsche 1969: 75). As post-war 'welfare states' in the West and centralized 'party states' in the East have come under challenge, contemporary political debate has become suffused by images of the state as malign and potentially monstrous. Only 'beyond the State', it appears, can a life worthy of free human individuals begin. Criticizing the excesses, inefficiencies and injustices of the extended state, alternatives have been posed in terms of the construction of a 'free market' and a 'civil society' in which a plurality of groups, organizations and individuals interact in liberty. This concern has been paralleled in social theory, where analysts have challenged liberal pluralist and economic determinist theories of power, and argued that the specific form of the state is of crucial importance, not only in understanding geo-political relations, but also in comprehending modern forms of exercise of power over national territories (e.g. Evans et al. 1985; Jessop 1990).

But the political vocabulary structured by oppositions between state and civil society, public and private, government and market, coercion and consent, sovereignty and autonomy, and the like, does not adequately characterize the diverse ways in which rule is exercised in advanced liberal democracies. Political power is exercised today through a profusion of shifting alliances between diverse authorities in projects to govern a multitude of facets of economic activity, social life and individual conduct. Power is not so much a matter of imposing constraints upon citizens as of 'making up' citizens capable of bearing a kind of regulated freedom.

Personal autonomy is not the antithesis of political power, but a key term in its exercise, the more so because most individuals are not merely the subjects of power but play a part in its operations.

Our aim here is to propose some ways of analysing these mobile mechanisms of contemporary political power. Our analysis relocates 'the state' within an investigation of *problematics of government*. As Foucault argued, the concepts that organize conventional ways of thinking about power cannot comprehend the exercise of power in modern societies: two centuries after the political revolutions that overthrew the absolutist monarchies of Europe, in the field of political thought we had not yet cut off the king's head (Foucault 1978: 88–9). In his remarks on 'governmentality' Foucault sketches an alternative analytic of political power (Foucault 1979; cf. Burchell et al. 1991). The term 'governmentality' sought to draw attention to a certain way of thinking and acting embodied in all those attempts to know and govern the wealth, health and happiness of populations. Foucault argued that, since the eighteenth century, this way of reflecting upon power and seeking to render it operable had achieved pre-eminence over other forms of political power. It was linked to the proliferation of a whole range of apparatuses pertaining to government and a complex body of knowledges and 'know-how' about government, the means of its exercise and the nature of those over whom it was to be exercised. From this perspective on political power, Foucault suggested, one might avoid overvaluing the 'problem of the State', seeing it either as a *'monstre froid'* confronting and dominating us, or as the essential and privileged fulfilment of a number of necessary social and economic functions. The state possessed neither the unity nor the functionality ascribed to it; it was a 'mythical abstraction' which has assumed a particular place within the field of government. For the present, perhaps, what is really important 'is not so much the State-domination of society, but the "governmentalization" of the State' (Foucault 1979: 20).

These schematic remarks form the starting point for the investigations of government proposed in this chapter. We propose an 'analytic' of problematics of government, and illustrate this through a preliminary investigation of 'liberalism', 'welfarism' and 'neo-liberalism'. The mentalities of government that we explore are not merely traces, signs, causes or effects of 'real' transformations in social relations. The terrain they constitute has a density and a significance of its own. Government is the historically constituted matrix within which are articulated all those dreams, schemes, strategies and manoeuvres of authorities that seek to shape the beliefs and conduct of others in desired directions by acting upon their will, their circumstances or their environment. It is in relation to this grid of government that specifically political forms of rule in the modern West define, delimit and relate themselves.

Central to the possibility of modern forms of government, we argue, are the associations formed between entities constituted as 'political' and the projects, plans and practices of those authorities – economic, legal, spiritual, medical, technical – who endeavour to administer the lives of others in the light of conceptions of what is good, healthy, normal, virtuous, efficient or profitable. Knowledge is thus central to these activities of government and to the very formation of its objects, for government is a domain of cognition, calculation, experimentation and evaluation. And, we argue, government is intrinsically linked to the activities of expertise, whose role is one not of weaving an all-pervasive web of 'social control', but of enacting assorted attempts at the calculated administration of diverse aspects of conduct through countless, often competing, local tactics of education, persuasion, inducement, management, incitement, motivation and encouragement.

Problematics of government may be analysed, first of all, in terms of their *political rationalities*, the changing discursive fields within which the exercise of power is conceptualized, the moral justifications for particular ways of exercising power by diverse authorities, notions of the appropriate forms, objects and limits of politics, and conceptions of the proper distribution of such tasks among secular, spiritual, military and familial sectors. But, we suggest, problematics of government should also be analysed in terms of their *governmental technologies*, the complex of mundane programmes, calculations, techniques, apparatuses, documents and procedures through which authorities seek to embody and give effect to governmental ambitions. Through an analysis of the intricate interdependencies between political rationalities and governmental technologies, we can begin to understand the multiple and delicate networks that connect the lives of individuals, groups and organizations to the aspirations of authorities in the advanced liberal democracies of the present.

Government versus the State

Many have recognized that the philosophical and constitutional images of the sovereign state are misleading. To the extent that the modern state 'rules', it does so on the basis of an elaborate network of relations formed amongst the complex of institutions, organizations and apparatuses that make it up, and between state and non-state institutions (cf. Harden and Lewis 1986; Schmitter 1974; Schmitter and Lehmbruch 1979). Sociological histories of state formation have shown that, in Europe for many centuries, economic activity was regulated, order was maintained, laws were promulgated and enforced, assistance was provided for the sick and needy, morality was inculcated, if at all, through practices that had little to do with the state. It was only in the eighteenth century that states began to be transformed from limited and circumscribed central apparatuses to embed themselves within an ensemble of institutions and procedures of rule over a national territory (Poggi 1978; Tilly 1975; see also Foucault 1980a).

Historical sociologists have analysed diverse mechanisms of state formation: the imposition of a national language and a level of literacy, a common coinage; the fusing of a territory into a single time-space system through innovations in transportation, communication and temporality; the unification of legal codes and authorities (Giddens 1985). Key practices of rule were institutionalized within a central, more or less permanent body of offices and agencies, given a certain more or less explicit constitutional form, endowed with the capacity to raise funds in the form of taxes, and backed with the virtual monopoly of the legitimate use of force over a defined territory. This coincidence of a defined territory of rule and a project and apparatus for administering the lives and activities of those within that territory, it is suggested, warrants us to speak of the modern nation-state as a centralized set of institutions and personnel wielding authoritative power over a nation (see, for example, Baechler et al. 1988; Hall 1986; Hall and Ikenberry 1989; Mann 1986, 1988). Further, it has been argued that geo-political relations and military conflicts have provoked and facilitated the centralization of domestic political power in the hands of a state apparatus. These considerations have led analysts to treat states as unified actors with considerable autonomy, ruling domestically and pursuing their interests upon the world stage by means of diplomacy and warfare (Giddens 1985; Mann 1988; Wallerstein 1984).

We argue that such a perspective obscures the characteristics of modern forms of political power. Within the problematics of government, one can be nominalistic about the state: it has no essential necessity or functionality. Rather, the state can be seen as a specific way in which the problem of government is discursively codified, a way of dividing a 'political sphere', with its particular characteristics of rule, from other 'non-political spheres' to which it must be related, and a way in which certain technologies of government are given a temporary institutional durability and brought into particular kinds of relations with one another. Posed from this perspective, the question is no longer one of accounting for government in terms of 'the power of the State', but one of ascertaining how, and to what extent, the state is articulated into the activity of government: what relations are established between political and other authorities; what funds, forces, persons, knowledge or legitimacy is utilized; and by means of what devices and techniques these different tactics are made operable.

Three differences between our approach and the new sociology of state formation are relevant here. The first concerns 'realism'. Historical sociologies of the state are realist in the sense that they seek to characterize the actual configurations of persons, organizations and events at particular historical periods, to classify the force relations that obtain between them, to identify determinants and explain transformations. Our studies of government eschew sociological realism and its burdens of explanation and causation. We do not try to characterize how social life *really* was and why. We do not seek to penetrate the surfaces of what people said to discover what they meant, what their real motives or interests were. Rather, we attend to the ways in which authorities in the past have posed themselves these questions: what is our power; to what ends should it be exercised; what effects has it produced; how can we know what we need to know, and do what we need to do in order to govern?

Second, language. An analysis of government takes as central not so much amounts of revenue, size of the court, expenditure on arms, miles marched by an army per day, as the discursive field within which these problems, sites and forms of visibility are delineated and accorded significance. It is in this discursive field that 'the State' itself emerges as an historically variable linguistic device for conceptualizing and articulating ways of ruling. The significance we accord to discourse does not arise from a concern with 'ideology'. Language is not merely contemplative or justificatory, it is performative. An analysis of political discourse helps us elucidate not only *the systems of thought* through which authorities have posed and specified the problems for government, but also the *systems of action* through which they have sought to give effect to government.

Third, knowledge. Knowledge here does not simply mean 'ideas', but refers to the vast assemblage of persons, theories, projects, experiments and techniques that has become such a central component of government. Theories from philosophy to medicine. Schemes from town planning to social insurance. Techniques from double-entry book-keeping to compulsory medical inspection of schoolchildren. Knowledgeable persons from generals to architects and accountants. Our concern, that is to say, is with the 'know-how' that has promised to make government possible.

Our analysis applies as much to geo-political issues as to those within any national territory. Inter-'national' relations are constituted in a military-diplomatic complex, through complex processes that empower particular agents and forces to speak and act in the name of a territory (Dillon 1989). These establish the limits and coherence of the domains of political authority, demarcate the geographical and conceptual spaces of political rule, constitute certain authorities as able to speak for a population, and place them in particular 'external' configurations with other 'states' and internal relations with events in particular locales. A 'geo-political' field is established, embodying diplomacy, envoys, treaties, agreements, borders, customs, and the like, at the same time as the writ of authorities is claimed over the subjects and activities composing a nation.

War, as a key aspect of such geo-political issues, is itself dependent upon certain practices of government: the elaboration of notions of national sovereignty over a territory unified by practices such as language or law; the development of administrative machineries of various types; and techniques for constituting persons as owing allegiance to a particular locus of identity and authority. Warfare and colonialism, as the exercise of rule from a centre over distant persons, places and goods, involve assembling subjects into military forces, disciplining them, inculcating skills and solidarities, producing, distributing and maintaining equipment and material as well as inventing the intellectual technologies required for strategy and planning. Warfare, that is to say, requires and inspires the invention of new practices of government: in geo-political relations too, we suggest, the state should first of all be understood as a complex and mobile resultant of the discourses and techniques of rule.

Political Rationalities and the Analysis of Liberalism

In what follows, building on our previous studies of specific domains, we elaborate some conceptual tools for an analysis of modern forms of government (see Miller 1986a; Miller and O'Leary 1987, 1989a; Miller and Rose 1986, 1988, 1990 [reproduced as chapter 2 of this volume]; Rose 1985, 1989a; see also Gordon 1980, 1987). Let us begin by considering the notion of political rationality. Political discourse is a domain for the formulation and justification of idealized schemata for representing reality, analysing it and rectifying it. Whilst it does not have the systematic and closed character of disciplined bodies of theoretical discourse, it is, nonetheless, possible to discern regularities that we term political rationalities. First, political rationalities have a characteristically *moral* form. They elaborate upon the fitting powers and duties for authorities. They address the proper distribution of tasks and actions between authorities of different types – political, spiritual, military, pedagogic, familial. They consider the ideals or principles to which government should be directed – freedom, justice, equality, mutual responsibility, citizenship, common sense, economic efficiency, prosperity, growth, fairness, rationality, and the like.

Second, political rationalities have what one might term an *epistemological* character. That is to say, they are articulated in relation to some conception of the nature of the objects governed – society, the nation, the population, the economy. In particular, they embody some account of the persons over whom government is to be exercised. As Paul Veyne has pointed out, these can be specified as members of a flock to be led, legal subjects with rights, children to be educated, a resource to be exploited, elements of a population to be managed (Veyne 1978, translation cited from Burchell 1991).

Third, political rationalities are articulated in a distinctive *idiom*. The language that constitutes political discourse is more than rhetoric (Miller and Rose 1990 [reproduced as chapter 2 of this volume]; see also Connelly 1987; McCloskey 1985; Nelson et al. 1987; Shapiro 1984; Taylor 1987). It should be seen, rather, as a kind of intellectual machinery or apparatus for rendering reality thinkable in such a way that it is amenable to political deliberations. It is here that a vocabulary of 'the State' has come to codify and contest the nature and limits of political power. Political rationalities, that is to say, are morally coloured, grounded upon knowledge, and made thinkable through language.

We can illustrate these three points if we consider the question of 'liberalism'. Liberalism is usually characterized as a political philosophy by the limits it places on the legitimate exercise of power by political authorities. During the second half of the eighteenth century the term 'civil society' ceased to designate a particular type of well-ordered political association, and came to signify, instead, a natural realm of freedoms and activities outside the legitimate sphere of politics (for discussion of the concept of civil society in these terms, and attempts to revive the principle for modern times, see Keane 1984, 1988a, 1988b). The scope of political authority was to be limited, and vigilance was to be exercised over it. Yet, simultaneously, government was to take as one of its obligations and legitimate tasks the fostering of the self-organizing capacities of civil society. Political rule was given the task of shaping and nurturing that very civil society that was to provide its counterweight and limit.

Liberalism, in this respect, marks the moment when the dystopian dream of a totally administered society was abandoned, and government was confronted with a domain that had its own naturalness, its own rules and processes, and its own internal forms of self-regulation (Foucault 1986). As Graham Burchell has pointed out, liberalism disqualifies the exercise of governmental reason in the form of *raison d'état*, in which a sovereign exercised his totalizing will across a national space (Burchell 1991). Power is confronted, on the one hand, with subjects equipped with rights that *must not* be interdicted by government. On the other hand, government addresses a realm of processes that it *cannot* govern by the exercise of sovereign will because it lacks the requisite knowledge and capacities. The objects, instruments and tasks of government must be reformulated with reference to this domain of civil society with the aim of promoting its maximal functioning.

The constitutional and legal codification and delimitation of the powers of political authorities did not so much 'free' a private realm from arbitrary interferences by power as constitute certain realms, such as those of market transactions, the family and the business undertaking, as 'non-political', defining their form and limits. Liberal doctrines on the limits of power and the freedom of subjects under the law were thus accompanied by the working out of a range of new technologies of government, not having the form of direct control by authorities, that sought to administer these 'private' realms, and to programme and shape them in desired directions.

This does not mean that liberalism was an ideology, disguising a state annexation of freedom. The inauguration of liberal societies in Europe accords a vital role to a key characteristic of modern government: *action at a distance* (as noted in the previous chapter, we adapt this term from Bruno Latour and Michel Callon: see Callon 1986; Callon and Latour 1981; Callon et al. 1986; cf. Miller and Rose 1990 [reproduced as chapter 2 of this volume]). Liberal mentalities of government do not conceive of the regulation of conduct as dependent only upon political actions: the imposition of law; the activities of state functionaries or publicly controlled bureaucracies; surveillance and discipline by an all-seeing police. Liberal government identifies a domain outside 'politics', and seeks to manage it without destroying its existence and its autonomy. This is made possible through the activities and calculations of a proliferation of independent agents, including philanthropists, doctors, hygienists, managers, planners, parents and social workers. And it is dependent upon the forging of alliances. This takes place, on the one hand, between political strategies and the activities of these authorities and, on the other, between these authorities and free citizens, in attempts to modulate events, decisions and actions in the economy, the family, the private firm, and the conduct of the individual person.

The elaboration of liberal doctrines of freedom went hand in hand with projects to make liberalism operable by producing the 'subjective' conditions under which its contractual notions of the mutual relations between citizen and society could work (Castel 1976; Foucault 1977). Those who could not carry out their contractual obligations were now to appear 'anti-social', and to be confined under a new legitimacy. The scandalous and bizarre were to be placed under a revised medical mandate, in asylums that promised to cure and not merely to incarcerate. Law-breakers and malefactors were no longer to have the status of bandits or rebels, but were to become transgressors of norms motivated by defects of character amenable to understanding and rectification.

The invention of the disciplinary institutions of prison and asylum was accompanied by the promulgation of a variety of programmes by lawyers, doctors, philanthropists and other experts, who claimed to know how to direct business activity, family life and personal morality onto the path of virtue. 'The State' was not the inspirer of these programmes of government, nor was it the necessary beneficiary. What one sees is not a uniform trend of 'State intervention' but rather the emergence, at a multitude of sites in the social body, of health and disease, of crime and punishment, of poverty and pauperism, of madness and family life as problems requiring some measure of collective response, and in relation to which political authorities play a variety of different roles (Foucault 1980a).

The domain of politics is thus simultaneously distinguished from other spheres of rule, and inextricably bound into them. Political forces have sought to utilize, instrumentalize and mobilize techniques and agents other than those of 'the State' in order to govern 'at a distance'; other authorities have sought to govern economic, familial and social arrangements according to their own programmes and to mobilize political resources for their own ends.

Programmes of Government

Government is a *problematizing* activity: it poses the obligations of rulers in terms of the problems they seek to address. The ideals of government are intrinsically linked to the problems around which it circulates, the failings it seeks to rectify, the ills it seeks to cure. Indeed, the history of government might well be written as a history of problematizations, in which politicians, intellectuals, philosophers, medics, military strategists, feminists and philanthropists have measured the real against the ideal and found it wanting. From the danger of de-population, the threats posed by pauperism or the forecasts of the decline of the race, through the problematization of urban unrest, industrial militancy, failures of productivity, to contemporary concerns with international competitiveness, the articulation of government has been bound to the constant identification of the difficulties and failures of government.

It is around these difficulties and failures that *programmes of government* have been elaborated. The programmatic is the realm of designs put forward by philosophers, political economists, physiocrats and philanthropists, government reports, committees of inquiry, White Papers, proposals and counterproposals by organizations of business, labour, finance, charities and professionals that seek to configure specific locales and relations in ways thought desirable. The relation between political rationalities and such programmes of government is one not of derivation or determination but of *translation* – both a movement from one space to another, and an expression of a particular concern in another modality. Thus in the early years of the twentieth century in Britain, the language of national efficiency served to articulate general political ideals concerning the ends to which government should be addressed, and provided a way of formulating a range of competing programmes and disputes from different political forces (Miller and O'Leary 1987; Rose 1985). Similarly, programmes for administering the enterprise in the USA in the inter-war period elaborated the basis of managerial authority in a way that was congruent with American ideals of personal freedom, initiative and democracy. A translatability was established between the ideals of American political culture and programmes for governing the newly emerged giant corporations with their professional managers (Miller and O'Leary 1989a, 1990; see also Miller 1991b). Such translatability between the moralities, epistemologies and idioms of political power, and the government of a specific problem space, establishes a mutuality between what is desirable and what can be made possible through the calculated activities of political forces (Miller and Rose 1988; Rose 1989a).

Programmes, as Colin Gordon has pointed out, are not simply formulations of wishes or intentions (Gordon 1980; see Miller and Rose 1989). First of all, programmes lay claim to a certain knowledge of the sphere or problem to be addressed – knowledges of the economy, or of the nature of health, or of the problem of poverty are essential elements in programmes that seek to exercise legitimate and calculated power over them. Governing a sphere requires that it can be represented, depicted in a way which both grasps its truth and re-presents it in a form in which it can enter the sphere of conscious political calculation. The theories of the social sciences, of economics, of sociology and of psychology, thus provide a kind of *intellectual machinery* for government, in the form of procedures for rendering the world thinkable, taming its intractable reality by subjecting it to the disciplined analyses of thought.

Theories and explanations therefore play an essential part in reversing the relations of power between the aspiring ruler and that over which rule is to be exercised. For example, as discussed in the previous chapter, before one can seek to manage a domain such as an economy it is first necessary to conceptualize a set of processes and relations as an economy which is amenable to management (Miller and O'Leary 1989a; see also Hopwood 1987; Thompson 1982; Tomlinson 1981a, 1983). In a very real sense, 'the economy' is brought into being by economic theories themselves, which define and individuate a set of characteristics, laws and processes designated economic rather than, say, political or natural. This enables 'the economy' to become something which politicians, academics, industrialists and others think can be governed and managed, evaluated and programmed, in order to increase wealth, profit, and the like. Similarly sociology, as a set of techniques and investigations that reveal the nation as a set of aggregated statistics with their regular fluctuations, and as knowable processes with their laws and cycles, has played a key role in the constitution of society and its diverse components and domains as a governable entity. Relations of reciprocity obtain between the social sciences and government. As government depends upon these sciences for its languages and calculations, so the social sciences thrive on the problems of government, the demand for solutions and the attraction of theories which have the plausibility of science and the promise of the rational disciplining and technologizing of the social field.

Programmes presuppose that the real is programmable, that it is a domain subject to certain determinants, rules, norms and processes that can be acted upon and improved by authorities. They make the objects of government thinkable in such a way that their ills appear susceptible to diagnosis, prescription and cure by calculating and normalizing intervention.

Technologies of Government

Government is a domain of strategies, techniques and procedures through which different forces seek to render programmes operable, and by means of which a multitude of connections are established between the aspirations of authorities and the activities of individuals and groups. These heterogeneous mechanisms we term *technologies of government* (Miller and Rose 1989). It is through technologies that political rationalities and the programmes of government that articulate them become capable of deployment. But this is not a matter of the 'implementation' of ideal schemes in the real, or of the extension of control from the seat of power into the minutiae of existence. Rather, it is a question of the complex assemblage of diverse forces – legal, architectural, professional, administrative, financial, judgemental – such that aspects of the decisions and actions of individuals, groups, organizations and populations come to be understood and regulated in relation to authoritative criteria. As noted in the previous chapter, we need to study the humble and mundane mechanisms by which authorities seek to instantiate government: techniques of notation, computation and calculation; procedures of examination and assessment; the invention of devices such as surveys and presentational forms such as tables; the standardization of systems for training and the inculcation of habits; the inauguration of professional specialisms and vocabularies; building designs and architectural forms – the list is heterogeneous and in principle unlimited.

Bruno Latour's reflections on power are suggestive here. Rather than considering power as the *explanation* of the success of authorities in composing a network of forces, Latour proposes a view of power as an *effect* of such a composition (Latour 1986, 1987b). A powerful actor, agent or institution is one that, in the particular circumstances obtaining at a given moment, is able successfully to enrol and mobilize persons, procedures and artefacts in the pursuit of its goals. Powers are stabilized in lasting networks only to the extent that the mechanisms of enrolment are materialized in various more or less persistent forms – machines, architecture, inscriptions, school curricula, books, obligations, techniques for documenting and calculating, and so forth. These stabilize networks partly because they act as potent resources in the local composition of forces. Thus architecture embodies certain relations between time, space, functions and persons – the separation of eating and sleeping, for example, or the hierarchical and lateral relations of the enterprise – not only materializing programmatic aspirations but also structuring the lives of those caught up in particular architectural regimes. Writing codifies customs and habits, normalizing them, both transforming them into repeatable instructions as to how to conduct oneself, and establishing authoritative means of judgement. 'Power' is the outcome of the affiliation of persons, spaces, communications and inscriptions into a durable form.

To speak of the 'power' of a government, a department of state, a local authority, a military commander or a manager in an enterprise is to substantialize that which arises from an assemblage of forces by which particular objectives and injunctions can shape the actions and calculations of others. Again, the notion of translation captures the process whereby this diversity is composed.[1] To the extent that actors have come to understand their situation according to a similar language and logic, to construe their goals and their fate as in some way inextricable, they are assembled into mobile and loosely affiliated networks. Shared interests are constructed in and through political discourses, persuasions, negotiations and bargains. Common modes of perception are formed, in which certain events and entities come to be visualized according to particular rhetorics of image or speech. Relations are established between the nature, character and causes of problems facing various individuals and groups – producers and shopkeepers, doctors and patients – such that the problems of one and those of another seem intrinsically linked in their basis and their solution.

These processes entail translation also in the literal sense of moving from one person, place or condition to another. Particular and local issues thus become tied to much larger ones. What starts out as a claim comes to be transformed into a matter of fact. The result of these and similar operations is that mobile and 'thixotropic' associations are established between a variety of agents, in which each seeks to enhance their powers by 'translating' the resources provided by the association so that they may function to their own advantage. Loose and flexible linkages are made between those who are separated spatially and temporally, and between events in spheres that remain formally distinct and autonomous. When each can translate the values of others into its own terms, such that they provide norms and standards for their own ambitions, judgements and conduct, a network has been composed that enables rule 'at a distance'.

Inscription and Calculation as Technologies of Government

In arguing against a 'state-centred' conception of political power, we do not mean to suggest that government does not produce centres. But centres of government are multiple: it is a question not of the power of the centralized state, but of how, in relation to what mentalities and devices, by means of what intrigues, alliances and flows – this locale or that is able to act as a centre.

Consider, first of all, the notion of statistics. Eighteenth-century European conceptions of government articulated a notion of statistics, or science of state, in which the operation of government was to be made possible by the accumulation and tabulation of facts about the domain to be governed. From this statistical project, through the requirements imposed upon firms to keep account books and make tax returns, through censuses and surveys, the investigations of Victorian social reformers, the records kept by the newly formed police forces and the school inspectors, through the calculations of such things as gross national products, growth rates of different economies, rates of inflation and the money supply, government inspires and depends upon a huge labour of inscription which renders reality into a calculable form. Written reports, drawings, pictures, numbers, charts, graphs and statistics are some of the ways in which this is achieved (Gigerenzer et al. 1989; Hacking 1982, 1990; Porter 1986; Rose 1991).

The 'representation' of that which is to be governed is an active, technical process. Government has inaugurated a huge labour of inquiry to transform events and phenomena into information: births, illnesses and deaths, marriages and divorces, levels of income and types of diet, forms of employment and want of employment. We can utilize Latour's notion of *inscription devices* to characterize these material conditions which enable thought to work upon an object (Latour 1987a; see also Rose 1988; Thevenot 1984). By means of inscription, reality is made stable, mobile, comparable, combinable. It is rendered in a form in which it can be debated and diagnosed. Information in this sense is not the outcome of a neutral recording function. It is itself a way of acting upon the real, a way of devising techniques for inscribing it in such a way as to make the domain in question susceptible to evaluation, calculation and intervention.

The inscription of reality in these mobile, combinable traces enables the formation of what we can call, following Latour, *centres of calculation* (Latour 1987a). Government depends upon calculations in one place about how to affect things in another. Information – concerning types of goods, ages of persons, health, criminality, etc. – must be transported and accumulated in locales – the manager's office, the war room, the case conference, and so forth – so that it can be utilized in calculation. The accumulation of inscriptions in certain locales, by certain persons or groups, makes them powerful in the sense that it confers upon them the capacity to engage in certain calculations and to lay a claim to legitimacy for their plans and strategies because they are, in a real sense, *in* the *know* about that which they seek to govern. The inscriptions of the world which an individual or a group can compile, consult or control play a key role in the powers they can exercise over those whose role is to be entries in these charts.

Figures transform the domain to which government is applied. In enabling events to be aggregated across space and time, they reveal and construct norms and processes to which evaluations can be attached and upon which interventions can be targeted. The figures themselves are mechanisms that enable relations to be established between different phenomena, rendering 'the population', 'the economy', 'public opinion', 'the divorce rate' into thought as calculable entities with a solidity and a density that appears all their own.

The complex interdependencies between inscription, calculation and government in France in the second half of the seventeenth century illustrate these processes clearly. During the first two decades of the reign of Louis XIV, Colbert, Superintendent of Commerce and Controller of Finance, Superintendent of Buildings and Secretary of State for Marine, can index the formation of a novel programme of government through inscription (P. Miller 1990). This involved innovations in calculative technologies for private enterprise: legal regulation in the Ordinance of 1673; publication of numerous textbooks explaining and commenting on this Ordinance and providing general advice to merchants; the elaboration of rationales for understanding these innovations; and the emergence of new pedagogic mechanisms for instructing merchants in the techniques of accounting. It also involved a significant strengthening and extension of the role of the intendants as all-purpose local administrators, and the construction of more systematic, regular and refined information flows from the provinces to the centre, frequently by means of large-scale inquiries.

The component parts of this technology of government were not all new, but when connected together they occupied a decisive role within a programme of government that elevated a desire to know the nation and its subjects in fine detail into an essential resource of political rule. Distance, delays arising as a result of lengthy travel and other factors such as establishing the local relays and networks upon which information and cooperation depended undoubtedly frustrated and disrupted this ideal machinery of 'government through inquiry'. Nevertheless the Colbert period illustrates the formation of a technology for governing a nation by exerting a kind of intellectual mastery over it. Establishing a network of conduits for the detailed and systematic flow of information from individual locales of production and trade to a centre helped constitute a single economic domain whose constituent elements could be known and regulated 'at a distance'.

From the invention of double-entry book-keeping to the contemporary deployment of accounting techniques such as Discounted Cash Flow analyses (see chapter 2), events in the internal realm of the 'private' enterprise have been opened up to government in this way (Miller 1991a; cf. Burchell et al. 1985; Hopwood 1987; Hoskin and Macve 1988; Loft 1986; Whitley 1986). Government here works by installing what one might term a calculative technology in the heart of the 'private' sphere, producing new ways of rendering economic activity into thought, conferring new visibilities upon the components of profit and loss, embedding new methods of calculation and hence linking private decisions and public objectives in a new way – through the medium of knowledge. Mechanisms such as this, as we have shown elsewhere, problematize the distinction between centrally planned and market economies: for example, the problems and techniques in the regulation of 'nationalized' enterprises in the UK following World War II were of a similar modality to those used to encourage efficiency and profitability in 'private' enterprise (Miller and Rose 1990 [reproduced as chapter 2 of this volume]).

Inscription itself can be a form of action at a distance. Installing a calculative technology in the enterprise, in the hospital, in the school or the family enjoins those within these locales to work out 'where they are', calibrate themselves in relation to 'where they should be', and devise ways of getting from one state to the other. Making people write things down and count them – register births, report incomes, fill in censuses – is itself a kind of government of them, an incitement to individuals to construe their lives according to such norms. By such mechanisms, authorities can act upon and enrol those distant from them in space and time in the pursuit of social, political or economic objectives without encroaching on their 'freedom' or 'autonomy' – indeed often precisely by offering to maximize it by turning blind habit into calculated freedom to choose. Such mechanisms, we argue later, have come to assume considerable importance in contemporary modes of government.

Expertise and Government

There are a number of versions of the process by which the personage of the expert, embodying neutrality, authority and skill in a wise figure, operating according to an ethical code 'beyond good and evil', has become so significant in our society (e.g. MacIntyre 1981; Perkin 1989). In our argument the rise of expertise is linked to a transformation in the rationalities and technologies of government. Expertise emerged as a possible solution to a problem that confronted liberal mentalities of government. How might one reconcile the principle that the domain of the political must be restricted, with the recognition of the vital political implications of formally private activities? The 'private' enterprise was to become a vital locale for the government of the economic life of the nation; the 'private' family was to be a resource for the government of social life. Each was a complex multivalent machine with internal relations which could be understood and administered and external consequences which could be identified and programmed. The inhabitants of these private domains – bosses, managers and workers; parents and children – were to be simultaneously the locus of private hopes, ambitions and disappointments, the source of varied types of social difficulties and the basis of all sorts of socially desirable objectives.

The vital links between socio-political objectives and the minutiae of daily existence in home and factory were to be established by expertise. Experts would enter into a kind of double alliance. On the one hand, they would ally themselves with political authorities, focusing upon their problems and problematizing new issues, translating political concerns about economic productivity, innovation, industrial unrest, social stability, law and order, normality and pathology, and so forth, into the vocabulary of management, accounting, medicine, social science and psychology. On the other hand, they would seek to form alliances with individuals themselves, translating their daily worries and decisions over investment, child rearing, factory organization or diet into a language claiming the power of truth, and offering to teach them the techniques by which they might manage better, earn more, bring up healthier or happier children, and much more besides.

Expertise nonetheless poses problems for political authority. Experts have the capacity to generate *enclosures*: relatively bounded locales or types of judgement within which their power and authority is concentrated, intensified and defended (cf. Giddens 1985: 13). Enclosures may be generated in governmental networks through the use of esoteric knowledge, technical skill or established position as crucial resources which others cannot easily countermand or appropriate. Of course, such enclosures are only provisional, and the claims of any particular expertise are always subject to contestation. But the example of the British National Health Service, which we discuss below, illustrates the ways in which doctors could deploy their expertise to translate the interests of civil servants and government ministers into their own. They managed to make their arguments and calculations the obligatory mode for the operation of the network as a whole, the lines of force flowing, as it were, from the operating theatre to the cabinet office, and not vice versa.

The complex of actors, powers, institutions and bodies of knowledge that comprise expertise has come to play a crucial role in establishing the possibility and legitimacy of government. Experts hold out the hope that problems of regulation can remove themselves from the disputed terrain of politics and relocate onto the tranquil yet seductive territory of truth. By means of expertise, self-regulatory techniques can be installed in citizens that will align their personal choices with the ends of government (Rose 1989a). The freedom and subjectivity of citizens can in such ways become an ally, and not a threat, to the orderly government of a polity and a society.

The Governmentalization of the State

The problematics of government offer a different perspective on the political phenomena conventionally addressed in terms of the state. The discursive, legislative, fiscal, organizational and other resources of the public powers have come to be linked in varying ways into networks of rule. Mobile divisions and relations have been established between political rule and other projects and techniques for the calculated administration of life. Diverse parts are played in technologies of rule by the political actors who hold elected office, make authoritative pronouncements as to policy and priorities, create legislation and get it enacted, calculate national budgets, raise taxes and adjust their levels and incidence, disburse benefits, give grants to industry and charities, command and direct bureaucratic staffs, set up regulatory bodies and organizations of all sorts, and, in certain cases, set in action the legitimate use of violence.

Such 'political' forces can only seek to operationalize *their* programmes of government by influencing, allying with or co-opting resources that they do not directly control – banks, financial institutions, enterprises, trade unions, professions, bureaucracies, families and individuals (see Ashford 1981: 57ff.; Harden and Lewis 1986: 155ff.). A 'centre' can only become such through its position within the complex of technologies, agents and agencies that make government possible. But, once established as a centre, a particular locale can ensure that certain resources only flow through and around these technologies and networks, reaching particular agents rather than others, by means of a passage through 'the centre'. Financial and economic controls established by central government set key dimensions of the environment in which private enterprises and other economic actors must calculate. Money, raised in taxes or public borrowing, is disbursed through the network, to certain local centres, but the continued supply of financial resources is conditional upon the conviction that an alignment of interests exists, that the local authorities, firms, and so on, will remain more or less faithful allies. Hence the threat of withholding of funds can be a powerful inducement to other actors to maintain themselves within the network, or an incentive for them to seek to convince the centre that their concerns and strategies are translatable and mutual.

The enactment of legislation is a powerful resource in the creation of centres, to the extent that law translates aspects of a governmental programme into mechanisms that establish, constrain or empower certain agents or entities and set some of the key terms of their deliberations. Imposing a regime of licensure, for example, empowers certain bodies to regulate those who seek to act in a certain professional capacity, both legitimating and regulating at the same time. Embodying the principle of 'the best interests of the child' in law may not *determine* the decisions of social workers and the courts, but it sets one of the terms within which those decisions must be calculated and justified. Programmes and strategies formulated at the centre may lead to attempts to establish regulatory or negotiating bodies, and may lead to more or less autonomy being granted to other aspects of the bureaucratic web of government such as departments of state or local authorities.

Yet entities and agents within governmental networks are not faithful relays, mere creatures of a controller situated in some central hub. They utilize and deploy whatever resources they have for their own purposes, and the extent to which they carry out the will of another is always conditional on the particular balance of force, energy and meaning at any time and at any point. Each actor, each locale, is the point of intersection between forces, and hence a point of potential resistance to any one way of thinking and acting, or a point of organization and promulgation of a different or oppositional programme. Entities may defect from a network, may refuse to be enrolled, or may bend their operations at certain points beyond all recognition. Budget holders will refuse to release sufficient funds, or recipients of funds will divert them to other purposes. Experts and academics will seize upon the tactical possibilities open to them and seek to deflect them to their own advantage. And professional groups will bargain, bicker and contest on the basis of quite different claims and objectives instead of meshing smoothly and with complete malleability in the idealized schemes of a programmatic logic.

Government is a congenitally failing operation: the sublime image of a perfect regulatory machine is internal to the mind of the programmers. The world of programmes is heterogeneous, and rivalrous. Programmes complexify the real, so solutions for one programme tend to be problems for another. Things, persons or events always appear to escape those bodies of knowledge that inform governmental programmes, refusing to respond according to the programmatic logic that seeks to govern them. Technologies produce unexpected problems, are utilized for their own ends by those who are supposed merely to operate them, are hampered by underfunding, professional rivalries and the impossibility of producing the technical conditions that would make them work – reliable statistics, efficient communication systems, clear lines of command, properly designed buildings, well-framed regulations, or whatever. Unplanned outcomes emerge from the intersection of one technology with another, or from the unexpected consequences of putting a technique to work. Contrariwise, techniques invented for one purpose may find their governmental role for another, and the unplanned conjunction of techniques and conditions arising from very different aspirations may allow something to work without or despite its explicit rationale. Whilst we inhabit a world of programmes, that world is not itself programmed. We do not live in a governed world so much as a world traversed by the 'will to govern', fuelled by the constant registration of 'failure', the discrepancy between ambition and outcome, and the constant injunction to do better next time.

Welfare and the Governmentalization of the State

Political commentators tend to agree that during the first half of the twentieth century, many Western societies became 'welfare states', in which the State tried to ensure high levels of employment, economic progress, social security, health and housing through the use of the tax system and investments, through state planning and intervention in the economy, and through the development of an extended and bureaucratically staffed apparatus for social administration. From our perspective, however, this is less the birth of a new form of state than a new mode of government of the economic, social and personal lives of citizens. This mode of government, which we term 'welfarism', is constituted by a political rationality embodying certain principles and ideals, and is based upon a particular conception of the nature of society and its inhabitants. This welfarist rationality is linked to an array of mutually translatable programmes, technologies and devices, ranging from tax regimes to social insurance, from management training to social casework, from employment exchanges to residential homes for the elderly.

We have discussed welfarism and the government of economic life elsewhere (Miller and Rose 1990 [reproduced as chapter 2 of this volume], 1991). Let us here consider welfarism and 'social' government. 'Social' does not refer in this instance to a given repertoire of social issues, but to a terrain brought into existence by government itself – the location of certain problems, the repository of specific hopes and fears, the target of programmes and the space traced out by a particular administrative machinery (Donzelot 1979a: 81).[2] The programmes of social government that proliferated in the nineteenth century involved complex alliances between private and professional agents – philanthropists, charitable organizations, medics, polemicists and others – and the state, formed around problems arising in a multitude of sites within the social body. From the latter half of the nineteenth century onwards, these programmes, and the schemes they gave rise to, were gradually linked up to the apparatus of the state. These connections were, no doubt, inspired by diverse aims and principles, but they appeared to offer the chance, or impose the obligation, for political authorities to calculate and calibrate social, economic and moral affairs and seek to govern them. Yet the state apparatus did not, could not, eliminate all other centres of power or decision, or reduce them to its creatures, whether through the mechanisms of command and obedience or by subjecting everyone to perpetual surveillance and normalization. Welfarism is not so much a matter of the rise of an interventionist state as the assembling of diverse mechanisms and arguments through which political forces seek to secure social and economic objectives by linking up a plethora of networks with aspirations to know, programme and transform the social field.

Governing the Networks of Welfare

The English example illustrates three key features of welfarism. The first concerns the relations between political rationalities and the formation of networks of government. As a political rationality, welfarism is structured by the wish to encourage national growth and well-being through the promotion of social responsibility and the mutuality of social risk. This rationality was articulated in a number of different ways. The Beveridge Report was framed in terms of a kind of contract between the state and its citizens, in which both parties had their needs and their duties (Beveridge 1942). The state would accept responsibility to attack the 'five giants of Want, Disease, Idleness, Ignorance and Squalor' through a nationalized health service, a commitment to full employment and a social insurance system which would prevent the social demoralization and other harmful effects of periods of want by redistributing income across the life-cycle. In return, the citizen would respect his or her obligations to be thrifty, industrious and socially responsible. The Labour Party, on the other hand, articulated this rationality in terms of the just and equal treatment for each and for all, to be realized by planned, rationalized and universal state dispensation of security, health, housing and education (Craig 1975; Morgan 1984).

The rationality of welfarism was programmatically elaborated in relation to a range of specific problematizations: the declining birthrate; delinquency and anti-social behaviour; the problem family; the social consequences of ill health and the advantages conferred by a healthy population; and the integration of citizens into the community. These were not novel problems, but in the post-war period they were to be problematized by a multitude of official and unofficial experts and, crucially, were to be governed in new ways. The key innovations of welfarism lay in the attempts to link the fiscal, calculative and bureaucratic capacities of the apparatus of the state to the government of social life. The social devices of the pre-war period consisted of a tangle of machinery for the surveillance and regulation of the social, familial and personal conduct of the problematic sectors of the population. The personnel, procedures, techniques and calculations that made up these devices were attached to specific locales and organizations: the courts, the reformatories, the schools and the clinics. Welfarism sought to articulate these varied elements into a network and to direct them in the light of centralized calculations as to resources, services and needs.

However, welfare was not a coherent mechanism that would enable the unfolding of a central plan. The networks were assembled from diverse and often antagonistic components, from warring Whitehall departments to peripheral and *ad hoc* agencies (Bulpitt 1986). This was no 'state apparatus', but a composition of fragile and mobile relationships and dependencies making diverse attempts to link the aspirations of authorities with the lives of individuals. Assembling and maintaining such networks entailed struggles, alliances and competitions between different groups for resources, recognition and power. The problem posed for the next thirty years, for those aspiring to form a 'centre' from which the welfare apparatus could be governed, was one of regulating those who claimed discretionary powers because of their professional or bureaucratic expertise.

The example of health illustrates these difficulties (our account draws on Klein 1983; see also Pollitt 1984; Starr and Immergut 1987). How was one to make administrable the multitude of hourly and daily individual decisions by physicians, consultants, general practitioners, nurses, dentists, pharmacists and others? Each of these agents claimed and practised their rights to make decisions not on the basis of an externally imposed plan, or according to criteria reaching them from elsewhere, but according to professional codes, training, habit, moral allegiances and institutional demands. The problem was one of connecting them instead to the calculations and deliberations of other authorities.

Between the Ministry of Health and the practitioners of the cure during the 1950s, a complex administrative structure was assembled. In the hospital sector alone this comprised 14 Regional Hospital Boards, 36 Boards of Governance for Teaching Hospitals and some 380 Hospital Management Committees. To govern this system in a 'rational and effective' manner as envisaged in the 1944 White Paper posed a problem of information: even the most basic information about the number and distribution of doctors was lacking at the periphery let alone the centre. This 'lack' was to be the start of a massive attempt to transform the activities of healers into figures that would make medicine calculable. The initial problematization was financial, for the new technology displaced earlier ways of relating medical care to money. A series of studies lamented the limited information possessed by the Ministry on the financial administration of hospitals, the absence of costing yardsticks to judge the relative efficiency or extravagance of administration of various hospitals, and hence the invidious alternatives of accepting the plans of medical agents wholesale as submitted without amendment, or applying overall cuts in a more or less indiscriminate manner (see Public Records Office 1950, quoted in Klein 1983: 48–9).

Diverse programmes sought to transform the health apparatus into a calculable universe in which entities and activities would be mapped, enumerated, translated into information, transmitted to a centre, accumulated, compared, evaluated and programmed. The duties of each actor and locale would be relayed back to them down the network in the form of norms, standards and constraints. The problems of calculability were to be raised again and again over the next thirty years, and in relation to differing political rationalities and programmes. But in the 1950s, Ministry of Health policy making was more or less limited to operating by exhortatory circular – an average of 120 a year throughout the decade – and political exhortations can be ignored. For the medical profession established the NHS as a medical enclosure. Medics drew on a profound optimism concerning the ability of medical science to alleviate illness and promote health, in a variety of tactics that succeeded both in shaping the 'policy agenda' concerning health and in placing certain issues out of bounds for non-professionals (Klein 1983: 27). Furthermore, medics came to dominate the administrative networks of health, forming a medico-administrative bloc that appeared resistant to all attempts to make it calculable in a non-medical vocabulary.

By the 1960s, the technological questions of how the machinery of health was to be governed were re-posed within a more general shift of governmental rationalities. The notion that efficiency and rationality could be achieved through mechanisms of planning crossed the boundaries of economic and social policy and the bounds of political party. The Plowden Report of 1961 called for the use of public expenditure control as a means to stable long-term planning, with greater emphasis on the 'wider application of mathematical techniques, statistics and accountancy' (Chancellor of the Exchequer 1961, quoted in Klein 1983: 65). A range of new techniques were invented by which civil servants and administrators might calculate and hence control public expenditure: the Public Expenditure Survey Committee (PESC), the use of cost benefit analysis, of PPB (Planning, Programming, Budgeting) and PAR (Programme Analysis Review). And official documents like the Fulton Report envisaged these as gaining their hold upon the machinery of government through their inculcation into a professional corps of administrative experts, specialists both in techniques of management and in those of numeracy (Committee of the Civil Service 1968).

Management, mathematics and monetarization were to tame the wild excesses of a governmental complex in danger of running out of control. The Ministry of Health set up its Advisory Committee for Management Efficiency in 1959 and expenditure on 'hospital efficiency studies' rose from £8,000 in 1963–4 to £250,000 in 1966–7. Health economists invented themselves and installed themselves in the Ministry of Health and outside it, articulating a new vocabulary for defining problems and programming solutions (Office of Health Economics 1967). Yet for some fifteen years these new mechanisms for central planning according to rational criteria appeared destined to fail.

It was in the 1970s that the medico-administrative enclosure of health was to be breached. Politicians and planners began to speak of the insatiability of the demand for medical services and hence the need to impose some politically acceptable limits upon national provision. The very success of medics in promoting high-tech medicine had vastly increased the cost of treatment. Sociologists and demographers issued dire predictions about the consequences of the ageing population and increases in life expectancy for demands on the health apparatus. Further, the medical monopoly over the internal working of the health apparatus began to fragment. General practitioners and consultants began to stake rival claims for dominance. New actors proliferated – nurses, physios, occupational therapists – and began to organize themselves into 'professional' forces, claiming special skills based upon their own esoteric knowledge and training, demanding a say in the administration of health, contesting the superiority of medical expertise. Ancillary workers became unionized and pressed for better wages. The conflicts between rational planning and expert powers became more evident. As the health apparatus threatened to become ungovernable, a new form of rational expertise, grounded in the discourse of health economics, began to provide resources for those who wished to challenge the prerogatives of doctors. New devices began to be developed for evaluating the costs and benefits of different treatments and decisions, rendering them amenable to non-clinical judgements made neither by doctors nor by local politicians, but by managers (Ashmore et al. 1989).

Further, the health consumer was transformed, partly by developments in medical thought itself, from a passive patient, gratefully receiving the ministrations of the medics, to a person who was to be actively engaged in the administration of health if the treatment was to be effective and prevention assured. The patient was now to voice his or her experiences in the consulting room if diagnosis was to be accurate and remedies were to be effective. The patient was also to be actively enrolled in the government of health, educated and persuaded to exercise a continual informed scrutiny of the health consequences of diet, lifestyle and work. And patients, reciprocally, were to organize and represent themselves in the struggles over health. By 1979, 230 organizations for patients and disabled people could be listed in a directory, providing forums for sufferers of particular conditions and their relatives, pressing for increased resources for problems ranging from migraine to kidney transplants, demanding their say in decisions concerning everything from the place of birth to the management of death. Out of this concatenation of programmes, strategies and resistances, a new 'neo-liberal' mode of government of health was to take shape.

Welfare and Responsible Citizenship

Welfarism embodies a particular conception of the relation between the citizen and the public powers. As the 'contractual' language of Beveridge's programme indicates, welfarism is a 'responsibilizing' mode of government. Social insurance, which Beveridge made the centrepiece of his report, can illustrate this (Rose 1980; on insurance see Defert 1991 and Ewald 1991). Insurance fundamentally transforms the mechanisms that bind the citizen into the social order. A certain measure of individual security is provided against loss or interruption of earnings through sickness, unemployment, injury, disablement, widowhood or retirement. Yet simultaneously the subjects of these dangers are constituted as the locus of social responsibility and located within a nexus of social risk.

Prior to insurance, perhaps the principal socially regulated relationship was between the employer and the employee. The technology of insurance not only entails the direct intervention of the state as third party into the contract of employment, it also articulates this relation within a different but complementary contract between the insured individual and society, introducing a relation of mutual obligation in which both parties have their rights and their duties. Programmes of insurance did not merely aspire to the prevention of hardship and want. They also sought to reduce the social and political consequences of economic events such as unemployment by ensuring that, whether working or not, individuals were in effect employees of society. Within the political rationality of welfarism, insurance constituted individuals as citizens bound into a system of solidarity and mutual interdependency. Insurantial technology did not compose a mechanism where premiums were adjusted to risk or contributions were accumulated in order to provide for future benefits. Rather, the vocabulary of insurance and the technique of contribution were chosen in the belief that this would constitute the insured citizen in a definite moral form: payment would qualify an individual to receive benefits, would draw the distinction between earned and unearned benefits, and teach the lessons of contractual obligation, thrift and responsibility.

Welfarism and the Technicization of Politics

The system of social insurance embodied definite politico-ethical aspirations. However, it had the paradoxical effect of expelling certain issues and problems from the political to the technical domain. This illustrates a third key feature of welfarism: the role accorded to expertise. By incorporating expertise into a centrally directed network, welfarism creates domains in which political decisions are dominated by technical calculations.

In most European societies, sickness and insurance funds were developed by voluntary associations, trade unions, political parties and religious groups. They had an immediate 'political' form, in that they allowed for some participation by the insured in decisions over the administration of these benefits, provided a base for workers' organizations, served as a resource for the creation of collective identities and the mobilization of members for issues such as elections and strikes. Such issues can be 'de-politicized' in two ways: either by relocating them as 'private' matters to be resolved by individual market transactions, or by transforming them into technical, professional or administrative matters to be resolved by the application of rational knowledge and professional expertise in relation to objective and apparently neutral criteria (Starr and Immergut 1987).

Even such a perceptive commentator as T. H. Marshall was to write of social insurance that 'This new sophistication was a scientific not a political phenomenon . . . applying techniques, which were of universal validity, to problems that were an intrinsic part of modern industrial society' (Marshall 1975: 69). Yet as Jacques Donzelot suggests, insurance de-dramatizes social conflicts, through 'eliding the questions of assigning *responsibility* for the origin of "social evils" and shifting the issue to the different technical options regarding variations in different parameters required to "optimise" employment, wages, allowances etc.' (Donzelot 1979b: 9).

And, at the same time, insurance creates a form of passive solidarity amongst its recipients, de-emphasizing both their active engagement in collective mechanisms of providing for hard times such as trade unions or friendly societies and their individual striving for self-protection through savings. Insurance is certainly a 'technical' option, but it is a technology that redraws the social domain and simultaneously readjusts the territory of the political, on the one hand – struggles, contestations, repressions – and the economic, on the other – wage labour, the role of the market, subsistence and poverty.

If the 'crisis' of welfare as a rationality of government arose, in part, out of the difficulties engendered by the technologies that sought to opera-tionalize it, the possibility of supplanting welfare by a new rationality arose out of the proliferation of other, more indirect means for regulating the activities of private agents. This entailed the implantation of technologies of calculation and the development of techniques for attaching actual or psychological rewards to certain decisions and making others financially or culturally less attractive. Government was to be vested in the entre-preneurial activities of producers of goods and suppliers of services, the expertise of managers equipped with new modes of calculation, the opera-tion of a market that would align the activities of producers and providers with the choices of consumers, actively seeking to maximize their 'life-styles' and their 'quality of life'.

From Welfare to Neo-Liberalism

Let us return to the political challenges to the extended state with which we began. For some thirty years following the publication of *The Road to Serfdom* (Hayek 1944), neo-liberal hostility to the 'interventionist state' seemed eccentric to the main lines of political debate (Friedman 1962; Hayek 1960). From the mid-seventies onwards, in the USA, Britain and elsewhere in Europe, neo-liberal analyses began to underpin the appeal of conservative political programmes and pronouncements. The political mentality of neo-liberalism breaks with welfarism at the level of moralities, explanations and vocabularies. Against the assumption that the ills of social and economic life are to be addressed by the activities of government, it warns against the arrogance of government overreach and overload. It counterposes the inefficiencies of planned economies to the strength of the market in picking winners. It claims that Keynesian demand management sets in motion a vicious spiral of inflationary expectations and currency debasement. It suggests that big government is not only inefficient but also malign: parties are pushed into making lavish promises in their competition for votes, fuelling rising expectations which can only be met by public borrowing on a grand scale (cf. Schumpeter 1950). Because 'the welfare state' depends on bureaucracy, it is subject to constant pressure from bureaucrats to expand their own empires, again fuelling an expensive and inefficient extension of the governmental machine. Because it cultivates the view that it is the role of the state to provide for the individual, the welfare state has a morally damaging effect upon citizens, producing 'a culture of dependency' based on expectations that government will do what in reality only individuals can.

Neo-liberalism reactivates liberal principles: scepticism over the capacities of political authorities to govern everything for the best; vigilance over the attempts of political authorities to seek to govern. Its language is familiar and needs little rehearsal. Markets are to replace planning as regulators of economic activity. Those aspects of government that welfare construed as political responsibilities are, as far as possible, to be transformed into commodified forms and regulated according to market principles. Economic entrepreneurship is to replace regulation, as active agents seeking to maximize their own advantage are both the legitimate locus of decisions about their own affairs and the most effective in calculating actions and outcomes. And more generally, active entrepreneurship is to replace the passivity and dependency of responsible solidarity as individuals are encouraged to strive to optimize their own quality of life and that of their families.

Neo-liberalism re-codes the place of the state in the discourse of politics. The state must be strong to defend the interests of the nation in the international sphere, and must ensure order by providing a legal framework for social and economic life. But within this framework, autonomous actors – commercial concerns, families, individuals – are to go freely about their business, making their own decisions and controlling their own destinies. Neo-liberal political rationalities weave these philosophical themes into an operative political discourse. A rhetoric of the traditional greatness of the nation, the family, the virtues of law and order, and the respect for tradition provides a translatability between neo-liberalism and traditional right-wing values, and simultaneously opens a complex space for the elaboration of governmental programmes.

Whatever its rhetoric, within the problematics of government, neo-liberalism is not rendered intelligible by counterposing a non-interventionist to an interventionist state. Rather, it should be seen as a reorganization of political rationalities that brings them into a kind of alignment with contemporary technologies of government. The new political initiatives often take the form of an attempted 'autonomization' of entities from the state, or, rather, an autonomization of the state from direct controls over, and responsibility for, the actions and calculations of businesses, welfare organizations, and so forth. They entail the adoption by the centre of a range of devices which seek both to create a distance between the formal institutions of the state and other social actors, *and* to act upon them in a different manner.

One of the central mechanisms of neo-liberalism is the proliferation of strategies to create and sustain a 'market', to reshape the forms of economic exchange on the basis of contractual exchange. The privatization programmes of the new politics have formed perhaps the most visible strand of such strategies, and one most aligned with the political ideals of markets versus state. But in terms of economic regulation at least, a rigid distinction between nationalized and private enterprises is misleading. On the one hand, the degree of political direction over the activities of nationalized companies was variable but small – perhaps the principal form that intervention took was the provision or refusal of investment capital. On the other hand, private sector enterprise is opened, in so many ways, to the action-at-a-distance mechanisms that have proliferated in advanced liberal democracies, with the rise of managers as an intermediary between expert knowledge, economic policy and business decisions. Of course, 'market forces' intersect in different ways with investment decisions and the like when businesses are no longer formally owned by the state, as do the imperatives to profit. But we might consider that this reconstruction of the form of economic regulation is less a revolution against the real failures of central planning than a rejection of the ideals of knowledge, power and the effectivity of planning that such rationalities embodied.

At the rhetorical and programmatic level, neo-liberalism also embodies a profound transformation in the mechanisms for governing social life. In place of collective provision and social solidarity the new rationality of government proposes notions of security provided through the private purchase of insurance schemes, health care purchased by individuals and provided by the health industry, housing offered through the private sector and efficiency secured through the discipline of competition within the market. The public provision of welfare and social security no longer appears as a vital part of a programme for political stability and social efficiency.

Monetarization has played a key role in breaching the enclosures of expertise within the machinery of welfare. For example, when contemporary British hospitals are required to translate their therapeutic activities, from operating theatres to laundry rooms, into cash equivalents, a new form of visibility is conferred upon them, new relations are established and new procedures of decision making are made possible. As we have already argued, making people write things down, and the nature of the things people are made to write down, is itself a kind of government of them, urging them to think about and note certain aspects of their activities according to certain norms. Power flows to the centre or agent who determines the inscriptions, accumulates them, contemplates them in their aggregated form and hence can compare and evaluate the activities of others who are merely entries on the chart. Managers rather than consultants become the powerful actors in this new network, and power flows from the cabinet office to the operating theatre via a multitude of calculative and managerial locales, rather than in the other direction. This is an attempt not to impose a power where previously none existed, but to transform the terms of calculation from medical to financial, and hence to shift the fulcrum of the health network. Far from autonomizing the health apparatus, these new modes of action at a distance increase the possibilities of governing it. Similarly, relocating aspects of welfare in the 'private' or 'voluntary' sector does not necessarily render them less governable. To be sure, different procedures of translation and alliance are entailed when 'political' institutions are 'de-centred' in networks of power. But the opposition between state and non-state is inadequate to characterize these transformations.

Neo-liberalism also entails a reorganization of programmes for the government of personal life. The language of the entrepreneurial individual, endowed with freedom and autonomy, has come to predominate over almost any other in evaluations of the ethical claims of political power and programmes of government. A sphere of freedom is to be (re-)established, where autonomous agents make their decisions, pursue their preferences and seek to maximize the quality of their lives. For neo-liberalism the political subject is less a social citizen with powers and obligations deriving from membership of a collective body than an individual whose citizenship is active. This citizenship is to be manifested not in the receipt of public largesse, but in the energetic pursuit of personal fulfilment and the incessant calculations that are to enable this to be achieved (Gordon 1986; Meyer 1986a).

Neo-liberalism forges a kind of alignment between political rationalities and the technologies for the regulation of the self that took shape during the decades of the 1960s and 1970s. No doubt this alignment is not the only one possible, or the most desirable. Nonetheless, neo-liberal programmes for the reform of welfare drew support from their consonance with a range of other challenges to the mechanisms of social government that emerged during these same decades from civil libertarians, feminists, radicals, socialists, sociologists and others. These reorganized programmes of government utilize and instrumentalize the multitude of experts of management, of family life, of lifestyle who have proliferated at the points of intersection of socio-political aspirations and private desires for self-advancement. Through this loose assemblage of agents, calculations, techniques, images and commodities, individuals can be governed through their freedom to choose.

Conclusion

Much of the analysis above is preliminary, but its central point is a simple one. The language of political philosophy – state and civil society, freedom and constraint, sovereignty and democracy, public and private – plays a key role in the organization of modern political power. However, it cannot provide the intellectual tools for analysing the problematics of government in the present. Unless we adopt different ways of thinking about the exercise of political power, we will find contemporary forms of rule hard to understand. It will thus be difficult to make proper judgement of the alternatives on offer.

Notes

1.   We adapt this from Callon and Latour (e.g. Callon and Latour 1981), but free it from the 'will to power' that motivates acts of translation in their account.

2. The division of social and economic is purely expositional: 'economic' problems were to be solved by 'social' means – as in the use of the family and the family wage in engendering the requirement of regular labour – and 'social' problems were to be solved 'economically' – as in attempts to resolve crime and urban unrest through decreasing the numbers of those in want of employment.

4

The Death of the Social?
Re-figuring the Territory of Government

Over the last two decades of the twentieth century, in almost all advanced industrial countries, from Sweden to New Zealand, the old certainties of 'the welfare state' came under attack, and welfare systems underwent transformation.[1] One saw the privatization of public utilities and welfare functions, the marketization of health services, social insurance and pension schemes, educational reforms to introduce competition between schools and colleges, the introduction of new forms of management into the civil service modelled upon an image of methods in the private sector, new contractual relations between agencies and service providers and between professionals and clients, a new emphasis on the personal responsibilities of individuals, their families and their communities for their own future well-being and upon their own obligation to take active steps to secure this. At the level of 'governmentality' – the deliberations, strategies, tactics and devices employed by authorities for making up and acting upon a population and its constituents to ensure good and avert ill – it seemed as if we were seeing the emergence of a range of rationalities and techniques that seek to govern without governing society, to govern through regulated choices made by discrete and autonomous actors in the context of their particular commitments to families and communities (Rose 1993b, 1994). These shifts in policy appear to be paralleled in a shift within the social sciences, where the object 'society', in the sense that began to be accorded to it in the nineteenth century (the sum of the bonds and relations between individuals and events – economic, moral, political – within a more or less bounded territory governed by its own laws), has also begun to lose its self-evidence, and 'sociology', as the field of knowledge which ratified the existence of this territory, is undergoing something of a crisis of identity.

While the destabilization of social theory was pioneered by those who would describe themselves as progressives, the relation of those on the left to the transformations in the welfare state has been almost entirely negative. This is not surprising, given the intimate relations between socialism, as a rationality for politics, and the proliferation of social devices that made up welfare: the social state, social insurance, social service, the social wage, social protection, and the rest. But we need to interrogate this opposition, in which the forces of progress seem obliged to take the side of the social against the forces of reaction which stand for individualism, competition, the market, and the like. To begin such a task, we might start by interrogating the notion of 'the social' itself. Are we witnessing not just a temporary shift in political and theoretical fashions but an event: 'the death of the social'?

Government from 'the Social Point of View'[2]

When, at the start of the 1980s, Jean Baudrillard diagnosed 'the end of the social' (Baudrillard 1983), he offered his readers three propositions: that *the social has never existed*, but has always been a kind of simulation of a social relation that has now undergone a de-simulation, a disintegration of what was, in any event, an imaginary space of reference and play of mirrors; that *the social has really existed and now invests everything*, has extended from a process of the rational control of residues – vagrants, lunatics, the sick – to a state in which everyone is completely excluded and taken in charge for a project of functional integration sanctified by the social sciences; *that the social has existed in the past but has ceased to do so* – the sociality of the contract, of the relation of state to civil society, of the dialectic of the social and the individual has been destroyed by the fragmentations of the media, information, computer simulation and the rise of the simulacrum. Baudrillard concluded with a tender recollection of 'the unbelievable naivety of social and socialist thinking, for thus having been able to reify as universal and to elevate as ideal of transparency such a totally ambiguous and contradictory – worse, such a residual or imaginary – worse, such an already abolished in its very simulation "reality": the social' (Baudrillard 1983: 86).

This diagnosis undoubtedly catches something significant, despite its characteristically apocalyptic tone and opaque field of reference. It reminds us, if we should need reminding, that 'the social' is invented by history and cathected by political passions: we should be wary of embracing it as an inevitable horizon for our thought or standard for our evaluations. Gilles Deleuze, in his introduction to Jacques Donzelot's *The Policing of Families*, puts the issue in rather more sober terms: 'Clearly it is not a question of the adjective that qualifies the set of phenomena which sociology deals with: the social refers to a particular sector in which quite diverse problems and special cases can be grouped together, a sector comprising specific institutions and an entire body of qualified personnel' (Deleuze 1979: ix). 'The social', that is to say, does not represent an eternal existential sphere of human sociality. Rather, within a limited geographical and temporal field, it set the terms for the way in which human intellectual, political and moral authorities, in certain places and contexts, thought about and acted upon their collective experience. This novel plane of territorialization existed within, across, in tension with other spatializations: blood and territory; race and religion; town, region and nation. A host of lines of organization and intervention cast across most European nations and in North America over the nineteenth century and the first half of the twentieth intersected, connected and entangled in this hybrid zone of 'the social'.[3] Social statistics, then sociology, and all the social sciences, would play their part in stabilizing the social as a domain *sui generis*, whose reality could no longer be ignored. Simultaneously, political forces would now articulate their demand upon the state *in the name of the social*: the nation must be governed in the interests of social protection, social justice, social rights and social solidarity.

By the early decades of the twentieth century, politicians in different national contexts in Europe and North America had been forced to accept that government of at least some aspects of this social domain should be added to the responsibilities of the political apparatus and its officials. One sees a rejection of the totalizing claims of political economy to prescribe and delimit the legitimate means to be used for the government of economic life. Simultaneously, law can no longer be the sole and sufficient legitimate political means for achieving order and security; indeed law itself must answer to the demands of social government. The political rationalities that played so great a part in the twentieth century – socialism, social democracy, social liberalism – may have differed on many things, but on this they agreed: the nation must be governed, but one must pose the question of how to govern from 'the social point of view' (cf. Procacci 1989; for France, see Donzelot 1984; for England, see Clarke 1979; Collini 1979). 'The social' became a kind of '*a priori*' of political thought: order would have to be social or it would cease to exist.

To speak of 'the death of the social' is undoubtedly misleading. Indeed, 'social' policies are increasingly articulated at a supra-national level through international bodies such as the Organization of Economic Cooperation and Development, the World Health Organization, the United Nations and the European Union. But, despite the undoubted persistence of the theme of society and social cohesion in contemporary political argument, 'the social' in the sense in which it has been understood for about a century is nonetheless undergoing a mutation. The conditions for this mutation, and the correlative emergence and proliferation of 'advanced liberal' programmes of government under a variety of different national political regimes, are heterogeneous and dispersed. Economic arguments have placed in question the idea of a national economy, whose formation in the nineteenth century was a key condition for the delineation of a social territory. Economic relations have come to be understood, not just as transnational, not in terms of relations among discrete national economies, but as connecting up components of one national population with components of another – economic competition is between cities, between sectors, between specialized markets within economic relations that do not respect national political boundaries. The problem of national economic government is now posed differently: while ruling parties still have to manage national populations with the territorialized political machinery available to them, they no longer conceive of themselves as operating upon a naturally functioning and systemically integrated national population whose 'social' coherence is a condition for its economic security (cf. Hindess 1994b).[4]

The logics of social government were also problematized in other ways. As Hirschman (1991) has pointed out, there was a proliferation of 'rhetorics of reaction' about the paradoxical dis-welfares of the welfare state – its costs, its burdens, its injustices – which came from different parts of the political spectrum. There were also diverse criticisms of the expert powers installed by welfare states, and the discretionary scope that welfare systems accorded to professionals and bureaucrats (I have discussed these in detail elsewhere: Rose 1993b, 1993c). While these criticisms of social government were heterogeneous, they nonetheless have a certain 'family resemblance'. In particular, arguments made by libertarians of left and right, progressives, humanists, proponents of civil rights and advocates of empowerment shared a changed specification of the subjects of government. The human beings who were to be governed – men and women, rich and poor – were now conceived as individuals who were to be active in their own government. And their responsibility was no longer to be understood as a relation of obligation between citizen and society enacted and regulated through the mediating party of the State; rather, it was to be a relation of allegiance and responsibility to those one cared about the most and to whom one's destiny was linked. Each subject was now located in a variety of heterogeneous and overlapping networks of personal concern and investment – for oneself, one's family, one's neighbourhood, one's community, one's workplace. Central to the ethos of the novel mentalities and strategies of government that I have termed 'advanced liberal' is a new relationship between strategies for the government of others and techniques for the government of the self, situated within new relations of mutual obligation: the community.

The Birth of the Community

Until recently, the apparently 'a-moral' language of the market captured most attention in debates over changes in welfare – privatization, competition, financial calculation, and so forth. But contemporary political rationalities also think in terms of another language which is just as important, which is highly morally invested and which intersects with markets, contracts and consumption in complex and surprising ways: 'community'. Consider the contemporary salience of the vocabulary of community care, community homes, community workers, community safety, for example. Consider the emergence of the idea of risk communities – drug abusers, gay men, carriers of particular genes, youth at risk. Consider the prominence of the language of community in debates over multi-culturalism and the problems posed for politicians, psychiatrists, police and others working in conditions of cultural, ethical and religious pluralism. All these seem to signal that 'the social' may be giving way to 'the community' as a new territory for the administration of individual and collective existence, a new plane or surface upon which micro-moral relations among persons are conceptualized and administered. I do not think this is merely a matter of changing professional jargon: it is indicative of a mutation, rather profound, if still uncertain, in the ways of thinking and acting that used to be conducted in a 'social' language. It is this mutation that also seems to lie at the heart of the recent prominence accorded to the language of community in political discourse from all shades of the political spectrum, and in the programmatic statements of political philosophers and advocates of the different versions of communitarianism. These new political languages are embodied in the ways in which a whole series of issues are problematized – made amenable to authoritative action *in terms of* features of communities and their strengths, cultures, pathologies. They shape the strategies and programmes that address such problems by seeking to *act upon* the dynamics of communities. They configure the *imagined territory* upon which these strategies should act – such as community mental health. And they extend to the *specification of the subjects* of government as individuals who are also, actually or potentially, the subjects of allegiance to a particular set of community values, beliefs and commitments.

We should not seek any single origin or cause of this reconfiguration of the territory of government. The social formed as a complex plane of interconnection among diverse minor lines of force, shifts in knowledge, in devices for charting populations and their vicissitudes, in practices of regulation and the pathways of action and calculation they traced out, contingent problematizations and ethical and political reformulations. Contemporary deployments of community are similarly heterogeneous, complex and mobile resultants of revised ways of representing, problematizing and intervening in a whole number of different arenas.[5] The term 'community', of course, has long been salient in political thought; it becomes governmental, however, when it is made technical. By the 1960s, community was already being invoked by sociologists as a possible antidote to the loneliness and isolation of the individual generated by 'mass society'. This idea of community as lost authenticity and common belonging was initially deployed in the social field as part of the language of critique and opposition directed against remote bureaucracy. Community activists were to identify not with a welfare system that they saw as degrading, policing and controlling, but with those who were the subjects of that system – the inhabitants of the housing estates, projects and ghettos. More or less simultaneously, the language of community was utilized by authorities such as the police to comprehend the problems they encountered in dealing with difficult zones – 'the West Indian community', the criminal community. Community here is a point of penetration of a kind of ethnographic sociology into the vocabularies and classifications of authorities; reciprocally, sociology itself intensified its investigations of collective life in terms of community and its anatomizing of the bonds of culture and the ties of locality that were thought to be essential conditions for its moral order. Within a rather short period, what began as a language of resistance and critique was transformed, no doubt for the best of motives, into an expert discourse and a professional vocation – community is now something to be programmed by Community Development Programmes, developed by Community Development Officers, policed by Community Police, guarded by Community Safety Programmes and rendered knowable by sociologists pursuing 'community studies'. Communities became zones to be investigated, mapped, classified, documented, interpreted, their vectors explained to enlightened professionals-to-be in countless college courses and to be taken into account in numberless encounters between professionals and their clients, whose individual conduct is now to be made intelligible in terms of the beliefs and values of 'their community'.

No doubt a whole range of other local shifts in vocabulary in diverse sites contributed to the emergence of community as a valorized alternative, antidote or even cure to the ills that the social had not been able to address – or even to the ills of the social itself. What began to take shape here was a new way of demarcating a sector for government, a sector whose vectors and forces could be mobilized, enrolled, deployed in novel programmes and techniques which operated through the instrumentalization of personal allegiances and active responsibilities: *government through community*. It is this sense of community that has come to the fore in recent political arguments (e.g. Etzioni 1993; Grey 1996). Society is to be regenerated, and social justice to be maximized, through the building of responsible communities, prepared to invest in themselves (Commission on Social Justice 1994). As the leader of the Labour Party, Tony Blair, put it in 1996, 'the search is on to reinvent community for a modern age, true to core values of fairness, co-operation and responsibility'.[6]

The re-figuring of the territory of government in terms of community has a number of significant features. The first is spatial: a kind of 'de-totalization'. The social, overarching all its stratifications and variations, was imagined as a single space, territorialized across a nation. Correlatively, government 'from the social point of view' posited a single matrix of solidarity, a relation between an organically interconnected society and all the individuals contained therein, given a politico-ethical form in the notion of social citizenship. Today, in contrast, a diversity of 'communities' is thought, actually or potentially, to command our allegiance: moral communities (religious, ecological, feminist, etc.), lifestyle communities (defined in terms of tastes, styles of dress and modes of life), communities of commitment (to disability, problems of health, local activism), and so forth. Such communities are construed as localized, heterogeneous, overlapping and multiple. Sometimes they are defined in terms of the geographical co-ordinates of a micro-locale. Sometimes they are 'virtual communities' associated neither in 'real' space nor in 'real' time but through a network of relays of communication, symbols, images, styles of dress and other devices of identification: the gay community, the disabled community, the Asian community (cf. Barry 1996; Barry et al. 1996). Such virtual communities are 'diasporic': they exist only to the extent that their constituents are linked together through identifications constructed in the non-geographic spaces of activist discourses, cultural products and media images.[7] And, while the language of community often locates discrete communities within a larger collectivity – a nation, a society, the planet itself – the nature of this superordinate allegiance is now most frequently posed as a problem. Hence arguments over 'multi-culturalism', the rise of political controversies over the implications of 'pluralism' – of ethnicity, religion, of sexuality, of ability and disability – together with conflicts over the competing and mutually exclusive 'rights' and 'values' of different communities.

A second significant feature of the birth of community is its changed ethical character. The social was an order of collective being and collective responsibilities and obligations. While the policies and programmes of the social accorded individuals personal responsibility for their conduct, this individual responsibility was always traversed by external determinations: the advantages or disadvantages conferred by family background, social class, life history, located within a wider array of social and economic forces such as changes in the labour market, booms, slumps, industrial cycles, the exigencies of urban environments, problems of housing supply. Of course, the extent to which such external determinants could or should mitigate personal responsibility was subject to continual dispute, as was the extent to which they could or should be compensated for in education, in the decisions of the criminal court, and so forth. Nevertheless, this configuration of ethical vectors is reorganized under the sign of community. The subject is addressed as a moral individual with bonds of obligation and responsibilities for conduct that are assembled in a new way – the individual in his or her community is both self-responsible and subject to certain emotional bonds of affinity to a circumscribed 'network' of other individuals unified by family ties, by locality, by moral commitment to environmental protection or animal welfare. Conduct is retrieved from a social order of determination into a new ethical perception of the individualized and autonomized actor, each of whom has unique, localized and specific ties to their particular family and to a particular moral community. Here we can locate the proliferation of debates on moral pluralism, and its diverse interpretations – as a relativistic threat to a necessary social agreement on moral absolutes or as the birth of a new era of enhanced ethical seriousness based upon individually sought and chosen allegiances in a cosmopolitan moral universe.

A third key aspect of the birth of community concerns the role of identification. The practices that assembled the social certainly entailed 'identification projects': programmes of mass schooling, of public housing, of public broadcasting, of social insurance, and so forth, had at their heart an image and a goal of the socially identified citizen, the person who, above all, understood themselves to be a member of a single integrated national society. The vocabulary of community also implicates a psychology of identification; indeed the very condition of possibility for a community to be imagined is its actual or potential existence as a fulcrum of personal identity. Yet these lines of identification are configured differently. Community proposes a relation that appears less 'remote', more 'direct', one which occurs not in the 'artificial' political space of society, but in matrices of affinity that appear more natural. One's communities are nothing more – or less – than those networks of allegiance with which one identifies existentially, traditionally, emotionally or spontaneously, seemingly beyond and above any calculated assessment of self-interest. Hence, like so many other similar loci of allegiance – class, civil society, ethnicity – arguments about community employ a Janus-faced logic (cf. Hindess 1993). Each assertion of community refers itself to something that already exists and has a claim on us: our common fate as gay men, as women of colour, as people with AIDS, as members of an ethnic group, as residents in a village or a suburb, as people with a disability. Yet our allegiance to each of these particular communities is something that we have to be made aware of, requiring the work of educators, campaigns, activists, manipulators of symbols, narratives and identifications. Within such a style of thought, community exists and is to be achieved, yet the achievement is nothing more than the birth-to-presence of a form of being which pre-exists.

'Government through community' involves a variety of strategies for inventing and instrumentalizing these dimensions of allegiance between individuals and communities in the service of projects of regulation, reform or mobilization. We can consider two examples which illustrate the complexity of these new governmental technologies.

My first example is security. Within social rationalities of government, a domain of collective security was envisaged to be maintained by the State on behalf of all citizens, through universal measures ranging from social insurance to the enforcement of the criminal law by a unified and socially funded police force. Today, this social image – and the practices to which it was linked – is displaced by a variety of different ways of imagining security, each of which mobilizes a particular sense of community. One image is of the 'gated city' preserving the security of its own residents, of the shopping mall policed by private security guards: that is to say, of a diversity of zones each circumscribing a community assuming – or being forced to assume – responsibility for 'its own' health, happiness, wealth and security (O'Malley 1992; Shearing 1995). The collective logics of community are brought into alliance with the individualized ethos of neo-liberal politics: choice, personal responsibility, control over one's own fate, self-promotion and self-government. A second image is of community as an antidote to the combined depredations of market forces, remote central government, insensitive local authorities in new programmes for the regeneration of delimited locales – paradigmatically areas of disadvantaged inner cities (Atkinson 1994; Etzioni 1993). New modes of neighbourhood participation, local empowerment and engagement of residents in decisions over their own lives will, it is thought, reactivate self-motivation, self-responsibility and self-reliance in the form of active citizenship within a self-governing community.[8] Government through the activation of individual commitments, energies and choices, through personal morality within a community setting, is counterposed to centralizing, patronizing and disabling social government. These opposed versions of security utilize similar images of subjects as active and responsible agents in the securing of security for themselves and those to whom they are or should be affiliated. Equally, they envision the space of government in similar ways, no longer territorialized across a national space, but organized in terms of the relations of identification between the person and 'their community' – the particular collectivity to which each person is bound by kinship, religion, residence, shared plight or moral affinity. In each case, community is not simply the territory of government, but a *means* of government: its ties, bonds, forces and affiliations are to be celebrated, encouraged, nurtured, shaped and instrumentalized in the hope of producing consequences that are desirable for all and for each.

My second example concerns the health promotion programmes that have taken shape around HIV and AIDS. Gay communities of allegiance and identification pre-existed the HIV epidemic in the West, constructed most recently through the campaigning activities and lifestyle politics of gay activists; it was largely in response to the political activism of these communities that national governments prioritized research and policies for HIV and AIDS (Ballard 1992). Gay organizations, first on their own, then in alliance with government health promotion campaigns, played a key role in the dissemination of new norms of sexual ethics and codes of sexual conduct to those who were 'at risk'. Not only in the publicity and health promotion materials, but also in the mass of social research into sexual attitudes and practices, identity and identification came to play a key role in the way in which sexual activity was rendered intelligible and in the development of strategies for its regulation – not only those targeted upon 'the gay community', but also those targeted upon other 'at risk groups'. Health promotion strategies were linked into the work of activist and self-help organizations, each strongly committed to the formation and valorization of the identity of its users and their communities. This established new forms of exclusion (Watts 1994) and new ways of problematizing the subjects to be governed (Bartos 1994). Government through community, even when it works upon pre-existing bonds of allegiance, transforms them, invests them with new values, affiliates them to expertise and reconfigures relations of exclusion. This does not make 'communities' in some sense false. But it should alert us to the work entailed in the construction of community, and the implications of the logics of inclusion and exclusion, of responsibilization and autonomization, that they inescapably entail.

We can thus be governed *through* our allegiance to particular communities of morality and identity. Many programmes of government now operate upon the presupposition of such communities, even where the allegiances presupposed do not immediately appear to exist. Programmes of urban renewal, for example, imagine the plight of the inner city in terms of the loss of a 'spirit of community', with all the capacities of self-reliance, entrepreneurship and communal pride which such a spirit evokes. They attempt to 'empower' the inhabitants of particular inner-city locales by constituting those who reside in a certain locality as 'a' community, by seeking out 'community groups' who can claim to speak 'in the name of community', and by linking them in new ways into the political apparatus in order to enact programmes which seek to regenerate the economic and human fabric of an area by reactivating in 'the community' these 'natural' virtues which it has temporarily lost. Complementarily, imagined communities, created by the activity of local activists or emerging as the reciprocal, as it were, of such governmental projects, can form the locus of the articulation of demands upon political authorities and resistance to such authorities: the language of community and the identity which is its referent becomes the site of new contestations. Hence community mobilization can be for causes as diverse as the demand for funding for HIV research and services, the blocking of a new road driven through a residential area, the protesting of racial harassment and opposition to policies for housing within 'our' community those who do not belong – black, mad, disabled, or whatever. These contradictions of community establish a new and agonistic territory for the organization of political and ethical conflicts.

This mutation, in which collective relations have been re-figured in such a way as to reduce the salience of 'the social' in favour of 'the community', has been accompanied by mutations along a number of other dimensions. In the remainder of this chapter, I want to discuss three of these, which are linked in different ways to the birth of the community. Along the first, one sees a reshaping of strategies for governing economic life, decoupling the relations that previously existed between social welfare and economic strength. Along a second, one sees the subjects of government specified in new ways, in terms of an ethic of activity which establishes new divisions between those who are considered to be competent citizens and those who are not. Along a third, one sees a reshaping of the relations between expertise and politics, and the emergence of a range of new expert technologies for governing expertise.

A De-socialization of Economic Government

A new configuration is taking shape for the government of economic life, in which techniques for the maximization of social welfare no longer appear necessary to secure economic well-being in a market constituted largely by private enterprises. The formation of the notion of a national economy was a key condition for the delineation of a distinct social domain. Classical political economy effected a separation of a domain of 'economic' events with their own laws and processes from a 'moral' domain. Economic events were territorialized within a national space, seen as governed by laws and relations whose scope and limits seemed to map onto the territory of political rule. As they crystallized within nineteenth-century thought, 'economies' were organized within nations, limited by borders, customs and other restrictions on imports and exports, unified through a single supply of money, characterized by a set of functional relations between their components, and these unities were located in a wider space within which they could engage in 'foreign trade' with other national economies. The responsibility of the political authorities for the security of a nation, a state and a people came to be understood in terms of their capacity to nurture natural economic processes to ensure national economic well-being (see the discussion in Tribe 1978). Further, over the course of the nineteenth century and into the twentieth, the solidity of these national economies was increased by the regular publication of various national indicators of economic performance, and by the gradual tracing out of a plane of 'economic policy', which concerned itself with the proper ways in which the strengths of such an economic system could be enhanced: action on the money supply, on the labour market, together with tariffs and restrictions on imports, and so forth, especially as national wealth came to be understood in terms of competition between discrete economies and their struggle to gain access to sources of cheap raw materials, cheap labour or lucrative markets outside their own territorial bounds.

In the strategies of government that developed over the course of the twentieth century, the domains of the economic and the social were distinguished, but governed according to a principle of joint optimization. Economic activity, in the form of wage labour, was given a new set of social responsibilities, seen as a mechanism which would link males into the social order, and which would establish a proper relationship between the familial, the social and the economic orders (Meuret 1981; Miller and Rose 1990 [reproduced as chapter 2 of this volume]; Rose 1989a; Rose and Miller 1992 [reproduced as chapter 3 of this volume]; Walters 1994). Simultaneously, the privacy of the wage contract was weakened, as politicians came to accept that conditions of labour and pay should be regulated in the name of social peace. The production of a labour market itself became part of the responsibilities of economic government, and a range of interventions into the social would maximize the economic efficacy of the population as a work-force, from vocational guidance and labour exchanges to various methods of maintaining the social habits of labour among the unemployed. Gradually, over the next six decades, new indexes

of economic activity were invented that would render the economy amenable to management, and new technologies of macro-economic regulations were brought into being. Through mechanisms of social insurance –
unemployment benefit, accident insurance, health and safety legislation,
and so forth – and through an array of forms of economic government – tax
regimes, interest rates and other techniques of 'demand management' – the
state assumed responsibility for the management of a whole variety of risks
– to individuals, to employers, to the state itself –in the name of society.

But the perception of 'the economy' which underpinned such endeavours is now undergoing a mutation (Hindess 1994b). 'An economy' is no
longer so easily imagined as naturally co-extensive with the realm of a
nation-state, with different 'national economies' inhabiting a wider
common field in which they traded, competed, exploited one another.
Theorists and practitioners alike now construe economic relations as
'globalized', and this new spatialization of the economy is coupled with
arguments to the effect that flexible economic relations need to be established in particular localities (Hirst and Thompson 1992; Reich 1992; both
cited and discussed in Hindess 1994b). Overlaying this 'dialectic of the
global and the local' are other trans-national spatializations of economic
relations, such as the argument that there is a 'global economy' of 'world
cities', in which Birmingham, Sydney, Baltimore, Budapest, compete
among one another for the economic benefit of company location, conferences, sporting events, tourism (Lash and Urry 1994; Zukin 1991).

Irrespective of the accuracy with which these trends are identified and
portrayed, the economic problems of government are being re-thought in
terms of a revised image of economic space and the means by which it
can be acted upon. It appears that, while national governments still have
to manage a national population, the economic well-being of the nation
and of its population can no longer be so easily mapped upon one another
and governed according to principles of mutual maximization. Government of the social in the name of the national economy gives way to
government of particular zones – regions, towns, sectors, communities – in
the interests of economic circuits which flow between regions and
across national boundaries. The economic fates of citizens within a national
territory are uncoupled from one another, and are now understood and
governed as a function of their own particular levels of enterprise,
skill, inventiveness and flexibility.

This is coupled with a shift in rationalities and techniques for the government of employment and unemployment. Unemployment is now understood as a phenomenon to be governed – both at the macro-economic level
and at the level of the conduct of the unemployed person him- or herself
through enhancing the activity of the individual in search of work, and

obliging the individual to engage in a constant and active search for employment and for the skills that will provide employment. On the one hand, the general problem of unemployment is re-conceived in terms of the respective competitiveness of different labour forces, understood at least in part in terms of the psychological, dispositional and aspirational capacities of those that make them up. On the other, individuals are solicited as allies of economic success through ensuring that they invest in the management, presentation, promotion and enhancement of their own economic capital as a capacity of their selves and as a lifelong project (Dean 1995; Walters 1994).

This emphasis upon the individuals as active agents in their own economic governance through the capitalization of their own existence is paralleled in a whole new set of vocabularies and devices for managing individuals within the workplace in terms of the enhancement of their own skills, capacities and entrepreneurship. These attempt an alliance between the desires of the worker or manager for self-enhancement and actualization through work and the perceived need of the enterprise to become flexible, competitive, agile, creative, and so forth. In labour, too, work is no longer to be construed as a social obligation, or its efficiency to be enhanced through maximizing the social benefits that the labourer finds in the workplace, or its primary role to be one of binding the individual into the collective through the socializing effects of the habit of work. Rather, the workplace itself – for labourers and for managers – is to be an area of self-promotion and the government of work is to be undertaken in terms of the enhancement of the active capacities of the entrepreneurial individual. No doubt, too, one could identify similar logics at work in the attempts to regenerate local economies, especially in urban areas: economic decline is to be halted through a range of devices that will enhance the activity of entrepreneurial individuals with skills and flexibility, and aspirations of self-promotion – exemplified, again, in the strategies for urban renewal pursued by UK governments in the 1980s and 1990s.

In short, one could suggest that, within those strategies of government that I have termed 'advanced liberal', one finds the emergence of a new way of conceptualizing and acting upon the relations between the government of economic life and the self-government of the individual: the economy is no longer to be governed in the name of the social, nor is the economy to be the justification for the government of a whole range of other sectors in a social form. The social and the economic are now seen as antagonistic, and the former is to be fragmented in order to transform the moral and psychological obligations of economic citizenship in the direction of active self-advancement. Simultaneously, government of a whole range of previously social apparatuses is to be restructured according to a particular image of the economic – the market. Economic government is to be de-socialized in the name of maximizing the entre-preneurial comportment of the individual.

The Subjects of Government

This transformation in the government of economic life links to a more general mutation in arrangements for the government of conduct. New ways are taking shape for understanding, classifying and acting upon the subjects of government, entailing new relations between the ways in which people are governed by others and the ways in which they are advised to govern themselves. Fundamental to this general field is a re-coding of dividing practices, revising the distinctions between the *affiliated* and the *marginalized*. By the affiliated I mean those who are considered 'included': the individuals and families who have the financial, educational and moral means to 'pass' in their role as active citizens in responsible communities. To remain affiliated one must 'enterprise' one's life through active choice, within authoritative terms and limits that have become integrated within all the practices of everyday life, sustained by a heterogeneous array of 'civilized' images and devices for lifestyle promotion. In rearing children, in schooling, in training and employment, in ceaseless consumption, the included must calculate their actions in terms of a kind of 'investment' in themselves, in their families, and maximize this investment with reference to the codes of their own particular communities. But the marginal are those who cannot be considered affiliated to such sanctioned and civilized cultural communities. Either they are not considered as affiliated to *any* collectivity by virtue of their incapacity to manage themselves as subjects or they are considered affiliated to some kind of 'anti-community' whose morality, lifestyle or comportment is considered a threat or a reproach to public contentment and political order. On this division between the affili-ated and the marginalized are articulated two rather different sets of debates, and two rather different governmental strategies, neither of which seem to be undertaken from 'the social point of view'.

The problem of risk provides us with a point of entry for an investiga-tion of these 'post-social' strategies for governing conduct. Sociologists have suggested that the prevalence of the language of risk is a consequence of changes in the contemporary existential condition of humans and their world (Beck 1992). In contrast, genealogical studies have analysed risk as part of a *particular style of thinking* born during the nineteenth century (Ewald 1991). This entailed new ways of understanding and acting upon misfortune *in terms of risk*: risk thinking brought the future into the present and made it calculable, using the statistical intelligibility that the collective laws of large numbers seemed to provide (Hacking 1991). Most significant for present purposes have been genealogies of social insurance that have traced the ways in which, over the course of the twentieth century, security against risk was socialized.

In the late nineteenth century, the respectable working man was urged to be *prudent*, an obligation which required him to take a range of active steps to secure himself, his family and his dependants against future misfortune: joining insurance schemes provided by trade associations or friendly societies, personal involvement in the selection of benefits and the making of regular payments, and so forth (Defert 1991). These schemes established quite direct connections between the individual responsibility of each member and the mutuality of the responsibility that was shared among the members as a whole. These mutualized relations of prudence were relatively short-lived. By the end of the nineteenth century in Britain, Australia and the United States they were already being displaced by commercialized operations in which security was secured through individuals contracting into private insurance schemes run for profit (O'Malley 1995). At the turn of the century, in most European countries, these voluntary relations of prudence – mutual or commercial – were further transformed with the implementation of national schemes of compulsory social insurance. There were many different forces at work here, including political worries about the viability and integrity of the schemes, and concerns about the consequences to, and of, those who were left uninsured through failure of companies or through unwillingness or inability to be thrifty. But, as Ewald puts it, 'Insurance becomes *social* . . . because European societies come to analyse themselves and their problems in terms of the generalised technology of risk' (1991: 210): risk, responsibility and thrift became vectors of social government.

Social insurance was acquired as a benefit of citizenship. As is well known, schemes were structured with the aim that they would not 'demoralize' those who were their members through the inculcation of dependency, but, on the contrary, produce moral effects of responsibility, regularity of habits of labour and social obligation in those who were their beneficiaries (Gilbert 1966). Of course, the injunction to personal prudence on one's own behalf and that of one's dependants did not disappear over the twentieth century. But nonetheless, today, a strategic shift is occurring in the politics of security. Individuals are, once again, being urged by politicians and others to *take upon themselves* the responsibility for their own security and that of their families: to insure against the costs of ill health through private medical insurance, to make provision for their future through private pensions, to take an active role in securing themselves against all that could possibly threaten the security of their chosen style of life. This 'new prudentialism' (O'Malley 1992) uses the technologies of consumption – advertising, market research, niche marketing, and so forth – to exacerbate anxieties about one's own future and that of one's loved ones, to encourage us to subdue these risks and to tame our fate by purchasing insurance designed especially for us and our individual situation. There is obviously an industry of risk here, seeking out and creating markets for products in the interests of its own profit. But there is also a politics of risk, as politicians warn about the future of social pension and insurance schemes, and exhort responsible individuals to take primary responsibility for the management of risks to their own security and that of their families by disposing of their current income in the interests of their own future comfort. Thus, as in other technologies of consumption, a hybrid arrangement of forces and devices has been assembled together which acts to govern choice in the supposedly mutually reinforcing interests of personal security, private profit and public good.

This contemporary prudentialism differs from its nineteenth-century forebear in a number of ways. The person who is to be made prudent is no longer mutualized but autonomized. Thrift is recast as investment in a future lifestyle of freedom. Insurantial expertise is no longer a matter of actuarial wisdom, the assurance of stability and probity, and the personal relation with the contributions collector, but works through amplifying the very anxieties against which security is to protect and promoting the dreams of tranquillity and a golden future which insurance can provide, through the use of all the techniques of advertising and marketing. Further, insurance agents now offer themselves as versatile advisers in the techniques of risk reduction and risk management. As risk is simultaneously proliferated and rendered potentially manageable, the private market for 'security' extends: not merely personal pension schemes and private health insurance, but burglar alarms, devices that monitor sleeping children, home testing kits for cholesterol levels, and much more. Protection against risk through an investment in security becomes part of the responsibilities of each active individual, if they are not to feel guilt at failing to protect themselves and their loved ones against future misfortunes. The ethics of lifestyle maximization, coupled with a logic in which someone must be held to blame for any event that threatens an individual's 'quality of life', generates a relentless imperative of risk management not simply in relation to contracting for insurance, but also through daily lifestyle management, choices of where to live and shop, what to eat and drink, stress management, exercise, and so forth. Of course, this inaugurates a virtually endless spiral of amplification of risk – as risk is managed in certain zones and forms of conduct (e.g. shopping in malls scanned by security cameras;

foetal monitoring; low-fat diets and heart disease), the perceived riskiness of other unprotected zones is exacerbated (high streets; unsupervised pregnancies; the uneducated dietary habits of children and the poor). These arrangements within which the individual is re-responsibilized for the management of his or her own risk produce a field characterized by uncertainty, plurality and anxiety, thus continually open to the construction of new problems and the marketing of new solutions.

These new logics of risk management not only multiply the points at which normative calculation and intervention are required, but also fragment the social space of welfare into a multitude of diverse pockets, zones, folds of riskiness, each comprised of a linking of specific current activities and conducts and general probabilities of their consequences. In this new configuration, 'social insurance' is no longer a key technical component for a general rationality of social solidarity: taxation for the purposes of welfare becomes, instead, the minimum price that respectable individuals and communities are prepared to pay for insuring themselves against the riskiness now seen to be concentrated within certain problematic sectors.

This discussion highlights more general features of the new 'post-social' technologies of governing conduct which are taking shape. Under the rationalities of welfare, social technologies were to civilize individuals, render them as citizens with obligations to conduct themselves with prudence in exchange for certain guarantees against uncertainty. In the new prudential regimes, individuals, educated through the mechanisms of marketing and the pedagogies of consumption and lifestyle, are to gain access to previously 'social' benefits such as educational advantage, health status and contentment in old age through purchase in a competitive market. Promotion of private insurance in these ways thus exemplifies a more widespread shift which has given consumption markets a central role in the shaping of conduct. These are not guided by a political logic, but they nonetheless make it possible to transform political technologies for the government of subjectivity. Affiliation to communities of lifestyle through the practices of consumption displaces older devices of habit formation that enjoined obligations upon citizens as part of their social responsibilities. Consider, for example, the way in which advertising and marketing have transformed the role of the technologies invented in the early years of the twentieth century that targeted mothers – potential future mothers in the schools, new mothers by health visitors, mothers as the guardians of hygienic and healthy homes by doctors and other experts in domesticity. Consumption regimes now operate as highly managed and carefully calibrated domains for the calculated regulation of the minutiae of private conduct through personal acts of choice. The contemporary politics of conduct, at least in part, is conducted by means of the selective amplification of passions, anxieties, allegiances and identities intrinsic to the commercial struggle to sell goods and maximize profits.

The commodification of identities and the instrumentalization of passions to which it is linked opens a heterogeneous and risky field – identities may become identified with forms of conduct that themselves call forth demands for new areas of regulation. Techniques of commodification of identities can be utilized by political authorities in calculated strategies such as those to reduce the spread of HIV, the use of drugs or the prevalence of drunken driving, but they can also be used in the spread of evangelical religions or pornography. The alliances forged here are always risky, provisional and revisable; nonetheless, from this point onwards, projects for the government of conduct will operate on a territory marked out by the vectors of identity, choice, consumption and lifestyle.

Governing the Margins

It would certainly be misleading to interpret the contemporary redrawing of the boundaries of the political as merely a 'reduction of the role of the State in society'. On the one hand, we have seen the spread of the mechanisms which Deleuze characterized under the rubric of 'societies of control', where conduct is continually monitored and reshaped by logics immanent within all networks of practice. In such practices we are continually subject to processes of functional integration: 'life-long learning', 'continual retraining', 'constant job readiness', ceaseless consumption (Deleuze 1995). But these processes of continuous modulation of conduct have been accompanied by the intensification of direct, disciplinary, often coercive and carceral, political interventions in relation to particular zones and persons. As civility is understood as affiliation by consumption, dividing practices are reconfigured to problematize certain 'abjected' persons, sectors and locales for specific reformatory attention: the underclass, the excluded, the marginal.

It would be unwise to overstate the novelty of these divisions. One could write the history of the government of conduct in terms of its successive taxonomies and forms of division: the eighteenth-century division of poverty and pauperism; the Victorian proliferation of institutions for specific groups: fallen women, sailors out of work, blind children. At the end of the nineteenth century, there was a tension between those who would *unify* the social problem in terms of a degenerate constitution and those, in England most notably the Webbs, who would see the major requirement of a system of administration as a practice of *distinction*: the classification of socially problematic individuals into precise categories, each requiring its own distinct form of intervention. It would be foolish to deny the continued presence of these diagnostic and classificatory imperatives within the social machinery of the welfare state as it assembled over the middle decades of the twentieth century. Unlike France, where the language of social right provided a unifying milieu within which conflicting political positions could engage with one another, in England, social legislation, industrial tribunals, social security tribunals and many other apparatuses operated in terms of precise yet diverse criteria of eligibility and allowances. Nevertheless, at the programmatic level, codifiers such as Beveridge and Marshall constructed a vision in which security against hardship, like hardship itself, was social and to be provided by measures of benefit and insurance that, in name at least, were to be termed 'universal', including all within a unified 'social citizenship'.

Of course, even within this unified vision there were concerns with those who eluded the bonds of citizenship – one only has to consider the debate in the 1960s over the 'cycle of deprivation'. But the emergence of the notion of an 'underclass' in the United States at the end of the 1970s does seem to mark a moment in which the social vision of a continuous *quantitative* variability in levels of civility becomes re-coded as a *qualitative* distinction.

> Behind the [ghetto's] crumbling walls lives a large group of people who are more intractable, more socially alien and more hostile than almost anyone had imagined. . . . Their bleak environment nurtures values that are often at odds with those of the majority – even the majority of the poor. Thus the underclass produces a highly disproportionate number of the nation's juvenile delinquents, school dropouts, drug addicts and welfare mothers, and much of the adult crime, family disruption, urban decay and demand for social expenditures. (*Time*, 29 August 1977, quoted in Katz 1993: 4)

The underclass was a heady mixture of long-term welfare recipients, hostile street criminals, hustlers in an alternative underground economy, traumatized alcoholics, vagrants and de-institutionalized psychiatric patients dominating the wastelands in the decaying industrial heartland of the cities of North America. In the UK, a less lurid picture was painted, but one in which the recipients of welfare were still portrayed in terms of a moral problematization: those lured into welfare dependency by the regimes of social security themselves, those unable to accept their moral responsibilities as citizens for reasons of psychological or other personal incapacity, those who might be enterprising, but who wilfully refused to operate within the values of civility and responsible self-management, such as New Age travellers or drug abusers.

Of course these essentially moral characterizations, in terms of dependency, danger or depravity, were contested by social liberals and those on the left. Initially these contestations were posed in the familiar logics of social causation and social welfare. Yet, since the 1980s, within British and European rationalities of social democracy, a new style of thought has taken shape, in which the old problems of inequality and social justice are analysed in a distinctive and recurring fashion. It is suggested that secular economic changes, exacerbated by policies which have sought to reduce welfare expenditure in the name of competitive tax regimes and the like, have led to the rise of a 'two-thirds, one-third' society, producing a widening gap between the 'included' majority who are seeing their standard of living rising and impoverished minorities who are 'excluded' (Levitas 1996). Thus, the European Commission, in a chapter entitled 'Social policy and protection – an active society for all', in its White Paper on 'European Social Policy: a Way Forward for the Union', argues that 'with more than 52 million people in the Union living below the poverty line, social exclusion is an endemic phenomenon . . . which threatens the social cohesion of each Member State and of the Union as a whole. . . . The marginalization of major social groups is a challenge to the social cohesion of the Union' (European Commission 1994: 49; cf. Commission on Social Justice 1994; Hutton 1995; Joseph Rowntree Foundation 1995).

Despite their great differences in notions of economic causation and personal responsibility, these rationalities operate with a surprisingly consonant picture of the abjected persons and groups that are their object. On the one hand, they are dispersed. They are no longer seen as part of a single group with common social characteristics, to be managed by a unified 'social service' and 'generic social workers' who can recognize the common roots of all social problems. The marginalized, the excluded, the underclass, are fragmented and divided; their particular difficulties thus need to be addressed through the activities of a variety of specialists each of whom is an expert in a particular problem – training schemes for those excluded through unemployment, specialist agencies working with those with disabilities, rehabilitation of addicts undertaken by specialist drug workers, education in social skills by workers with the single homeless, specialized hostels for battered women, for alcoholics, and so forth. Yet, on the other hand, these abjected subjects are re-unified ethically and spatially. Ethically, in that they are accorded a new active relation to their status in terms of their strategies and capacities for the management of themselves: they have either refused the bonds of civility and self-responsibility or they aspire to them but have not been given the skills, capacities and means. And spatially, in that the unified space of the social is reconfigured, and the abjected are relocated, in both imagination and strategy, in 'marginalized' spaces: in the decaying council estate, in the chaotic lone-parent family, in the shop doorways of inner-city streets. It appears as if, outside the communities of inclusion, outside the control society, there exists an array of micro-sectors, comprised of those who are unable or unwilling to enterprise their lives or manage their own risk, incapable of exercising responsible self-government, attached either to no moral community or to a community of anti-morality.

It is in this sense that it is possible to argue that new territory is emerging, after the welfare state, for the management of these micro-sectors, traced out by a plethora of quasi-autonomous agencies working within the 'savage spaces', in the 'anti-communities' on the margins, or with those abjected by virtue of their lack of competence or capacity for responsible ethical self-management: 'voluntary' endeavours (often run by users, survivors or philanthropists but funded by various grant regimes) – drug projects, disability organizations, self-help groups, concept houses, and so forth (oppositional forces transformed into service providers). Private and for-profit organizations – old people's homes, hostels, and so forth – make their money from private insurance or from the collection of the state benefits given to their individual inmates. In the huge and murky industry of 'training', unemployment is re-problematized as a matter of the lack of individual and marketable skills among the unemployed themselves, to be countered by a multitude of training organizations that are private and compete in a market for public contracts and public funds. Within this new territory of exclusion, the social logics of welfare bureaucracies are replaced by new logics of competition, market segmentation and service management: the management of misery and misfortune can become, once more, a potentially profitable activity.

Experts of Activity

I have suggested that the contemporary politics of competence construes subjects as, actually or potentially, active elements in their own self-government. This perception extends to those whom I have termed the abjected. Whether they be construed as excluded by socio-economic forces, marginalized by virtue of personal incapacity or pathology or morally alien on account of their dependency, depravity or delinquency, their alienation is to be reversed by equipping them with certain active subjective capacities: they must take responsibility, they must show themselves capable of calculated action and choice, they must shape their lives according to a moral code of individual responsibility and community obligation.

I have argued elsewhere that in 'control societies', market mechanisms are increasingly utilized to link the active individual and family to expertise, and I have suggested that this opens new possibilities for questioning expertise as shown in the rise of consumers' and users' organizations of various sorts (Rose 1994). For those who are to be the subjects of expert attention, similar 'active' policies are being set in place, but this injunction to activity allows far fewer opportunities for contesting expert authority. Take the example of unemployment, which I have already discussed. In the UK, in the policies of the Organization for Economic Cooperation and Development and in Australia, the unemployed person is now portrayed as a 'job-seeker', whose 'job readiness' is the key point at issue, where a lapse into long-term unemployment is to be avoided by emphasizing the requirement for an 'active' programme of income support, and who is to be trained in the active skills of 'job search' (cf. Dean 1995; Walters 1994). The injunction to activity here limits the possibilities of resistance. Jobseeking conduct is to be continually subject to individualized evaluation and judgement, and failure to manifest appropriately energetic conduct as specified in the manuals and criteria results in peremptory loss of benefit.

This injunction to activity extends to practices that might be thought more caring and progressive. Consider, for example, the widespread utilization of notions such as empowerment in the formulation of practices for a diversity of problematic categories (Baistow 1995; Cruikshank 1994). Experts still relate to their clients in a pedagogic and responsibilizing form. However, the emphasis has shifted. While clients were typically regarded as damaged individuals, with a personal pathology that may well have been triggered or sustained by social factors, hence requiring diagnosis and insight, the professional gaze has become more 'superficial': it now focuses upon conduct itself and the cognitive and moral organization of perception, intention, action and evaluation. In these new forms of practice, which are of course by no means universal but are spreading fast, the subject of expertise is now understood, at least for the purposes at hand, as an individual who lacks the cognitive, emotional, practical and ethical skills to take personal responsibility for rational self-management. Of course, this empowerment, and the activity it is to generate, are located not within a closed disciplinary space, but upon the governable territory of cultural community. Empowerment, then, is a matter of experts teaching, coaxing, requiring their clients to conduct themselves within particular cultural communities of ethics and lifestyle, according to certain specified arts of active personal responsibility. Empowerment, with all its emphasis on strengthening the capacity of the individual to play the role of actor in his or her own life, has come to encompass a range of interventions to transmit, under tutelage, certain professionally ratified mental, ethical and practical techniques for active self-management. Under the sign of empowerment, one thus can observe the redeployment of the whole panoply of psychological technologies for reforming conduct in relation to particular norms, from individual psychotherapy in various rational and cognitive forms, through the use of programmed behavioural techniques to group work. In line with the 'superficial' gaze of the new experts of conduct, however, these techniques are re-conceptualized so that they can be seen as having visible, identifiable and specifiable behavioural or mental outputs, leading to target behaviours that seem to be amenable to measurement and calculation. And, as we shall see, this emphasis on goals, targets and measurements is part of a new way not only of managing professional–client relations, but of managing professionals themselves.

Risk, Community and Expertise

The notion of risk once more provides a useful point of entry into the revised relations of expertise taking shape on the territory of community. In part this is because the capacity for personal 'power', or the lack of it, which is the object of empowerment technologies is itself re-thought in terms of the relations of risk and community which I discussed earlier: the risks posed to the individual themselves if they cannot adequately manage their life within the community, the risks the individual may pose to the community on account of their failure to govern themselves. It is also because the responsibilities of experts are themselves being re-formulated in terms of risk and community. In a range of domains, social workers, psychiatrists, doctors and others have been allocated accountability not so much for the cure or reform of clients, patients and other problematic individuals, but for their administration according to a logic of risk minimization (cf. Castel 1991; Rose 1996a). The novel intellectual techniques of risk identification, risk assessment and risk management bring into existence a whole new set of professional obligations: the obligation that each individual professional should calculate and reduce the risk of their professional conduct, instruct the subjects under their authority in the riskiness of the practices and procedures in which they are engaged and manage their clients in the light of the imperative to reduce the risk they may pose to others – their children, members of 'the general public'. Experts are thus increasingly required to undertake not so much an identification of a condition as a calculation of the riskiness of an individual or an event, with the obligation to take (legal, moral, professional, financial) responsibility for the calculations that they make, the advice that they give and the success of the strategies that they put into place to monitor and manage that risk. This is only one of the ways in which the reconfiguring of the territory of government has been linked to new roles for experts in the government of the conduct of active individuals within their communities.

Social government was expert government. The devices of 'the welfare state' opened a multitude of new locales for the operation of expert judgements, based on knowledge, training, professional and bureaucratic ethics and specialist skills: bureaux of various types, benefit, social security and unemployment offices, dossiers, case records, case conferences and tribunals. In each of these locales, experts and their judgements were not only vital relays in the links between political objectives and personal conduct, they also had considerable capacities to 'enclose' themselves and their judgements, to make demands in terms of their own perceptions of their interests and the requirements of the apparatuses they operated – in short to deploy a range of tactics to render themselves difficult for politicians to govern, if not actually 'ungovernable'. While the problems posed by experts were bemoaned over many years and from many different perspectives, a number of new technologies are currently being deployed through which experts can be linked into the devices for the conduct of conduct. Locales and activities that were previously part of the assemblages of the 'social' are being autonomized from the machinery of politics and novel devices are being used to govern the activities of those who work within them. In a plethora of quasi-autonomous units, associations and 'intermediate organizations', experts are allocated new responsibilities and new mechanisms are developed for the management of professional expertise 'at a distance', that is, outside the machinery of bureaucracy that previously bound experts into devices for the government of 'the social'. Previously 'social' experts such as social workers, benefit officers, doctors, social service bureaucrats and others now operate within a whole variety of quasi-private regulatory organizations: in the UK situation one could point to the Next Steps Initiative in the fragmentation and contractualization of the civil service; the establishment of 'agencies' to run even apparatuses previously considered to be essential to 'the State' such as the prison service; the proliferation of such hybrid public/private entities as Training and Enterprise Boards; the purchaser–provider split and case management techniques in social services, the fragmentation of health services into autonomous trusts and a range of other shifts popularly termed 'the quango-ization of the state'.[9] Three aspects are worth highlighting.

First, in the UK situation at least, there is a renewed emphasis upon the potential of a variety of legal and quasi-legal mechanisms to meet political obligations to address 'problems' – from discharged psychiatric patients to insider dealing – while refusing an extension of the politico-administrative machinery of the state. I am thinking here of the use of such statutorily specified and legally enforceable criteria as those governing minimum service standards and contracts specifying performance targets and outputs – numbers of patients to be treated, length of time a case must wait until dealt with, obligations for the relations between case managers, their clients and the providing organization, and so forth. This should not be seen as the expansion of 'law' as a 'system' and its capture by a political apparatus. The mechanisms of legal regulation are complex and fragmented. Politicians, professionals and consumer groups organize around the production of codes of professional conduct which specify various rights for users and clients. A new 'litigious mentality' ensures that 'the shadow of the law' becomes a means of managing professional activity through the self-regulation of decisions and actions in relation to such formally promulgated codes and standards. Struggles over the regulation of expertise occur not only in the courts, but in campus sexual harassment offices, human rights committees and commissions, review bodies for appealing welfare decisions and in many new and diverse forums. These legal procedures are not in themselves new. Nonetheless, the widespread utilization of these forms of regulation renders the actions and judgements of professionals governable in new ways – and, in the process, changes the very terms in which these judgements themselves are construed, prioritized, justified and enacted.

Perhaps even more significant has been the spreading of modes of financial calculation and budgetary obligations to areas which were previously governed according to bureaucratic, professional or other norms. The allocation of budgetary responsibilities to professionals – doctors, educationalists, civil servants, those working with excluded groups – requires them to calculate their actions not in the esoteric languages of their own expertise, but by translating them into costs and benefits that can be given an accounting value. Coupled with the raft of other elements sometimes referred to as 'the new public management', this has transformed the governability of professional activity while, at the same time, apparently devolving more decisional power to those actually involved in devising and delivering services in local sites (cf. Hood 1991). Again, on the one hand, this has punctured the enclosures within which many forms of expertise were able to insulate themselves from 'political interference'. On the other, it has done so at the price of shifting powers to other forms of expertise – those of accountants and managers – and of changing the very terms in which experts calculate and enact their expertise.

Finally, it is worth remarking upon the ways in which the mechanisms of audit have become versatile means of purporting to render accountable and judgeable the activity of professionals, managers, business people, politicians and many others (Power 1994). Audits of various sorts come to replace the trust that social government invested in professional wisdom and the decisions and actions of specialists. In a whole variety of practices – educational, medical, economic, organizational – audits hold out the promise – however specious – of new distantiated forms of control between political centres of decision and the autonomized loci – schools, hospitals, firms – who now have the responsibility for the government of health, wealth and happiness. Like the utilization of legal codes, and the allocation of budgetary responsibilities, government by audit transforms that which is to be governed: rendering something auditable shapes the processes that are to be audited, and the logics and technical requirements of audit displace the internal logics of expertise. Thus the emphasis on defined and measurable goals and targets in the work that professionals do with their abjected clients is an element within a much wider reconfiguration of methods for the government of specialist activities. These arrangements retain the formal independence of professionals while utilizing new techniques of accountability to render their decisions visible, calculable and amenable to evaluation. No doubt many different factors converged to accord political priority to attempts to open up expertise to visibility and judgement according to criteria that purport to be publicly intelligible, rather than logics that are the esoteric preserve of the specialists themselves. And no doubt the consequences have frequently been costly and bureaucratic. But a politics of expertise also needs to recognize that such mechanisms may perhaps contain some innovative possibilities for contesting and reshaping the relations of power between experts and their subjects.

Conclusions

Many of the transformations to which I have drawn attention are themselves linked to a shift within the field of politics, in the ways in which political discourse itself configures the limits of the political and its relations with other domains. Confronted by supra-national associations and trans-national ecological movements, rival nationalisms fighting across a single geographical terrain, federalism, the politics of ethnic, cultural and linguistic minorities and multi-culturalism, it is no longer easy for political thought to territorialize itself in an apparently 'natural' geo-political space in which the nation is coextensive with and delimited by a unified polity of social citizens (cf. Tully 1995). In the face of such 'strange multiplicities', to adopt Tully's term, in a variety of national contexts and from a variety of political positions, 'anti-political motifs' are on the rise within political discourse (Hindess 1994a). These motifs not only stress the corruption and ineffectiveness of the political classes but, more fundamentally, are based upon a sense of the limits of any politics that sees itself as omni-competent and articulates itself in terms of overarching political programmes. These 'anti-political' motifs have recently alighted upon 'community'– which formerly had been a part of the mundane vocabulary of social policy and sociological investigation, valorized only by a small band of communitarian political philosophers and romantic or eccentric activists – as the space in which powers and responsibilities previously allocated to politicians might be relocated. Each of these emergent political rationalities – civic republicanism, associationalism, communitarian liberalism – in its different way, seeks a way of governing, not through the politically directed, nationally territorialized, bureaucratically staffed and programmatically rationalized projects of a centrally concentrated state, but through instrumentalizing the self-governing properties of the subjects of government themselves in a whole variety of locales and localities – enterprises, associations, neighbourhoods, interest groups and, of course, communities. Of course, it would be absurd to suggest that a politics of community is itself novel: as Tully points out, communitarianism may be regarded as one of the traditional themes of modern constitutional thought (along with nationalism and liberalism). But in these contemporary political rationalities, community is made calculable by a whole variety of reports, investigations and statistical inquiries, is the premise and objective of a range of governmental technologies, and is to be acted upon in a multitude of authoritative practices and professional encounters. Community, that is to say, is to be governmentalized: it cannot be understood outside the other shifts to which I have tried to draw attention in this chapter. What are of interest, therefore, are the problematizations through which collective existence has come to offer itself to thought in the form of community, and the new representations, techniques, powers and ethical relations that have been invented in the process.

It is too early to gauge the durability of these new ways of thinking about politics and government. For present purposes, their significance lies less in their success than in the evidence that they provide of an imperative felt at the heart of politics to fashion a revised way of governing, one which can not only make itself consistent with the heterogeneity of the forms in which struggles are now carried out – nationalist, ethnic, religious, moral, environmental – but also connect up with the new conceptions of subjectivity through which the subjects of government increasingly have come to understand and relate to themselves. It is, of course, not a question of the replacement of 'the social' by 'the community': the spatialization and territorialization of political thought does not proceed in such linear sequences.

Nonetheless, the hold of 'the social' over our political imagination is weakening. While the social has no doubt been seen as a zone of failure since its birth, the solution to these failures is no longer automatically seen to be reinvention of the social. While our political, professional, moral and cultural authorities still speak happily of 'society', the very meaning and ethical salience of this term is under question as 'society' is perceived as dissociated into a variety of ethical and cultural communities with incompatible allegiances and incommensurable obligations.

We have still to begin the task of anatomizing the new relations of power brought into play on this new multiple and fragmented territory of government. In doing so, we should not assume that all is for the worst in this 'post-social' age. We need not simply to condemn the injustices and disadvantages entailed in the de-socialization of government, but also to engage inventively with the possibilities opened up by the imperatives of activity and the images of plural affinities. The role of such analyses should not be to praise or to blame, but to diagnose, to identify the points of weakness that might be exploited if we are to maximize the capacity of individuals and collectivities to shape the knowledges, contest the authorities and configure the practices that will govern them in the name of their freedoms and commitments.

Notes

1. This piece was originally written in 1993. In revising it for publication in this collection, some tenses and formulations have been modified where they specifically refer to events that are now some fifteen years in the past.
2. This phrase is taken from Procacci (1989), but here it is used slightly differently.
3. On 'lines', see Deleuze and Parnet (1987: 124–47).
4. Paul Hirst and Grahame Thompson (1996) have argued forcefully that the analysts and commentators have got it wrong, that economic relations were, in many ways, more 'globalized' in previous times than they are today, and that it is misleading and pernicious to argue that national governments are powerless. For the purposes of our argument, however, the truth effects of discourses of economic globalization are somewhat independent of the veracity of the analysis,
5. Obviously there are similarities between this argument and that concerning the construction of nations and identities in the form of 'imagined communities', which cannot be discussed here (cf. Anderson, 1991).
6. In an article in the Guardian newspaper of 29 January 1996, timed to coincide with a speech to mark the tenth anniversary of the report of the Archbishop of Canterbury's Special Commission on Urban Priority areas, Faith in the City.

7. The term 'diaspora' which is sometimes employed here is interesting, imply-
    ing that what is currently dispersed was once together – an essential unity
    scattered by the hand of fate or politics.

8. There are, of course, many other versions of this, most notably in the revival
    of civic republicanism. The 'advanced liberal' ethos of much contemporary
    civic republicanism is pointed out in Burchell (1995).

9. Quango is an acronym for quasi-autonomous non-governmental
    organization.

5

Mobilizing the Consumer
Assembling the Subject of Consumption

Many diagnoses of our 'post-modern condition' hinge upon debates about consumption: has consumption replaced production as the key to the intelligibility of our present; did the previous emphasis on production in social thought overlook the dependence of an economy of commodity exchange upon the simultaneous constitution of consuming pleasures; have consumption sub-cultures replaced class, region, religion, generation and gender as sources of interests and identifications? Alongside these debates has been an argument about subjectivity. It has been suggested that the perspective of consumption reveals features of our experience that were undervalued in most classical social theory – the active arts though which individuals shape their everyday lives with the materials provided for them by dominant economic, social and cultural forces; the role of subjectivities, pleasures and desires in the history of our present which is so often painted in the monotonous and sombre tones of state, domination, ideology and hegemony (see, e.g., Bocock 1993; Featherstone 1991; Shields 1992a).

Yet there is a deep ambivalence underpinning many diagnoses, at least as they come to bear upon 'the subject of consumption', the individual who is imagined and acted upon by the imperative to consume. On the one hand, it is claimed that human beings, in engaging in acts of consumption and the relations surrounding consumption, achieve pleasures, exert powers, find meanings, construct diverse subjectivities and enact sociality in a creative and innovative manner (e.g. Shields 1992b). On the other hand, it appears that – to the extent that all these are construed as individual achievements, organized in a field whose dynamic is the quest for profit, structured in terms of wealth, culture and gender, shaped by a power relationship in which producers and their agents impose their meanings and values upon others – the pleasures, powers and meanings produced are, in crucial respects, false. The collective socialities are enacted at the price of turning a blind eye to the regimes of exploitation, illusion and exclusion that foster consumption, and the subjectivities so constructed are enfeebled or damaged. This latter theme reactivates the earlier melancholy 'aristocratic' disdain with which critics of 'mass society' regarded the rise of new consumer goods, advertising, and the like, which, as Featherstone puts it, viewed these as giving rise to 'an atomized, manipulated mass who participate in an *ersatz* mass-produced commodity culture targeted at the lowest common denominator' (Featherstone 1991: 14). In these respects the regime of consuming subjectivities is to be the target of a critique, its contradictions are to be exposed, the hidden costs – individual, political and cultural – of its surface pleasures are to be revealed (e.g. Langman 1992; Qualter 1991).

In this chapter, we do not wish to arbitrate between these two lines of argument, which we have undoubtedly caricatured. Indeed, many recent studies of consumption practices have served to deepen and enrich our understanding of the construction of what Frank Mort has termed 'the commercial domain' (Mort 1996). Our aim is to make a contribution to the empirical bases of such debates, by examining a number of ways in which different images of the subject of consumption have operated *internal* to one element of the new 'economy of consumption': the shaping and advertising of products. Making up the subject of consumption, we suggest, has been a complex technical process. To understand this process, it is necessary to look beyond general shifts in cultural understanding or the imperatives of profit, and examine the ways in which the understandings of human individuality, personality and psychology elaborated by the psychological sciences have played a key role in the construction of consumption technologies. For psychological expertise in advertising provides a site where we can explore the extent to which this has been less a matter of dominating or manipulating consumers than of 'mobilizing' them by forming connections between human passions, hopes and anxieties, and very specific features of goods enmeshed in particular consumption practices.

There have, of course, been innumerable studies of the rise of advertising and the vicissitudes of the industry, its relations with market research, with producers of goods, and of the techniques that advertising has deployed. While many of these are genial and essentially progressivist accounts, often written by insiders (e.g. Elliot 1962; Henry 1986; Nevett 1982; Pearson and Turner 1965), the tone of studies written by sociologists and cultural analysts has been one of deep unease about the nature of this profession (notably Ewen 1976; see also Qualter 1991; Schudson 1984).

This unease has extended to the symbiotic relations between business, advertisers and psychologists that have obtained at various moments in the history of the industry, encapsulated in Ewen's view of advertising as a 'tool of social order' steered by businessmen depicted as 'captains of consciousness' (Ewen 1976). Even when they are dubious about the efficacy of advertising, or of the extent to which it does, in fact, make much use of psychological techniques beyond relatively simple conceptions of attitudes and methods of attitude change, the general image portrayed is of a profession which treats consumers as largely irrational or foolish, to be manipulated through methods not far removed from those of political propaganda, with consequences for public culture and democracy that are largely deleterious (Qualter 1991).

Our own perspective differs. We abstain from a mode of analysis which links the unholy alliance of psychology, advertising and capitalism with a manipulation of desires in the name of private profit, social anaesthesia and commodity fetishism. We are concerned rather with what one might term the 'productive' features of these new techniques, the ways in which psychological knowledges have connected themselves up in complex ways with the technologies of advertising and marketing to make possible new kinds of relations that human beings can have with themselves and others through the medium of goods. In addition, while many of the existing studies have treated the USA and 'Madison Avenue' as their primary empirical focus, and tended to concentrate on the early periods of the utilization of psychology in advertising, our focus is on Britain, and upon the two decades following the end of World War II. In particular, we offer a detailed case study of one particular site at which changing psychological conceptions of the human being intersected with changing concerns of producers wishing to market their products and their advertising agents. This site is the Tavistock Institute of Human Relations (TIHR), a sister institution to the Tavistock Clinic, which was founded in the years immediately following the end of World War II and undertook a range of innovative investigations into such varied issues as workplace democracy, the psychoanalytic education of general practitioners, group relations training and marital therapy (Miller and Rose 1988, 1994 [reproduced as chapter 6], 1995a [reproduced as chapter 7]). While many of these initiatives have been discussed in the secondary literature, little attention has been paid to the work that was undertaken for advertisers by the TIHR, possibly because so much of this work remains unpublished or in archival form only. Yet, from the 1950s onwards, the TIHR was approached directly by many major companies about the development and marketing of their products. The TIHR worked extensively with the advertising agencies responsible for the development of many campaigns – including those for companies such as Cadburys, Shell-Mex and BP, Guinness and Birds Eye Foods. In the present chapter, drawing upon archival material from the TIHR, we trace some of the ways in which changing problematizations of the consumer were linked to changing technologies of investigation and to changing conceptions of the modes of interrelation between products, advertisements and individuals in choices of goods to purchase and in the acts of consumption themselves. We argue that a distinctive mode of 'mobilizing the consumer' can be traced to this particular moment in the assembling of the subject of consumption.

Our focus is upon a period where, like today, the relations between advertising and the subjectivity of the consumer were matters of intellectual concern and critique: the period from 1950 to 1970. Events across these twenty years are interesting for a number of reasons. In the first place, across these two decades a plethora of new objects for mass consumption within the home appeared, new advertising media including the television became widely available, and novel ways of representing and acting upon the consumer based on psychological and psychoanalytical knowledge were devised. We will suggest that, in the course of these events, a new way of governing the acts of consumption was invented, one that sought to link the individual to the act of consumption and to the object of consumption by means of a new form of 'psy' expertise. Advertising agencies and individual companies keen to promote their wares turned increasingly to this domain of human relations, which was seen to lurk unexplored in the multitude of choices individuals made between one product and another, choices that in themselves might appear trivial, but which could have a fundamental influence on the economic viability of a particular firm or even industry.

This period is of particular interest also because of the interplay between the construction of consumption technologies and their critique, an interplay that may hold lessons for our own period. Thus, in 1957, Vance Packard denounced the 'hidden persuaders', those who attempted, 'often with impressive success, to channel our unthinking habits, our purchasing decisions, and our thought processes by the use of insights gleaned from psychiatry and the social sciences' (our references are to the second edition: Packard 1960: 11). The word 'hidden' referred to the fact that such efforts typically took place 'beneath our level of awareness'. Existing marketing techniques were considered misguided because actual purchasing behaviour was only remotely connected with what people told interviewers: people did not know what they wanted; people did not tell the truth about their wants and dislikes even when they knew them; and one could not assume that individuals would behave in a rational way when selecting one commodity rather than another. These 'irrational' aspects of purchasing behaviour posed particular problems for companies trying to sell increasing quantities of goods in a more and more standardized market where differences between goods were trivial or non-existent. The answer, as the director of research at the *Chicago Tribune* acknowledged, was to turn to psychological and psychoanalytic devices as a way of seeking to understand and act upon consumer choices. For these experts, it appeared, knew more about the individual consumer than he or she knew about him- or herself. Professional persuaders seized upon 'mass psychoanalysis to guide campaigns of persuasion' that had become the basis of a multi-million-dollar industry. By reaching into the consumer's psyche, acts of consumption could be probed to try to figure out

> why we are afraid of banks; why we love those big fat cars; why we really buy homes: why men smoke cigars; why the kind of car we draw reveals the brand of gasoline we will buy; why housewives typically fall into a hypnoidal trance when they get into a supermarket; why men are drawn into auto showrooms by convertibles but end up buying sedans; why junior loves cereal that pops, snaps, and crackles. (Packard 1960: 12)

The 'professional persuaders' saw individuals as bundles of day-dreams, replete with 'misty hidden yearning, guilt complexes, irrational emotional blockages . . . image-lovers given to impulsive and compulsive acts' (Packard 1960: 14). Once such motivational characteristics were identified and understood, access could be gained to the unconscious or subconscious mind, thereby leading to an understanding of those factors that determined choices of which even the individual consumer was unaware. There was one aim only: to enable advertisers and producers to manipulate the choices and decisions of consumers for their own advantage.

There were, of course, more cautious assessments of the use and power of 'techniques of persuasion', especially in the light of the experience of World War II with propaganda, psychological warfare, moral campaigns and 'brainwashing', which had been bound up not only with much psychological innovation, but also with concerns about the differences between public opinion and the nature of consent in totalitarian and democratic regimes (e.g. Brown 1963). Nonetheless, Packard's populist critique was echoed at a more prestigious intellectual level in a reworking of the earlier theses of Adorno and Horkheimer by Herbert Marcuse. Marcuse, writing in 1964, announced the arrival of a 'one-dimensional society', a society characterized by a 'comfortable, smooth, reasonable, democratic unfreedom' (our references are to the 1968 edition: Marcuse 1968: 19). According to Marcuse, a one-dimensional society was typified by 'false needs', needs to 'behave and consume in accordance with the advertisements', needs that were the result of indoctrination and manipulation (Marcuse 1968: 22). In a one-dimensional society, individuals 'recognize themselves in their commodities; they find their soul in their automobile, hi-fi set, split-level home, kitchen equipment' (Marcuse 1968: 24). The prevailing technological rationality was one in which the 'irresistible output of the entertainment and information industry . . . bind[s] the consumers more or less pleasantly to the producers . . .' (Marcuse 1968: 26). Insofar as the resulting way of life extended, according to Marcuse, to all spheres of private and public existence, there was little cause for optimism. For Marcuse, the one-dimensional society was a totalitarian society, a society in which it became almost impossible to distinguish between the mass media as instruments of information and entertainment, and the mass media as agents of manipulation and indoctrination. The resulting *mimesis*, the identification of the individual with the prevailing system of mass production and distribution, meant that the chances of radical change were limited. Hence, for Marcuse, the possibilities of inaugurating a qualitatively new mode of existence characterized by Reason and Freedom were remote.

Culture critics such as Packard, Marcuse and others had a particular conception of the consumer (see also Mills 1956; Whyte 1956). Even where they themselves reasoned psychologically about the effects of mass society, they nonetheless conceived of the consumer as a passive being, acted upon by the vast advertising and cultural apparatus that invented desires, created false needs and manipulated individuals into identifying with objects that would otherwise have been alien to them. Paradoxically, however, it was not this image of the consumer that was deployed by those responsible for constructing the new technologies of advertising. Many psychologists and advertisers were aware of the criticisms of propaganda, manipulation and brainwashing and consciously sought to distance themselves from them, stressing the distinctiveness of their own techniques of commercial persuasion and the role of the free market and consumer choice. Critique here, as in many other areas, formed an internal element in the development of knowledge and practice. But more significantly, advertisers and psychologists held a different and more complex view of the 'subject of consumption'.

Making up the consumer in the post-war decades was thus no simple matter. The 'consumer' emerged as a highly problematic entity, by no means a passive tool of the manipulations of the advertisers, but someone to be known in detail, whose passions and desires were to be charted, for whom consumption was an activity bound into a whole form of life that must be anatomized and acted upon. At issue here was not so much the invention and imposition of 'false needs' as a delicate process of identification of the 'real needs' of consumers, of affiliating these needs with particular products, and in turn of linking these with the habits of their utilization. Making up the consumer entailed simultaneously making up the commodity and assembling the little rituals of everyday life which would give that commodity meaning and value. This is not a brute attempt to impose desires upon a plastic and undifferentiated mass, but an unprecedented and meticulous cartography – part imagined, part derived from novel forms of experimentation – of the everyday life of consumption and its little pleasures and anxieties.

A number of studies of advertisements have sought to interrogate the images of the person they rely upon, by 'decoding' them utilizing semiotic and psychoanalytic techniques (Williamson 1978; cf. Leiss et al. 1986: ch. 9) or by relating them to the changing attitudes towards the body, image and identity in potential consumers which they seek to engage and instrumentalize in order to sell goods (Mort 1988). But we can address conceptions of the human being held by advertisers and marketeers more directly. Indeed, between 1950 and 1970, it is possible, in one local site, to identify at least three distinct ways of understanding the consumer: psychoanalytical, social psychological and, for want of a better term, 'rational'. In what follows, we explore each of these three distinct conceptions of the consumer in turn as they were articulated in the work of members of the Tavistock Institute of Human Relations, in relation to the sale of such diverse products as ice cream, chocolate, soft toilet tissue, beer and stout, petrol and oil, mustard, biscuits, frozen fish-shapes, baby foods, vitamin-enriched drinks, diamond engagement rings, savoury drinks, holidays and shaving equipment.

Such detail may appear trivial or unimportant: are we not observing merely the local results of far-reaching changes in the social determinants and global social logics that shape consumption practices? At the least, we suggest, there is something to be gained in intelligibility by studying these transformations at a more local level. More boldly, we would argue that the changes articulated in terms of such global logics of consumption might better be understood as the resultants of the linkages and relays formed among all those practices that serve to mobilize the consumer. It is the consumer, understood as a being able to appreciate and act according to minute differences between virtually identical products, who lies at the heart of the much-vaunted 'global competitiveness' of contemporary capitalism. It is in terms of 'brand' images, product design, consumer loyalty and product life-cycles that contemporary competitiveness is seen to reside. Without the possibility of mobilizing the consumer according to psychological conceptions of the act of consumption, without 'lifestyle' being understood as something linking up a particular complex of subjective tastes and allegiances with a particular product, battles over the best way of linking the desires of individuals to the productive machine would take very different forms.

The Pleasure of Consumption

A mundane problem – how to increase ice cream sales in winter – can be taken as the starting point for the elaboration of a psychoanalytic notion of the consumer. This seems, at first sight, exactly the sort of endeavour attacked by the likes of Packard and Marcuse: the consumer industry, in an alliance with social scientists, was attempting to intrude on the sacrosanct domain of the private home and the psyche of the individual. Even in the privacy of the home, consumers were not to be free from the injunctions to consume according to certain patterns, to modify long-standing traditions to suit the revenue needs of corporations producing ever more standardized products, and to change the very nature of the individual to achieve such ends – in this case, to even out seasonal fluctuations in ice cream sales.

Isabel Menzies and Eric Trist sought to adapt the tools of psychoanalytic investigation that had already been developed at the 'Tavi' (as the Institute and Clinic were often collectively termed) for the study of the consumer – most notably the utilization of their newly discovered dynamics of 'the group' (Miller and Rose 1994 [reproduced as chapter 6 of this volume]; see, e.g., Menzies 1960: 95–121). As far as ice cream was concerned, they began with the initial assumption that the 'ordinary private home was . . . the most likely market in which to realise a substantial increase in winter sales in the short-term' (TIHR 1950: 1), and that this could be achieved by 'securing for ice cream an accepted and permanent place in the meal system of the family' (TIHR 1950: 1).

However, this initial assumption was quickly challenged once actual investigations were carried out. These used group discussions as technique of inquiry, a method broadly derived from the group work that had been pioneered at the Tavi by Wilfred Bion, and which was to be used not just for therapeutic purposes but in such diverse settings as the investigations of poor industrial relations in a factory, group relations training courses, and the education of general practitioners and marital therapists. A group of potential consumers of ice cream – selected in a rather *ad hoc* manner – were brought together and asked to discuss not this or that brand or product but ice cream in general; one investigator would sit with the group and prompt it, while another would take notes. Somewhat to the surprise of the investigators, the problem was not getting the group to start talking about the product, but getting them to stop – especially when the same technique was deployed later in the investigation of such things as motoring. And what was going on here, as the investigators perceived it, was a kind of free association, which began from practical questions, of course, but which later took off into the underlying unconscious and preconscious dynamics of consumption.

As far as the consumption of ice cream in the home was concerned, there were technological problems to begin with: only three per cent of homes had refrigerators, and virtually none had home freezers. This meant that there was a kind of teasing quality to ice cream advertisements encouraging the consumption of ice cream at home, since there was no practical way of getting it. 'Why are they tempting and teasing us?' complained one consumer interviewed in the study (Menzies and Trist, published in a revised version in Menzies Lyth 1989: 77). There were also problems concerning the consumption of ice cream in the 'family meal system' (TIHR 1950: 2). For the housewife, having ice cream with meals in the home 'was sometimes experienced as rather an assault on the role of the housewife as provider of food: she had to do nothing to prepare it; gave nothing of herself' (Menzies Lyth 1989: 76). Ice cream was a competitor to the custard the housewife made herself. The 'housewife's need to please her family by giving them what they wanted . . . was thus in conflict with her wish to sustain her feeding role' (Menzies Lyth 1989: 76).

A way of understanding these tensions and conflicts was needed if manufacturers were to avoid the anger and hostility that consumers were held to feel, and the possibility that this might lead them to dismiss the idea of ice cream in the home. The psychoanalytic notion of 'pleasure foods' met this need. The concept of pleasure foods, a fusion of Kurt Lewin's field theory and psychoanalysis, 'brought together the environmental influences, the "field" and the internal situation through which the consumer responded to field forces' (Menzies Lyth 1989: 72). Oral gratification, through the consumption of pleasure foods, was viewed as a way of alleviating current anxieties and depression, for such emotions were held to be derivatives of the infantile anxiety and depression connected with the loss of the breast. Compensation for the loss of the breast was sought in the consumption of substitute objects – the so-called 'pleasure foods'.

Ice cream, Menzies argued, was 'the pleasure food *par excellence*' (Menzies Lyth 1989: 73). The significance of ice cream stemmed 'from its symbolic closeness to the breast and the mother–child relationship' (Menzies Lyth 1989: 69). The very term 'ice cream' established a 'link with the breast, but better than that, a breast that gives cream', a theme sustained 'in the little round blobs in which ice cream is served in dishes and in the cones or cornets in which it is sold from shops, kiosks or barrows'. This encouraged one to lick or suck the ice cream, while 'the more 'sophisticated' children or childish adults bite off the narrow end of the cone and treat it as a nipple through which they suck down the ice cream' (Menzies Lyth 1989: 69–70). Ice cream has 'great power to act as a substitute for the breast, to wipe out anxieties and depression' (Menzies Lyth 1989: 73). The physical sensation of eating ice cream, when 'optimally experienced', is so complete that it is capable of blotting out all other concerns. As for the child at the breast, there are no bad things left, and 'reality consists only of the good substance and the pleasure it gives' (Menzies Lyth 1989: 73).

But there are potential pitfalls in this experience of eating ice cream. It can be too cold, in which case pleasure becomes neuralgic pain, good turns to bad. Also, if ice cream is not immediately available to satisfy the impulsive and infantile desire, it is likely that this will touch off 'violent infantile hostility against the ice cream manufacturers' (Menzies Lyth 1989: 75). The availability and condition of the ice cream supplied was thus crucial. Ice cream manufacturers were dealing with a dynamic that was much more complex than they had appreciated. They were, in effect, seeking to intervene in the mother–child relationship. For when the child is in a completely dependent position, food is love and security. In the mind of the child 'love is loving acts and good things, particularly the good breast' (Menzies Lyth 1989: 70). Deprivation of the breast can lead to 'aggressive omnipotent phantasies which are followed by guilt, depression and anxiety. The breast and the good food it gives have complete and immediate power to assuage these feelings' (Menzies Lyth 1989: 71). Ice cream eating was thus inextricably linked to deep-seated characteristics of human relations.

Even outside the home, the psychological significance of ice cream could not be ignored. Ice cream was already consumed in reasonably large quantities in cinemas, hospitals and in midday restaurants and industrial canteens. In the cinema, the 'solitary gluttony' of eating ice cream could be hidden, but the 'need for perfection, the anger at being teased and tantalized' if it was not immediately available were ever-present potential problems (Menzies Lyth 1989: 82). Because of the danger of arousing infantile reactions such as hostility and anger towards manufacturers, ice cream supplies in places such as cinemas should never run out, Menzies strongly recommended to the manufacturers. In institutions such as hospitals, where stress and anxiety are high for both staff and clients, ice cream could be particularly valuable, acting as a 'motherly' food, a 'sign that the hospital cared'. In midday restaurants and industrial canteens, pleasure foods act as compensation for having to eat away from home. This suggested that 'ice-cream consumption might be high in such places and could easily be stimulated' (Menzies Lyth 1989: 85).

Problems faced by manufacturers of other 'pleasure foods' could be readily fitted into this interpretive grid. A particular chocolate product – Toblerone – provided the starting point for further elaboration of this distinctive psychoanalytic conception of the consumer. Toblerone, a chocolate product unique in its design, had disappeared during and immediately after World War II, had then been in short supply, and, when fully reintroduced, met with only limited success. An approach to the Tavistock by the manufacturers provided the opportunity for a discussion of the concept of pleasure foods and a demonstration of the applicability of this concept to the particular product in question.

For the analysts at the TIHR, despite its distinctive appearance, Toblerone was part of a much wider phenomenon – the consumption of chocolate, and all that this meant to individuals. The intensity of the feelings about eating chocolate and other pleasure foods 'stems from conscious and unconscious memories in the individual of former experiences of feeding, ultimately and basically the early feeding-centred relationship with the mother' (TIHR 1959a: 5). For chocolate manufacturers, the psychological significance of consumption was double-edged. Eating chocolate could, as one woman said, provide 'company'; another described how the eating of pleasure foods enabled her to cope with an irritating elderly relative (TIHR 1959a: 7). Yet eating such foods could also give rise to anxiety, guilt and other problems. Moreover, pleasure foods play a significant role as 'sublimated social activities and more directly sexual activities' (TIHR 1959a: 11). Other problems included greed and attempts to control it. People were 'afraid of being too enticed and excited by the chocolate. . . . Fears of being possessed or compelled by sweets, especially chocolate and other rich sweets, were very common' (TIHR 1959a: 9). Spots, bad teeth and becoming fat were also stated as evidence of the effects of overindulgence in pleasure foods such as chocolate.

Without appreciating the role of chocolate-eating in the social, psychological and sexual make-up of the individual, manufacturers would not be able to understand the failure of sales to take off significantly in the 1950s. Insofar as food 'expresses social and sexual wishes, conveys social and sexual satisfactions, and deals with social and sexual anxieties', chocolate manufacturers would have to address such issues if they wished to increase the sales of their products (TIHR 1959a: 12). Marketing would thus need to embrace much more than the superficial characteristics of the product. It would ultimately depend upon the capacity of the manufacturers and advertisers to form an alliance between the properties offered by the product and the unconscious, yet nonetheless highly active, needs, desires and anxieties of the purchaser who would be the consumer.

The Psychological Meaning of Consumption

The choices that individuals make between products pose problems for manufacturers and advertising agencies keen to differentiate their products. As the 'consumer society' took shape in the post-war years, corporations began to ask novel questions about why a competitor's products sold when theirs did not. There was a growing demand for a body of knowledge to underpin the increasingly professionalized know-how of advertising and marketing. In part, this was of course simply an indication of the concern to maintain or improve profitability and market share. But it also helped provide the conditions for a shift in perception as to what drove individuals to purchase one product rather than another. The 'consumer' came to be viewed as differentiated by age, by gender, by class and by psychological type. For the TIHR, beset with financial problems at the expiry of its grant from the Rockefeller Foundation, such concerns provided a crucial point of attachment of their psychological expertise to the requirements of the novel consumption market. And in the process they elaborated conceptions of the consumer that were not so directly infused with psychoanalytic images.

One of the earliest opportunities that members of the Tavistock had to demonstrate the complexity of consumer wishes and needs was provided by a request to investigate the development and marketing of the 'Pin-Up' home perm. The report that was produced sought to establish the distinctive contribution that a social psychology of the consumer had to offer (TIHR 1951). For, rather than addressing a specific product and asking why it was used, and why other products were chosen in preference to it, the object of attention was much broader. The report was 'designed to study women's attitudes and behaviour towards their hair', with the aim of gaining 'an understanding of deeper feelings related to hair' (TIHR 1951: 1). The concern was to 'build up a body of information on the social and psychological aspects of hair and hair-doing', with the expectation that this would lead indirectly to results of value to the client firm (TIHR 1951: 1).

A social psychology of women's hair would provide manufacturers with a knowledge base for decisions concerning product development and advertising themes. This noted the strong pressures women are under to maintain a good appearance. These came partly from cultural expectations, and partly from 'forces internal to themselves' (TIHR 1951: 3). By achieving and maintaining a good appearance, 'a woman indicates both to herself and others that she has attained some degree of success in accepting the adult feminine role' (TIHR 1951: 3). This means that she has 'come to terms with the problem of her sexuality in a way that is within normal limits for our society, and has attained some belief in herself as a good sexual object and good mother, actual or to be' (TIHR 1951: 3). This image of the well-adjusted woman was thought not to be specific to particular social groups, but to be generally held. Even if questions of affordability of perms and other forms of hair care entered the picture for women from lower income groups, the point was that there was held to be a feminine role model that applied to women from all sectors of the population. The stereotype centred on 'waviness', itself associated with images of softness and naturalness, smoothness and sheen. Waviness connoted the 'feeling of a sensuous life', but in a socially acceptable form, a 'civilised rather than primitive naturalness' (TIHR 1951: 4). So rather than home perms inventing a new need, they 'played into one of the fundamental needs of women', and 'expanded the opportunities for expressing a fundamental wish' (TIHR 1951: 4). The invention of the home perm 'has provided the female community with a new tool to achieve the aim of wavy hair' (TIHR 1951: 8).

The researchers studied a variety of women involved in giving and receiving home perms, generally using long non-directive interviews. They studied 'gatekeepers', those who possessed a high degree of skill in hairdressing, without having any professional training. They studied 'solos', skilled persons who required no assistance in doing their own hair. They studied 'two-person relationships', hairdressing relationships that were either based on mutual dependence or non-reciprocal. And they studied shop permers and non-permers, in order to understand the reasons for having shop perms, and the reasons why some women were resistant to perming of any kind. These interviews focused not on what made people buy particular products, but rather upon the importance of hair to women. The researchers interpreted the responses of those they talked to in terms of the anxieties and fears associated with the potential loss or impairment of hair, arguing that 'there are within the feminine personality' certain deep anxieties about physical damage and loss linked to 'unconscious aggressive and destructive trends within the personality, which seem also to be associated with hair-doing activities' (TIHR 1951: 12). The existence of the so-called 'destructive tendencies' and their associated anxieties were held to provide the 'psychological basis of the ordeal aspects of hairdressing' (TIHR 1951: 12). Hair-doing, it was remarked, 'seems to satisfy obsessional tendencies in women', and such obsessional behaviour 'is recognised to be an indication of the existence of anxiety and at the same time is a mechanism which may serve to control it' (TIHR 1951: 13).

This image of women as beset by obsessional tendencies could provide the basis for practical recommendations to producers. Women, they argued, felt a need to see good results quickly. Since perming of any kind was experienced as a serious ordeal, and since women tended to postpone re-perming as long as possible, technical improvements in the home perm product were needed. A reduction in the time for the whole perming opera-tion would be a major benefit, particularly if this allowed the home perm operation to be 'undertaken and comfortably completed within one of the recognised divisions of the day, the afternoon or evening' (TIHR 1951: 18). An improvement in the smell of the waving lotion would help relieve anxieties associated with perming, both for those doing the perm or having it done to them, as well as for 'other members of the household, especially male members' (TIHR 1951: 19). And any written material accompanying the home perm should be regarded as 'objective and authoritative', as coming from a 'technical expert' in the field, one whose advice could be regarded as intrinsic to the services provided by the firm marketing the product. By means of such technical improvements, manufacturers might be able to combat the anxieties and 'ordeal aspects' of home perming, aspects accentuated 'by the fact that it is endured alone, and at the same time is necessarily made public to members of the household and is dis-turbing to them' (TIHR 1951: 13).

Technical improvements in the home perm were one way of addressing the issues. But there was a more far-reaching solution, one that built on the psychological meaning of consumption and sought to foster the devel-opment of a 'home perm culture'. Initially, home perms were regarded as substitutes for shop perms. They were used by those who could not afford shop perms, and they were often considered to be of lesser quality because they did not last as long. But home perms, when understood psychologi-cally, had positive attributes too. For the home perm 'produces soft, natural looking waves immediately, as contrasted with the hard, unnatural looking waves of the shop perm in its early stages' (TIHR 1951: 17). And even attributes that might appear to be unequivocally negative, such as the fact that home perms do not last as long, could be turned to advantage. What was needed was 'to develop a new pattern of usage of home perms', to develop a more frequent and regular usage of the home perm (TIHR 1951: 17). The objective – of interest in both psychological and marketing terms – was thus to 'facilitate the establishment of this new home perm culture' (TIHR 1951: 17).

This way of representing the psychological meaning of consumption was generalizable. It could be applied to other hair products, such as shampoo (TIHR 1960a). Group discussions with working-class and middle-class housewives sought to 'identify general factors in relation to shampoo' (TIHR 1960a: 1). In particular, as hair 'symbolises a good and attractive appearance', it 'is likely to be invested with anxieties and fears' (TIHR

1960a: 2). Those involved in producing and marketing shampoos were advised to recognize that it was not only the perceived qualities of sham- poos – smell, colour, viscosity, pleasantness in use, economy – that were at issue. For the 'image that a consumer has of any particular shampoo' is determined 'not only by the properties which she perceives as a result of using it but also by the advertisements with which it is associated' (TIHR 1960a: 5). This might well be true of all products, but it had a particular relevance to the advertising of shampoos, because 'women's expectations and frustrations are so high in relation to shampoo' (TIHR 1960a: 5).

One might believe that there is a world of difference between the washing and perming of hair and the cleansing of the body after defeca- tion. Such a distinction would be misleading, at least in terms of the ways in which acts of consumption were analysed by Tavistock researchers. In the mid-1950s, a new question was brought to the researchers of the TIHR, one that centred on the development and marketing of a new type of toilet tissue, 'soft' as opposed to 'hard' tissue (TIHR 1956a, 1956b). This was addressed by means of a number of regional studies carried out in 1956 – covering Yorkshire, Birmingham, Glasgow, Manchester and the south of England – that sought to understand long-term market trends, the 'total toilet tissue field', rather than soft tissues only. These studies demonstrated considerable regional variation, with Yorkshire standing out from the other areas studied. In Yorkshire, progress and a rise in standards of living were 'accompanied by a curious kind of traditionalism' in which 'changes are made in a spirit of regret for the past and little feeling of anticipation or interest or even real conviction about the possibility of a more pleasurable future' (TIHR 1956a: 1). In Yorkshire, 'Life should be a struggle, much strength of mind must be exercised to control one's desire for pleasure, and there is little capacity to admit . . . the possibility of pleasure connected with bodily functions' (TIHR 1956a: 1).

This had considerable implications for the marketing of a *soft* toilet tissue. For the 'qualities' associated with products were not simply chosen according to the functions they performed. First and foremost, they had psychological and sociological significance. While 'hard' was usually equated with bad, the converse equating of soft with good – at least in the case of toilet paper – was not so simple. 'Soft' papers 'were also viewed with great distrust and anxiety because they were not "reliable". They crumbled, they tore too easily, were pulpable, too absorbent, and so on' (TIHR 1956a: 1). Soft toilet tissue, at least in the Yorkshire area, thus had a contradictory position in relation to the psychological value placed on cleanliness: 'One feels almost that there is so much anxiety about cleanli- ness, associated with such vigorous cleaning that nothing soft could pos- sibly stand up to the way it would be used' (TIHR 1956a: 1). Underlying the protestations against softness, there was seen to lurk 'a great longing to have something more gentle, if only it were not felt to be almost immoral to have that kind of pleasure' (TIHR 1956a: 1). But this longing for 'softness' was outweighed by the 'Yorkshire conventions' that dictated that 'it is really not acceptable . . . to be discriminating about toilet papers' (TIHR 1956a: 4).

A number of recommendations arose from this extensive study of the qualities associated with toilet tissue. There was a description of the 'desired standard tissue'. This, it was argued, should convey an overall impression of a 'dignified, solid middle class comfort, but without, as it were, any direct approach to sensuality or even to luxury, and with great emphasis on reliability, good service and integrity' (TIHR 1956b: 6). This standard tissue should be associated with the quality of 'softness', but this should be a 'maximum softness compatible with protection from contamination, either by permeation through the paper or by breaking when the paper is used with a rubbing or scraping movement' (TIHR 1956b: 6). But there were dangers in over-emphasizing the quality of 'softness' for standard toilet tissue. For softness, as an absolute quality, 'seemed to provoke anxiety in standard tissue users', whereas 'smoothness and fineness are felt as compatible with safety' (TIHR 1956b: 6).

The recommendations for soft toilet tissue again focused on the qualities associated with it, and the potential anxieties it could provoke. It should be associated with qualities such as 'luxury and comfort', 'gentle, kind care' and a 'certain dignity or reserve' (TIHR 1956b: 6). It should 'grant the right to pleasure and satisfaction in the care of the body', and should suggest that it 'can reduce the tedium or inconvenience of essential personal, family or household tasks' (TIHR 1956b: 7). But while soft toilet tissue might be regarded as a luxury, it must 'give the impression of appreciating the seriousness of its tasks' and must 'never seem a frivolity' (TIHR 1956b: 7). The report concluded with a recommendation to the manufacturers that they should seek 'as quickly as possible' to establish a soft toilet tissue in the market (TIHR 1956b: 8).

Thus, over the 1950s and 1960s, consumers came to be viewed as diverse and complex actors, whose choices were nonetheless psychologically intelligible. As commercial television became one of the principal means of advertising, manufacturers and advertising agencies increasingly turned to psychological advice as to how to overcome problems with marketing, to market new products or to market old products more effectively. Of course, psychology itself was heterogeneous and conflictful, and the approach taken at the Tavi was only one line within this field. Nonetheless, the key point is that, through this relation of psy expertise, advertising, marketing and production, the very notion of consumer choice was transformed. Consumer choice was no longer to be regarded as a function of the product alone, of what it offered in and of itself. Nor was choice to be understood as something that might be influenced solely by the promise of status, glamour, happiness, and so forth. Indeed, in certain circumstances, this could even be counter-productive, suggesting something that was beyond the reach of ordinary individuals. Rather, the choice of particular products was to be intrinsically linked to the subjective meaning of consumption for the ordinary individual in his or her everyday life, however that psychological meaning was to be understood. The marketing of a home perm became a question of understanding the psychological and social aspects of hair, a matter of grasping the nature of the 'feminine psyche', and of analysing the 'obsessional tendencies in women' as they might be manifested in everyday behaviour. The simple act of purchase of shampoo had similarly to be understood in terms of deep-seated 'anxieties and fears'. The introduction of soft toilet tissue was also fraught with difficulties of a psychological order – the anxieties and fears associated with an apparently simple decision as to whether to purchase greater comfort. Even pet ownership, insofar as it brought another living being within the family, was a decision of psychological and social significance *par excellence* (Bridger 1970; TIHR 1965a). Albeit in different guises, a knowledge of the extraordinarily rich and complex psychological meaning of consumption as it obtained in the individual living of an ordinary life was to become a central feature in these new technologies for allying consumer choice with commercial objectives.

The Rational Consumer

But what if consumers were rational? What if individuals were not beset by anxieties, emotions, obsessive tendencies and a need for compensation for the loss of the breast? What if people chose to purchase products because of preferences for the objective qualities of a product that could not be explained away as *post hoc* rationalizations? This was the possibility explored by a group of researchers at the TIHR led by Fred Emery, who sought actively to mitigate the influence of psychodynamic models of the consumer in favour of those which regarded consumers as essentially rational actors making calculated choices.

The Rational Alcohol Drinker

The question of Guinness drinking – what kinds of people drink Guinness, and what kinds of people do not drink Guinness now, but might do so in the future – provided an ideal opportunity for Emery to elaborate this notion of the 'rational consumer' (TIHR 1960b). The problem was one of finding out what people think they are 'preferring and drinking' when they either accept or reject Guinness, of determining the 'product image' of Guinness. But this was not a question of identifying those idealized images contained in advertising that had been so fiercely attacked by the culture critics. The 'product image' referred rather to those 'real and discriminable qualities' that individuals sought when choosing an alcoholic drink. For when choosing between bitter, Mackeson and Guinness, drinkers were making comparisons that were 'rational and restrained' (TIHR 1960b: 1, 4). The choices made by drinkers followed 'from an awareness of the objective taste qualities of their drinks' (TIHR 1960b: 9).

On the basis of this image of the rational consumer, analyses such as the 'Semantic Differential Test' on taste qualities were conducted, diagrams were drawn of the 'Logical Structure of Guinness and Bitter Images', 'controlled taste experiments' were carried out on carefully selected samples of individuals, and graphs of changing preferences over the drinkers' lifetimes were constructed. The end point was the production in tabular form of the 'distinctive product images' of Guinness, Mackeson and bitter. This made it possible to conclude that the Guinness drinker 'differs in getting more steady satisfaction from the particular combination of properties and effects that characterise Guinness' (TIHR 1960b: 17). Rejecting explicitly the view that Guinness and non-Guinness drinkers have 'succumbed to nationally common delusions about their drinks', Emery argued instead that there is 'strong evidence for the hypothesis that it is the preference for these properties and effects that has to be explained not preference for Guinness as advertised or as fancifully or idiosyncratically perceived' (TIHR 1960b: 17). And from the 'logical structure of the product images' one might make predictions, such as the proposition that 'it seems likely that regular Bitter drinkers may develop into Guinness drinkers but unlikely that regular Mackeson drinkers would do so' (TIHR 1960b: 17).

But if individuals were rational, they were not all rational in exactly the same way. Consultants at the TIHR, like a number of contemporary economists, disputed the adequacy of the classical economic image of the universal rationality of the consumer in the market for understanding consumer choices (see Katona 1951 for an economic argument that comes close to Emery's notion of 'rational choice'). Just as one could identify 'product images', so too could one identify 'personality images'. Clearly, what was necessary was to map the one on to the other. Using a variation of the Semantic Differential technique, a picture of the Guinness drinker emerged as a 'solid citizen', 'friendly, responsible, hardworking, unaggressive, relaxed, sociable' (TIHR 1960b: 18). This self-definition of the Guinness drinker presented a relatively sharply defined personality type. This was in contrast to the picture of the bitter drinker that emerged, a picture typified in a negative fashion, as lacking the qualities other drinkers attributed to themselves. The sharply defined personality image of the Guinness drinker suggested, however, 'that a much closer fit exists between the product and the person it serves' (TIHR 1960b: 19). Indeed there was a 'striking parallel' between the 'logical structures' of the personality images and the product images (TIHR 1960b: 20).

But the notion of 'personality' was insufficient if one was to gain a 'first approximation to a theoretical understanding of the complex processes involved in alcohol drinking' (TIHR 1960b: 39). Drawing on an earlier paper (TIHR 1959b), Emery outlined three different aspects of an individual's 'life-space': the 'objective behavioural environment that presents him with a range of stimuli, cues, goals, etc.'; his 'subjective orientation to this life of his'; and 'his pattern of drinking preferences and habits' (TIHR 1960b: 23). Particular combinations of these different aspects of an individual's 'life-space' gave rise to a tripartite typology of drinking habits: *reparative*, *social* and *indulgent* drinking. It was these patterns of life conditions, philosophy of life and drinking habits that would, or so it was hoped, make possible an explanation of why certain individuals chose certain alcoholic drinks.

For Guinness, it was the 'reparative drinker' who was to be the principal focus of attention, since 'it is clear that the reparative drinker's self-image corresponds closely to that of the Guinness drinker' (TIHR 1960b: 27). Moreover, 'the product image of Guinness is very much like that which a reparative drinker would seek' (TIHR 1960b: 27). The fit was almost perfect: 'No other drink used by this sample corresponds as closely' (TIHR 1960b: 27). The reparative drinker is 'happy enough with his past and his present and confident that he can cope with problems as they arise' (TIHR 1960b: 24). Believing that there is little prospect of a major improvement in his circumstances, the reparative drinker will tend to see himself as someone who is 'well and truly settled down in his way of life, unimpressive in his achievements but worthy of repute as a hardworking, conscientious and stable member of the community' (TIHR 1960b: 24). The reparative drinker who seeks refuge in a club or a pub is seeking refuge from external conditions, not from himself as an indulgent drinker is. The reparative drinker will thus be drinking 'so as to be better able to return to and exercise real mastery over his work environment' (TIHR 1960b: 25).

This conception of the 'reparative' alcohol drinker had considerable implications for the advertising of Guinness. According to Emery, consumers were not duped by advertising into choosing things they would not otherwise have purchased. But this did not mean that advertising could not be successful if the images it used 'fitted' both the 'product image' and the 'life-spaces' of the reparative drinker. Thus, of three Guinness symbols – the zookeeper, the man with the girder, and the 'moon face' on the glass of stout – it is the 'girder man' who was considered to be the most appropriate symbol for the advertising of Guinness. While acknowledging that it is very difficult to control the meanings of pictorial symbols, Emery argued that the 'girder man' as an advertising symbol for Guinness symbolized that Guinness 'gives you that "something extra" needed for the extra effort' (TIHR 1960c: 5). Such a symbol might be 'appropriate for the young Bitter drinking man in his prime', while for the heavy Guinness drinker, 'the connotation should be a restoration of strength to go on doing the ordinary things of life' (TIHR 1960c: 5).

More generally, the notion that alcohol consumption was based on rational choices led to a particular role for the 'Flavour Profile' technique (see Cairncross and Sjostrom 1950). Individuals had to be carefully selected to participate in 'flavour panels', and placed in a small group setting. The group was to work in almost complete isolation for three-day stretches, with tasting done blind for the most part, and with a poet on hand to help access the sort of memories and experiences that individuals wished to articulate. From this experimental situation, composite flavour profiles could be constructed for a wide range of stouts, brown ales, lagers, light and pale ales, as well as bitters. The conclusion was dramatic: 'each had a profile as unique as a human fingerprint' (TIHR 1963a: 12). While the basic 'structural elements' might be common, the 'combinations of patterns' were different. All that remained for the manufacturer was to produce a drink that resided at the appropriate point on a continuum of 'basic taste patterns'.

Brands: The Psychological Cost of Choosing between Equivalents

The question of consumer choice is relatively simple if individuals make rational choices based on preferences for readily discernible objective qualities of products. Things are much more complicated if individuals are faced with products that are equivalent, or if they are faced with a choice of products whose differences they are unable to identify and assess. In these circumstances, there is a 'psychological cost' to those who seek to make a rational choice between alternatives. 'Brand loyalty' was the term that was coined to understand how individual consumers reduced such psychological cost to themselves (on the general question of brands in advertising, see Leiss et al. 1986: 107–11).

The case of petrol and oil purchase provided a particularly instructive example of such processes, for although it is individuals who purchase petrol, they do not 'consume' it in the sense that they consume Guinness, beer, lager, chocolate or ice cream. And the issue is further confounded since, as Tavistock researchers were quick to point out, the purchase of petrol for car drivers is closely tied to self-images (TIHR 1959c). It was these issues that were to be addressed when, in January 1959, the Tavistock Institute was commissioned by S. H. Benson Limited, on behalf of Shell Mex and BP Ltd, to undertake a 'long-term programme in which survey techniques would be employed as well as more intensive psychological and sociological approaches' (TIHR 1959c: 1). Work on the main part of the project began in April 1959, with a short inquiry into reactions to an abstract cinema film on BP. It proceeded to a series of individual and family interviews, group discussions and questionnaire work, discussions with consumers, as well as visits to garages and petrol stations.

The complexity of the issue began with the question of car ownership and driving, for the driver has a particular relationship to the car. When learning to drive, individuals go through 'phases of feeling inadequate in relation to the skills and knowledge required', progressing to a 'sense of triumph and achievement, a warmer feeling for the car and some growth of self-respect' with the acquisition of driving skill (TIHR 1959c: 2). Although this sense of achievement may diminish with experience, the car tends nonetheless to be 'incorporated in the driver's image of himself. It becomes an extension of his psychological image' (TIHR 1959c: 2). However, few people 'ever feel themselves completely masters of their vehicle' (TIHR 1959c: 2). Mechanical faults, traffic, weather, road surface conditions, the vagaries of other drivers, and so on, all remind the driver of the limitations of his or her skill and control.

This need for control over the vehicle has important implications for the purchase of petrol and oil. For, in order to purchase petrol, the driver has to interrupt the 'relationship between him and the car', provoking unfavourable reactions (TIHR 1959c: 3). This is not simply a matter of inconvenience, but arises because in stopping to purchase petrol 'he is reminded that the car's functioning is subject to circumstances outside his own control, that it is not an extension of himself and that he is diminished when it goes out of operation. He feels worried, silly and powerless or potentially powerless' (TIHR 1959c: 3). This is why, the Tavistock researchers argued, drivers 'feel tense between the moment when they decide to stop for petrol and oil', and the moment when they actually stop, resenting the need to stop, attempting to delay the stop, and finding reasons for not stopping at the first convenient place, promising themselves and their passengers a better stop, being critical of stations and attendants when they do stop, and so forth (TIHR 1959c: 3).

The notion of 'brand preference' was held to play an important role here. For brand preference affects where the driver actually stops, drivers preferring to keep to a preferred range of brands or to avoid others (TIHR 1959c: 3). And brand preference plays a further important role in handling the anxiety and conflict in deciding which petrol to purchase and when. Although drivers 'realize the importance of petrol they know little about it. Their beliefs are uneven and very often contradictory. Ignorance lies alongside an anxiety about the powers and potentiality of petrol' (TIHR 1959c: 10).

This 'conflict between the need to know about petrol brands and the difficulty of knowing' is, the Tavistock researchers argued, 'fundamental to the understanding of consumer behaviour in this market' (TIHR 1959c: 10). An acknowledgement that such a conflict exists 'helps one to understand why it is so frequently said that all the leading known brands of petrol are much the same' (TIHR 1959c: 10). For the theory that all petrol is much the same is accompanied by a 'fear that there really is a difference, that if only one knew enough about it one could choose the one petrol that would make all the difference' (TIHR 1959c: 10). The belief that all petrol is much the same is thus 'valuable to the individual as a way of dealing with the possibility that he is really missing something. Like many other of his beliefs it serves the function for him of warding off anxiety or doubt' (TIHR 1959c: 10). Brand preference, that is to say, could be understood as a way of handling psychological conflict. The Tavistock researchers were unequivocal: 'We regard the conflict between the need to know and the difficulty of knowing as a central factor . . . in the maintenance of brand preferences. *It is a rare consumer who makes his choice on realistic grounds*' (TIHR 1959c: 10, emphasis added).

This put advertising in a curious position with regard to brand preference. For if it is the case that 'one very important reason why a particular consumer sticks to a particular brand is to cope with the possibility that he might be missing something elsewhere' (TIHR 1959c: 10), then the consumer does not have to 'decide between the blandishments or technical arguments of advertisers' (TIHR 1959c: 10). The consumer can 'tell himself that if something is good his own brand will incorporate it' (TIHR 1959c: 10). It is 'probably partially true of brand preference in many fields' that 'consumers stick to brands because it is psychologically uneconomical to explore, experiment and learn about minor differences' (TIHR 1959c: 10). And this is particularly important in the case of petrol because of the 'technicalities, objective dangers and subjective anxieties associated with cars and motoring' (TIHR 1959c: 10).

But soon this notion of brand preference proved insufficient. In 1965, a report was prepared for Dynamar on the 'social and psychological factors involved in the choice of petrol and automotive lubricants' (TIHR 1965b: 1). In this report, the notions of 'brand preference' and 'brand choice' were declared inadequate as a way of designating the emotional significance attached to brands, and the notion of 'brand cathexis' was put forward as more appropriate (TIHR 1965b: 9). Feelings about brands of petrol were seen to be divided into two categories: positive and negative cathexis. The degree of intensity of 'positive feelings' was held to be indicated by the 'extent to which the habitual journey itself may be distorted . . . to get a particular brand of petrol' (TIHR 1965b: 10). One motorist had tried a particular brand, on the recommendation of a friend, to cure trouble with sticky valves in a secondhand car purchased in the early part of his career. The trouble having disappeared, this motorist continued to use the same brand for the following thirty-two years in a variety of vehicles. Other motorists, having kept detailed records when young concerning petrol consumption, developed a 'kind of persistent addiction to one brand of petrol', even though the 'kind of experimentation carried out might be extremely perfunctory' (TIHR 1965b: 10).

'Negative brand cathexis' was a kind of 'mirror image' to the positive side. There were those who had a 'specific aversion to one particular brand' that could be traced back to a 'particular bad experience with the petrol concerned', while the disapproval of a further group 'seems more directed against the company than its product' (TIHR 1965b: 14). On the whole, the report commented, 'more motorists were prepared to admit to and act upon negative brand cathexis than positive' (TIHR 1965b: 14). Genuine indifference to the brand of petrol – the complete absence of 'brand cathexis' – was not found: 'we have not met any in whom no feelings about brands could be detected at all' (TIHR 1965b: 14). While consumers were rational, then, the rationality expressed itself in very complex ways in the forms of life and habits of conduct within which their acts of consumption were assembled and reassembled.

An Avalanche of Consumers

The decade of the 1960s was the heyday for the rational consumer at the Tavistock. Almost anything, it appeared, could be an object of 'consumption'. If consumers were rational, but were nonetheless more complex entities than much conventional economic theory suggested, the concerns of corporations to maintain or improve market share, to introduce new products, or to counteract the long-term decline of a particular product could be aligned with the Tavistock's capacities to understand the psychological and sociological aspects of human conduct.

From 1960 on, there was an avalanche of requests to study a multitude of products and consumer reactions. There were concerns about the overall size of the future market for mustard, and the long-run decline in eating English mustards, expressed by Colman's. Semantic Differential scales were constructed to identify and explore the possible taste qualities of mustard, and how these related to the taste qualities of other foods and particularly meat. A similar method was used to evaluate a new small non-chocolate biscuit to be introduced to the market by Cadbury's Ltd. Preliminary investigations showed that biscuits were eaten for three purposes: as an adjunct to drinking; as a food; and for tension management. A test group of eighty housewives was asked to judge the taste qualities of three biscuits on nine dimensions, using a seven-point scale. From these tests, the crucial characteristic that emerged was 'appetizing', this dimension distinguishing clearly between the biscuits, and correlating highly with liking for the biscuit. There was an investigation into the 'attitudes of housewives to frozen fish-shapes' (TIHR 1959d). The 'social and psychological factors concerned in the introduction of a liquid scourer' were studied in terms of the 'more general social and psychological factors involved in household cleaning' as well as in terms of 'the more specific factors that might be involved in the use of scourers' (TIHR 1960d). The 'making of gravy', and the qualities people sought in gravy, were studied in order to assist in the formation of an advertising campaign to be mounted by Bisto in the autumn of 1962 (TIHR 1962a). The 'body surface' as a whole, as distinct from particular parts of the body such as the face and the hands, was taken as the object of study. Unstructured or depth interviews were used to encourage thirty-seven mothers to talk and express themselves freely on the subject of baby foods, the mental experience of them, the ways in which they come into contact with them, and what happens when they are finally consumed (TIHR 1962b). And flavour profiles for vitamin C drinks were constructed on the basis of a study of thirty-eight mothers, in an attempt to identify the 'ideal drink' for 5- to 15-year-olds (TIHR 1963b).

Nothing, it seemed, could escape this interpretive grid. A group of twenty-two women under the age of 25 who were 'going steady with a serious boy-friend' were asked to discuss and comment on advertising copy, illustrations and complete advertisements for diamond engagement rings (TIHR 1963c). They were also asked to discuss the process of getting engaged, deciding on rings, and the 'concept of a diamond' (TIHR 1963c: 1). On a more mundane topic, thirty-nine women were organized into four discussion groups to investigate views about the constituents and tastes of Bovril and Marmite, their uses (as drink, as spread, as flavouring agent) and their flavours (TIHR 1963d). As a way of understanding the 'often unconscious feelings involved in taking a holiday', eighty-two respondents were involved in group discussions or interviewed individually (TIHR 1965c). On behalf of S. H. Benson Ltd and the Gillette Co., some fifty respondents were divided into six groups to address the sociological and psychological aspects of shaving (TIHR 1961). And a more general study of 'hair care' addressed the 'characteristics and properties of hair-care practices and products . . . as *perceived* by *the consumers*, not by the producers or advertisers' (TIHR 1964: 6, emphasis in original).

Despite the diversity of products they studied, these researchers at the TIHR worked on the assumption that most consumer behaviour was rational, although this was not the perfect rationality invoked by most conventional economists. A social psychology of responses to advertising images showed that 'persuasion is an interpersonal process', and that 'it is necessary to bring back into our concept of psychological man, certain characteristics that have been stripped off in the search for fundamental laws of organism–object relation' (TIHR 1962c: 6). This placed the general issue of persuasion firmly back on the terrain of the rational individual choosing those items or qualities he or she valued. By drinking Guinness instead of bitter, by having mustard with certain meats, by purchasing Bisto rather than Oxo for making gravy, by liking small 'bite-sized' biscuits in certain settings, by selecting Bovril rather than Marmite or vice versa, and by dreaming of a diamond engagement ring, individuals were engaged in a consistent activity. They were making rational choices for objects or qualities they sought and valued. They were not seeking to alleviate infantile anxieties associated with loss of the breast, or experiencing unconscious memories of early feeding experiences. Nor was it necessary, in order to understand 'the consumer', to delve into the 'feminine psyche', or to posit 'obsessional tendencies' on the part of women. Instead, matters were relatively straightforward. It was a question of understanding 'what the consumer thinks and will do' (TIHR 1962d: 2). When seeking to determine the appropriate price for a new brand of a popular beverage, it was a question of mapping price and quality onto each other so as to understand what 'variation in price around the established standard will be noticed by the consumer or what variation in quality from the standard will be seen as worth a given price change' (TIHR 1962d: 2). Consumer behaviour with respect to prices might thus be understood by means of experimental studies of human judgement, rather than by recourse to psychoanalytical models.

The dream of providing a general theory of such processes was to prove largely elusive. But the power of such approaches, and their attraction to advertisers and producers, appears to reside precisely in their modesty and pragmatism, perhaps even their liberalism. Explicitly or implicitly, they rejected the illiberal potentials that underpinned those psychological theories of the total manipulability of human motivations that have most concerned cultural analysts. They simultaneously rendered consumer choice in a free market intelligible in terms of a complex and hybrid array of individualized psychological factors, and suggested that these could be understood and engaged with in a calculated manner. In the process, these psychological investigations elaborated a cartography of consumption that was unprecedented in its scope. From this time forward, the subjective everyday life of the consumer, the minutiae of the dreams, hopes, fears, doubts and affections that traversed our mundane existence, was to become a legitimate and respectable object that could be rationally calibrated and known.

Conclusion

What can be learned from all this varied consulting work undertaken for advertising agencies and manufacturers by a single, though influential, organization? It has not been our claim that the TIHR was typical of other organizations giving such advice, or that its shifting concerns can in some way be seen as representative. Nonetheless, it is clear that over this period its clients included some of the major producers of consumption goods in the UK, and it advised on advertising and marketing campaigns that had a high public profile. To that extent we suggest that the work done at the TIHR was exemplary of the intellectual and practical labour entailed in assembling the modern consumer. We have suggested that, at the very least, the psychologists working with advertisers were neither fools nor knaves; they did not treat consumers as passive automatons to be manipulated and equipped with false needs, nor did they treat the act of consumption as a matter of the sovereign will of the producer to which the consumer must succumb. It was by no means easy to 'make up' the consumer – neither a simple matter of the realization of a wish for profit or the invention of a psychological or 'imagological' fiction. Consumers themselves were construed as highly problematic entities, not so different, it appeared, from those who researched them or wanted to sell them goods. In order for a relation to be formed between the individual and the product, a complex and hybrid assemblage had to be inaugurated, in which forces and flows imagined to issue from within the psyche of persons of particular ages, genders or social sectors were linked up to possibilities and promises that might be discerned within particular commodities, as they were organized within a little set of everyday routines and habits of life. The desires of the individual, whether psychoanalytically derived or rationally modelled, were to be matched with the output of the productive machine. Only when such assemblages of persons, commodities and habits had been produced, and when this assemblage had become infused with psychological functions – whether these be infantile pleasures or adult self-reparations – would it be possible to overcome problems of resistance to purchasing particular types of goods.

In the process, what was entailed was an unprecedented and meticulous charting of the minutiae of the consuming passions by new techniques of group discussions, interviewing and testing. This charting does not merely uncover pre-existing desires or anxieties: it forces them into existence by new experimental situations such as the psychodynamically interpreted group discussion that enable them to be observed, it renders them thinkable by new techniques of calculation, classification and inscription such as 'flavour profiling' and hence makes them amenable to action and instrumentalization in the service of sales of goods. However, even from this limited study, one is struck by the diversity of potential images of the consumer that can be made available to those who wish to sell goods, and by the recognition that those who consume were to be considered, in a variety of different ways, as active agents in their own consumption patterns. The work of the TIHR is thus characteristic of a wider set of processes that were involved in shaping the 'commercial domain' in the mid-twentieth century.

No doubt it is ironic that the forms of knowledge and institutional projects gathered around the Tavistock Clinic and the Tavistock Institute of Human Relations, which had formerly understood themselves as emancipatory, or at the very least as bringing psychodynamic expertise to bear in order to mitigate the miseries of human relations, should dedicate themselves with such energy and seriousness to the problems of the market for soft toilet tissue or housewives' attitudes to frozen fish-shapes. However, from the 1960s onwards, as new political techniques for the government of conduct sought to utilize the apparent powers of advertising, the expertise of the Tavi was deployed in campaigns with more virtuous resonances: for example, using the psychodynamic group techniques developed to sell ice cream in studies for the Road Research Laboratory and the Ministry of Transport on methods to limit drink driving especially at Christmas, and to reduce the death toll among young male motorcyclists. Nonetheless, we would not dispute that many attempts to know and utilize the psychological needs, wants, envies and anxieties of potential consumers were cruder and more cynical than those we have described. And we would agree that advertising and marketing thrive, not merely by promising pleasures that mere goods could never deliver, but also on the inevitable dissatisfactions which they thereby engender: consumers spiralling through an interminable series in which they discard an item which they once thought indispensable, in order to acquire something that satisfies a desire which they did not previously know they had. Nonetheless, what is entailed here is more than the invention of 'false needs'. Rather, these human technologies should be understood as one element in the complex construction of our contemporary 'passional economy', the connections of human being and its corporeality into a regime of needs, desires, pleasures and terrors.

It would be pointless simply to denounce such a passional economy. Instead, perhaps, we might see these psychological projects for making the passions of the soul knowable and calculable as elements within a more general 'political economy of subjectification', in which consumption technologies, along with other quite different narrative forms such as television soap operas, establish not only what one might term a 'public habitat of images' for identification, but also a plurality of pedagogies of everyday life, which set out, in often meticulous if banal detail, the habits of conduct which might enable one to live a life that is personally pleasurable and socially acceptable. These offer new ethics and techniques of living that do not set self-gratification and civility in opposition, as in the ethical codes of the puritan sects that Weber considered so important in the early phases of capitalism, but affiliate them in an apparently virtuous liaison of happiness and profit. In engaging with these formulae, albeit in creative and innovative ways, individuals play their own part in the games of civilization that shape a style of life through participation in the world of goods (Rose 1994a).

6

On Therapeutic Authority
Psychoanalytical Expertise under Advanced Liberalism

In contemporary European and North American societies, authority has acquired a new therapeutic vocation, and the ethical warrant required to exercise authority over the conduct of one's fellow human beings has been reshaped. This has involved new ways of thinking and acting upon all those points where an individual's relations with others intersect with their relations with themselves. These novel ways of understanding life in small and large groups, orienting ourselves towards the most intimate of personal relations, have constructed a new density for the world we inhabit in the family, the factory, the school, the hospital, the office and everyday life.

In this chapter, we investigate the formation of this new species of authority through a case study of the Tavistock Clinic and the Tavistock Institute of Human Relations. But we suggest that this exemplifies something that proliferates widely through contemporary experience: a complex of loosely connected expertises, technologies and representations addressed to the management of problems of living, or the problematization of life from the perspective of its potential amenability to therapy.

Therapeutic authority has been brought into existence through shifts in three dimensions of experience: problematizing, diagnosing and intervening (Miller and Rose 1990; Rose and Miller 1992 [reproduced as chapters 2 and 3 of this volume, respectively]). Events and activities, difficulties and distress, have been problematized, that is to say, constituted as problems to be addressed and shaped into phenomena deemed to require expert intervention. A certain level of agreement has been reached that such phenomena should be conceptualized and addressed in terms of an inner world of psychological processes and an interpersonal world of human relations. This problematizing of incidents and issues is intrinsically linked to a new way of diagnosing. Old problems are reconfigured and new ones discovered, when life is rendered intelligible in terms of the languages and judgements of the 'psy' disciplines. The twin activities of problematizing and diagnosing are themselves linked to the project of intervening, that is to say, acting in a calculated way upon these psychological and inter-psychological realms and relations in order to improve them. Whether it is through marriage guidance or management consultancy, therapeutic authority is grounded in the associations established between problematizing, diagnosing and intervening.

Earlier cultural analysts, such as Phillip Rieff, Christopher Lasch and Richard Sennett, accounted for the rise of a therapeutic culture by pointing to the breakdown of collective values and solidarities, the decline of established transcendental authorities on the conduct of life and the resulting individualization and fragmentation of society (Lasch 1980, 1984; Rieff 1966; Sennett 1976). These cultural changes, it appeared, had produced a simultaneous valorization of privacy and its invasion by a kind of 'orthopaedics of the soul' promising happiness. More recent arguments explain the burgeoning of therapies in terms of the exacerbation of uncertainty and risk in contemporary societies, and a general rise of reflexivity, which extends to the emergence of a reflexive project of the self (Giddens 1991; Lash and Friedman 1992). According to this view, therapy represents an attempt at self-conscious planning of the life-course in conditions that constantly generate dilemmas, and where individuals must make choices of maximum significance in conditions of inadequate information and minimal predictability.

Such arguments seek to explain therapeutics by locating its origins in general social and cultural transformations. A concern with therapeutics as a form of authority, however, directs our attention to a more modest, mundane and operational level: to an analytical approach which asks not 'why' therapeutics, but 'how'. To ask 'how' is to attend not to global cultural transformations, but to more identifiable phenomena: how do specific features of conduct become problematized in particular sites; what theoretical codes make such problems thinkable and manageable; to what extent is the previously unproblematic now rendered problematic and with what consequences; how are remedial technologies invented to give these forms of thought the capacity to intervene and generate effects?

This ensemble of thinking, acting and governing in diverse locales and at numerous points of friction is less fragmented than it may appear. In their multiplicity, technologies of intervention form a kind of therapeutic machine – they are given an intelligibility and a rationality through their connections within an abstract, irreal machinery that lies at their heart (on the notion of 'machine', see Deleuze and Guattari 1980; Deleuze and Parnet 1987). Deleuze uses the notion of machine to designate the lines of visibility, tension and association that create a particular ensemble of relations of power: to speak of a therapeutic machine is to speak of a diagram or force field that is immanent in a range of practices that engage individuals and groups in their daily lives. Through tracing the links between a multiplicity of interventions and the abstract machine they presuppose and actualize, we can grasp the significance of all those therapeutic forms of expertise of human conduct: the ethical regime which they compose for the subjects of authority is simultaneously a new ethical regime for authority itself.

The life-history of 'the Tavi' is an exemplary condensation of these transformations (for very useful anthologies of the 'classic' papers, see Trist and Murray 1990, 1993). The Tavistock Square Clinic for the Treatment of Functional Nerve Disorders was set up by Hugh Crichton Miller in 1920 (Dicks 1970; cf. Miller and Rose 1988); since that time the institution has shown a remarkable capacity to link itself up to diverse perspectives of problematization of human conduct, to shift amongst diverse conceptual orientations, and to render itself technical in a whole variety of ways. It was one of a number of clinics established by participants in the mental hygiene movement, which saw minor problems of human conduct from bed-wetting to delinquency and industrial inefficiency as originating in the early experiences of the child within his or her family, and as remediable by early therapeutic intervention. From the 1920s to the outbreak of World War II, members of the Tavistock Clinic sought to utilize explanations and techniques derived from psychoanalysis and dynamic psychologies in order to explain and remedy problems of disturbed and delinquent children, and troubled adults, and in order to address the difficulties that confronted a wide range of professionals working with human beings – notably social workers and probation officers – and to train them in appropriate ways of understanding and intervening in difficulties of human conduct. During World War II, J. R. Rees, medical director of the Clinic, was appointed consulting psychiatrist to the army, and members of the Tavistock, as well as individuals who would later become affiliated to it, made key contributions to the war effort in the selection and training of troops, and in the rehabilitation of shell-shocked soldiers and returning prisoners of war. In the post-war period, the Clinic reoriented its conceptual bases and techniques in ways more directly linked to psychoanalysis, and played a key role in the development of the 'British school' of psychoanalysis. It sought to integrate psychoanalysis with approaches derived from sociology, social psychology and anthropology, and to 'apply' it to contexts that went beyond the classical therapeutic relationship of patient and analyst – working with couples, with groups, with families, and with a multitude of professionals of human conduct.

The Tavistock Institute of Human Relations (TIHR) was established after the war, when the Tavistock Clinic was incorporated into the National Health Service. The participants in the post-war 'Tavistock Mission' argued that the experience of wartime had demonstrated clearly the significance of psychological concerns not merely to individual mental welfare but also to the efficiency of organizations of all types, and to the understanding and treatment of wider social problems not currently accepted as within the area of mental health (see Trist and Murray's 'Historical Overview' in Trist and Murray 1990). In the succeeding years, the Institute developed such work, collaborating with government and industry in the analysis and attempted resolution of problems of productivity, industrial relations and organizational functioning. The Institute established the first group relations training procedures, and undertook long-term action research projects to democratize and humanize working life in a number of European countries. Meanwhile, the Clinic extended its work through innovative techniques of family therapy and marriage guidance, through new methods of adult and child therapy, and through training general practitioners, social workers and others in the 'helping professions' in the psychodynamic aspects of their work.

Of course, the Tavistock was not unique. It was only one of a number of institutions and academic departments established in the aftermath of World War II, in the United States as well as in a number of European countries, which had closely related intellectual and practical aspirations. Intellectually, institutions like the Yale Institute of Human Relations and the Department of Social Relations at Harvard built upon the engagement of American social scientists from diverse disciplinary backgrounds in common projects as part of the war effort, and sought to link sociology, anthropology, psychology and psychiatry into a general science of social relations: Parsons' general theory of action would be the most distinguished offspring of this liaison. Practically, these conceptual innovations were to be put at the service of understanding the human causes of social conflict, from the roots of crime to the effects of propaganda, seeking to resolve them in the service of social harmony and in ways consonant with the demands of political democracy, productivity and personal fulfilment (cf. Miller 1986b; Rose 1989a).

There were multiple relays between post-war developments in the United States and those in Britain. According to Eric Trist, one of the key figures in these developments, the Tavistock Institute of Human Relations was actually named after the one at Yale (Trist 1980: 147). As with the Yale Institute and many other similar ventures, financial support from the

Rockefeller Foundation made the TIHR viable in its earliest years. In 1945, the Rockefeller Foundation granted £22,000, to be spent over a period of three years, for 'work in social and preventive psychiatry' at the Tavi (Dicks 1970: 133). This was not the first time that the Rockefeller Foundation had supported the Tavi – in 1936 it had awarded a research fellowship to Tommy Wilson for psychosomatic studies to be conducted at the Tavistock. As Haraway says of Rockefeller's involvement in the developments at Yale, 'it was a type example of efforts to coordinate research on personality, development, social groups, culture, physiology and medicine, psychiatry, law and religion under the rubric of social harmony and personal adjustment' (Haraway 1989: 68; on Rockefeller, see Brown 1979; Fisher 1993; Sklar 1980).

Nonetheless, the Tavi is an exemplary focus for the study of therapeutic authoritiy because of its capacity to render itself technical, that is to say, to produce an 'effect'. It is this capacity to make itself technical, rather than the intellectual or social conditions for the birth of the institution, that provides our focus here. How can small and localized institutions such as the Tavi become bound in to a general and multiple 'effect'? We consider first the apparently innocuous mechanism of 'training' and the invention of a powerful new technology that transformed ways of understanding and utilizing the relations brought into being when individuals come together in a 'group'. We then examine two specific areas: group relations training, which was to be a versatile mechanism for reconceptualizing relations of authority; and marriage, or rather the birth of new ways of problematizing, diagnosing and remedying the domain of marital relations.

The Few and the Many

How can the few transform the many? How can a small number of people, confined to a handful of geographical sites, and with limited resources of time and money, change the ways of thinking, criteria of judgement and forms of conduct of others who are dispersed over wide areas, act independently and make decisions about a multitude of issues in a variety of contexts? How can a few 'make a difference'?

It seems that there are only so many ways in which the few can change the many. Most have been tried before: by churches seeking to spread the word of God (evangelism, missionaries, Sunday schools, Pray TV); by politicians seeking to spread norms of conduct and forms of national allegiance (legal codes, sumptuary laws, compulsory schooling, imposition of a common language); and by doctors seeking to diffuse hygienist principles (health 'visitors' – whose precursors were the lady missioners of the sanitary associations – baby books, domestic science teaching).

That is to say, you can regulate others, enmesh them in a web of codes and standards, coupling these with sanctions for transgression and/or rewards for obedience. You can captivate others, seduce them with your charms and powers, bind them to your values through the charismatic force of your persona. You can educate others, 'change their minds' as the saying goes, train, convince or persuade them to adopt particular ways of understanding, explaining, reasoning, evaluating, deciding, such that they will recast what they wish to achieve through reckoning in your terms. Or you can convert others, transform their personhood, their ways of experiencing themselves and their world so that they understand and explain the meaning and nature of life-conduct in fundamentally new ways.

Of these four ways of acting upon others, this last is undoubtedly the most potent. Whilst education transforms the intellectual technologies which individuals utilize to evaluate, reason and speak about their world, conversion transforms persons at the level of their subjectivity. Personhood itself is remade, producing new ways of being in the world, of experiencing and ascribing significance to that experience. This is a matter of transforming the ethical rationales and techniques according to which individuals relate to themselves, judge themselves and steer themselves in the multiplicity of their relations with others. When addressed to those who will have to exercise authority, it poses, in a particularly potent way, the relation between what one is and what one should do, that is to say, between one's exercise of authority over others and one's own practices of the self (cf. Foucault 1988). It is here that the techniques of the Tavistock can be related to the generation and spread of radically new ways in which authorities reflect upon and interpret their conduct and decisions.

Acting upon individuals by endowing them with new ethical regimes, new ways of experiencing, judging and acting, removes the onus of having to calculate for all eventualities. A variety of ways of behaving, of reacting and of comporting oneself are possible in each situation. But these ways of understanding one's circumstances and seeking to act upon them take place within a field of actions that has been transfigured. The domain of possibilities that opens up in each and every instance is thus shaped by a programme learned elsewhere, and yet it is also extended and refashioned in a multitude of sites and in relation to a multitude of local problems. The few may exert power over the many by preaching, educating, legislating, seducing, rewarding and punishing persons. But attempts to act upon the actions of others work best by reshaping persons at the level of their subjectivity, so that they exercise their newfound capacities and attributes freely.

To understand these ways of changing others is to understand something about power. For power is more than a matter of bending others to your will, suppressing, controlling or dominating them: it is best seen as action on the actions of others (cf. Foucault 1982). And such power implies freedom, it presupposes rather than annuls individuals' capacities as agents, and works best through shaping the ways in which others construe and enact their freedom. A whole field of possible reactions, results and inventions is opened up through the operation of such relations of power. When conducted according to a more or less common set of principles centred on a particular institutional locale, the force of this mechanism is that it aligns the ways of thinking and acting of those transformed with those of a centre. Its mode of functioning is molecular, the relations of force and action that it brings into play existing as dispersed activities that achieve all the more strength insofar as they operate only in the detail and the fine segmentation of life. Far from a mechanism for rendering individuals passive and docile, this is a question of endowing individuals with new competencies, aptitudes and qualities. And these new attributes can in turn be conveyed to others, so that there exists a kind of 'multiplier effect', the generation of a surplus through each empirical injection of ideas and techniques.

The Tavi was to engage itself explicitly with the problem of how the few could change the many. The methods which it adopted were diverse, but its central means was through a transformation of the authority of authorities – through working upon the proliferation of 'professionals' that came to inhabit the devices and practices of the post-war 'welfare state'. For, in the aftermath of World War II, it appeared that you could not produce a state of welfare without producing experts who would set up and administer the various devices that connected citizens to welfare services. Knowledge was required to work out which devices were needed, to design them, and to choose between different possibilities in the light of a rationalized judgement as to their likely efficacy. Expertise was required to deliver the devices to the appropriate persons and locales, to scrutinize and diagnose, to select and refer, to advise and treat. In short, the apparatus could be assembled only through enrolling the actions and judgements of authorities.

What some have referred to as 'the professional society' is characterized by more than simply the growth of a professional sector and its increasing power as a political force (cf. Perkin 1989). It entails a radically new set of rationalities as to the appropriate goals and means of authoritative government of life, a new dispensation of powers between politicians, judicial agents and those accredited with expertise, a new way of dividing and relating the political and the non-political spheres of life (Rose and Miller

1992 [reproduced as chapter 3 of this volume]). And it entails also the invention of a range of new ways of 'being professional'. Whilst the Tavi would engage itself along all these dimensions, its most direct contribution was to this last question. Most of the professionals now inhabiting the apparatus of welfare were engaged, in one way or another, in shaping the conduct of others. The Tavi would contribute to a decisive transformation of what it meant to be 'a professional' of the conduct of human conduct.

The emergence of professionals in the conduct of conduct, professionals whose expertise lies in the shaping of the self-steering mechanisms of others in relation to certain norms grounded in positive knowledge, may be seen as a decisive event in the genealogy of authority. It poses in a new way an old problem in the exercise of authority – the relation between authority over others and authority over the self (for a much earlier example, see Oestreich 1982). By what right, and through what techniques, may one legitimately exercise authority over the intimate details of another's personal and interpersonal life? The answer was not merely an 'intellectual' matter – new codes of knowledge, grids of classification, criteria of judgement and procedures for action. It was also a 'moral' matter. We are familiar with the criticism of professionals for the space of discretion which always seems to be created for their own moral criteria to enter into their expert judgement: criticism, that is to say, of the moral basis and legitimacy of the powers which they are accorded to interfere in the personal affairs of others. What is less frequently discussed is the extent to which this becomes a question which professionals pose to themselves in the forms of political culture that are liberal, democratic and pluralistic. To be a professional of the conduct of conduct thus entailed more than the learning of a few techniques or the acceptance of a moral code of propriety. The Tavi promulgated a mode of professional conduct which appeared both ethically and technically appropriate to spheres as diverse as medicine, social work, probation and nursing. These disparate domains would come to be seen as having something in common. And this 'something in common' was an ethico-technical style of professional authority that was fabricated out of varying combinations of elements derived from orthodox psychoanalysis, object relations theory and systems theory. This style of professional authority, this way of formulating what we might term, after Max Weber, 'professionalism as a vocation', articulates a particular way of being an authority in the conduct of conduct, of coping with the difficulties and demands of working life, as well as a way of accessing and addressing the problems of clients, patients or employees.

The success of the Tavistock derived from its capacity to make this way of understanding authority technical, that is to say, to link a certain resolution of the problem of the professional vocation with a technology that would make the creation of such a professional more than just a dream or a norm. This technology went under the prosaic title of training. At the minimum, such training would educate professionals, providing them with an additional way of understanding the variety of human relations they entered into in the course of their public – and private – lives. But in its ideal form, to engage with this technology of training would be a trans-figurative experience, one that would restructure their personalities such that their lives would have to be conducted in new terms. Those profes-sionals so transfigured would themselves enact what the post-war leaders of the Tavi referred to as the Tavistock Mission – they would enact it not through obeying a set of instructions contained in some central plan, but through the inventiveness with which they developed and extended their own work. And many would set up sister or daughter institutions of the Tavi, they would 'bud off' to form nodes in a national and international network of training institutions whose links with the Tavistock were not formal or hierarchical, but those of kinship.

Training had been offered by the Tavistock Clinic from very early on: in child guidance, in psychiatric social work and in those elements of clinical or educational psychology that then existed. During the 1930s, as the perspectives of mental hygiene spread, general practitioners, magis-trates, probation officers and ministers of religion began to come to the Tavistock Clinic to be educated through lectures, intensive weekends, and the like. But the war put a stop to most of the training activities of the Clinic.

Training was certainly central to the post-war Tavi: by 1970, training of social workers, probation officers and others in work with 'marital problems' was undertaken by the Family Discussion Bureau. There was training of general practitioners, through the GP seminars begun by Michael Balint in 1953, and continued after his retirement by Robert Gosling, serving some fifty general practitioners at any given time. There were seminars for medical officers of health, chiefly in the Children's Department. There was the Introductory Psychotherapy Course for psy-chiatrists. There were several different kinds of course for probation offi-cers. There were courses for dermatologists, for Borstal assistant governors and prison officers, for medical officers of health and health visitors in community psychiatry. There were external courses for educational psy-chologists, and for the staff of schools for maladjusted children. And there were the regular 'Leicester Conferences' run by Tavi staff from 1957 onwards, attended by professionals from industry, the civil service, the churches and many others. In addition there were innumerable conferences and one-off courses.

At one level, what distinguished the training emphases of the post-war period from the pre-war activities was the priority accorded to psychoanalysis. Psychoanalysis, especially object relations psychoanalysis as developed by Melanie Klein, formed the common conceptual matrix within which almost all organizational life, personal distress and professional activity was to be rethought. But, perhaps more significant, what differentiated training in the post-war period was the use made of the technology of 'the group'. For enrolling professionals would not be a simple matter of instructing them through traditional forms of lectures, reading, essay-writing, seminars, and the like. This might equip them with a language, but it would not engage them at the level of their personality and their experience. To reach these depths of the person, a new form of learning was required: 'experiential learning'. The inventors of the two key modes in which this could occur were Wilfred Bion and Michael Balint.

Experiences in Groups

What happens when people gather together? When six, sixteen or twenty-six individuals assemble in a seminar room, a schoolroom, a business meeting, a workplace? They remain, after all, just individuals. Surely, to speak of anything more, to talk in terms of a collective entity, something supra-individual, is to invoke the metaphysical. There are, in reality, only individuals. In the 1930s, social psychology had not developed much beyond such a conception. But, according to Wilfred Bion, groups are not just aggregates of individuals: in the group, something happens (Bion 1948–51; Bion and Rickman 1943 – both reprinted in Bion 1961).

When Le Bon had talked in the late nineteenth century of mass phenomena occurring in the crowd, he had placed himself within a long tradition of speculation on what happens when people get together (Le Bon 1895; cf. McDougall 1920; for the history of studies of the crowd, see Moscovici 1988; Van Ginneken 1992). This had usually been understood as an opportunity for all sorts of uncivilized conduct to occur once the layers of control on individual conduct had been swept away in the tumult of collective forces. But, by the 1930s, this way of thinking had lost its persuasiveness, and with it were discarded the familiar tropes of accounts of 'group phenomena' – the propensities of humans when gathered together to panic, their susceptibility to being swayed and led, the reduction of individuals' capacity to reason and to utilize the higher intellectual functions in such circumstances, the fickleness in belief, and the impulsive and emotional nature of actions that characterized assemblies of persons.

The American social psychologists of the 1920s and 1930s viewed the crowd as no more than an aggregate of the behaviours and dispositions of individuals in social situations, in short, a nexus of individual attitudes (cf. F. H. Allport 1924), although these attitudes were endowed with all the emotions of longing, hatred, passion and prejudice that could explain loyalty, patriotism, propaganda, and the like (cf. G. Allport 1935). By disaggregating crowds into individual attitudes, collective phenomena could be disciplined: broken into constituent elements that could be charted through attitude surveys, measured through attitude scales, and managed through the use of techniques of leadership and communication. When, in 1921, Freud addressed the issues of 'group psychology', he effected a kind of reconciliation of the perspectives of individual and group. On the one hand, the group was formed out of forces arising within the individual unconscious, ties of identification with others not altogether different from the forms of identification or object-cathexis that we know within sexual life. It was these libidinal ties that bound the individual to the group leader (Christ, the commander in chief . . .) and to other members of the group (Freud 1955: 116). Humans, that is to say, do not have a 'herd instinct', as Wilfred Trotter had postulated (Trotter 1916), but were 'horde animals', seeking situations in which they can identify themselves with one another and with a single person superior to all.

But there remained the question of how the phenomena that arise in a specific assembly of persons could be rendered intelligible and acted upon. J. L. Moreno and Kurt Lewin had invented a diagram of the group in which the forces that traversed it could be visualized upon a single plane – producing what Moreno termed 'sociometry' and Lewin termed 'field theory'. Each provided a means of charting the dynamic ties that grouped individuals into collective entities. Field theory produced a complex topography of group forces, and rendered substantial such speculative phenomena as group atmosphere, group values and 'we-feeling' through topographical charts of the vectors traversing human relational space (Lewin 1946; Moreno 1934). Lewin's notion of the group was simultaneously normative and practicable. It could be translated into instructions for the production of well-functioning groups, and for the diagnosis and resolution of group pathologies. The Tavi group would share with Lewin this attribute of practicability, but not his optimistic normativity. It would portray the group in more sombre tones. Yet, paradoxically, it would be this more troubling group that would be the most amenable to being acted upon.

Wilfred Bion had experienced groups at war, having been a tank commander in World War I. But Bion's contribution was more than that of reaffirming the reality of the group as an entity *sui generis*, it was his demonstration that one could act upon and through the group and its processes. Initially involved in the War Office Selection Boards, Bion had been instrumental in the invention of the method of officer selection known as the 'leaderless group tests', where the leadership qualities of potential officers were made manifest by observing how they operated in groups in which authority structures and external direction were absent (Bion 1946; cf. Ahrenfeldt 1958; Rees 1945). Drafted in 1942 to command the training wing of the Northfield Military Hospital in Birmingham, and enjoined to discover 'forms of treatment that would enable as many of the neurotic casualties of war as possible to be returned to military duties rather than being discharged to civilian life' (Bridger 1990: 68), Bion sought to deal with the unruly conditions on the Northfield training wing through the mechanism of the group. This entailed not only understanding the problems of the wing in terms of the relations amongst the patients and staff, but also trying to utilize the relations amongst all the persons in the institution in the service of therapy. It was, Bion argued, a kind of collective neurosis that accounted for the disruptive behaviour of the men in the ward, a phenomenon that arose as a consequence of a kind of collective psychological character that had been acquired in the ward, and that could be tackled by getting the group itself to recognize and attack its own neurotic characteristics (Bion and Rickman 1943; cf. Kraupl Taylor 1958). The 'First Northfield Experiment', as it was termed, lasted only six weeks before it was terminated by the Directorate of Army Psychiatry – the chaos created was apparently intolerable to other staff at the hospital and Bion was posted elsewhere (for an account of the Northfield experiments and their role in the invention of the 'therapeutic community', see Bridger 1990; see also Main 1989: ch. 8). However, something more durable had been brought into existence: the understanding that the group and its dynamics could be used to reveal and to transform the individuals who comprised it.

In Britain and in the USA, the management of military personnel in World War II provided an array of laboratory settings for the psychiatric visualization of group life (cf. Rose 1996a). Maxwell Jones invented his version of the therapeutic community in the Mill Hill Neurosis Unit established for the treatment of soldiers suffering from 'effort syndrome', and later refined it in an industrial neurosis unit set up to rehabilitate a hard core of inefficient or maladjusted individuals unable to settle back into the peacetime rigours of industrial labour (cf. Rose 1989a: 50–2). Tom Main, later medical director of the Cassel Hospital, was himself sent to Northfield Hospital in 1945, where he transformed Bion's initial dangerous experiment into an organized technique in which all aspects of the institution's regime and personnel were to be instrumentalized with 'the eventual aim of the resocialization of the neurotic individual for life in ordinary society'

(Main 1946, reprinted in Main 1989: 8). Wartime forged intellectual and personal alliances between those who were to refound the Tavi in the post-war period, convinced more than ever of the powerful benefits that psychoanalytically informed interventions on group life could have for individual well-being and organizational efficiency (Dicks 1970). Ronald Hargreaves, of the pre-war Tavistock Clinic, played a variety of key roles in military administration, working to bring Tavi perspectives into as many aspects of military life as was feasible. Eric Trist and Jock Sutherland worked with the War Office Selection Boards. John Rickman, Michael Foulkes, Joshua Bierer and Harold Bridger all worked at Northfield – Bridger developing some of the key techniques. Henry Dicks worked on the psychological foundations of the Wehrmacht and Nazi culture and was seconded to examine Rudolf Hess. Tommy Wilson and John Kelnar developed 'transitional communities' for the resettlement of returning soldiers and prisoners of war. A new territory of interpersonal relations had been invented which would underpin a powerful way of problematizing conduct in social settings, and of formulating technologies of intervention and therapy.

In the immediate post-war period a further and decisive step was taken in rendering the 'something' that happens in groups more readily utilizable. As elsewhere in the scientific experience, the moment of the experiment was decisive, here crystallizing a way of construing the forces operating between people in groups that was to be enduring and practicable. In his groups at the Tavi, Bion created a kind of experimental apparatus for the production and observation of group mentality and group culture, one that could isolate and intensify group phenomena sufficiently to force them out into the open where they could first be felt, and then seen and named. For Bion, group psychology and individual psychology were not distinct, but 'the group provides an intelligible field of study for certain aspects of individual psychology, and in doing so brings into prominence phenomena that appear alien to an observer unaccustomed to using the group' (Bion 1961: 134). The apparatus that was to bring group phenomena to light, and to train a whole generation of observers, was the unorganized group.

In 1948, Bion was asked by the Professional Committee of the clinic to 'take' some 'therapeutic groups' (cf. Bion 1961). With characteristic modesty, he suggests that the expectation that patients could be 'cured' in such settings was theirs, not his. What distinguished these groups from others that had preceded them is captured, in part, in the notion that they were 'unorganized'. What were they there for? The members of the group, if one can call them that, look to Bion to tell them. But he refuses. Or, rather, he points out to them that they are expecting him to do something: they have some good expectations of him and are disappointed to find out that he is not living up to his reputation as a 'taker' of groups. They demur, but he suggests that they remain persuaded that they are correct in their expectations, and that they regard him as being wilfully provocative and deliberately disappointing. After a while, the atmosphere changes. Someone else, Mr X, 'takes charge of the group' and, being anxious for its welfare, turns its attention to Bion – clearly the source of the trouble. He asks Bion to explain himself. Bion remarks that, unfortunately, he can throw little light on Mr X's problems.

Mr X, understandably, finds this reply most unsatisfactory. He turns to question other members of the group about their motives for attending. He has success with some, but meets unexpected resistance from others. Bion suggests that what the group really wants to know is his motives for being present, and, since these have not been discovered, it is not satisfied with any substitute. It is clear, at least to Bion, that this interpretation is not welcome: his view is either ignored, or taken as evidence of his own warped outlook.

The group is in an uncomfortable emotional state. Another member steps in and seeks to repair the situation. He assures the group that Bion must, after all, have good reason for taking the line he does. The group relaxes, and Bion feels tempted to respond to this friendly change with an explanation of his behaviour. He does not; rather he points out that the group now appears to want to coax him to mend his ways in order to conform to their expectations. The group becomes extremely annoyed: Bion remarks that he feels his interpretations are disturbing the group. The group, it appears, will reinterpret any contribution within it to suit its desires. Means of communication within a group are so tenuous that Bion thinks it might be better if each member spoke a language unknown to the others – at least then we would not assume we understood what any individual said.

The group turns to another member, and Bion gets the impression that it is looking to him to be a leader without the conviction that he can be. Bion remarks that it seems that the group is determined to have a leader, and that successive individuals are tried out and their characteristics matched against what the group knows it wants. But why, he asks, do we want a leader? We have no decisions to make, our situation is stable. Yet the group wants something, its processes are not intellectual ones, and 'Whatever it may appear to be on the surface, the situation is charged with emotions which exert a powerful, and frequently unobserved, influence on the individual' (Bion 1961: 39–40).

But it is not enough simply to draw attention to this complex realm of phenomena which subverts the capacity of individuals in collective situations to think clearly, act rationally and combine effectively. On its own, it would be more likely to plunge us into despair than to give rise to new opportunities: once warned of these swirling currents beneath the smooth surface of social encounters, it would be understandable if one sought to avoid them. For as an experimental apparatus, the group isolates and intensifies phenomena. This makes it possible to try out different approaches. When used correctly, it allows the creation and stabilization of something previously inchoate and elusive. But to create and stabilize, it was necessary to go further. Bion did this by stating that whatever is happening is taking place at the level of the group itself. The group has something – call it a group mentality, or a group culture – that interacts with the individual, that draws the individual into its sway. Yet despite its changeability, this something is not infinitely variable; it has patterns. And it was in naming and limiting these patterns that the group could be grasped.

Bion found the term: the group held assumptions. At any one time, it appears to have a 'basic assumption' about the kind of group it is. Under the sway of this assumption, it acts as if there could be no other possible reason for its existence than this. There turned out to be rather few of these basic assumptions: the group assumes that it is there for pairing (baP); to protect itself against threats and dangers by fight or flight (baF); to depend upon another, a leader, whom it desperately wishes will provide it with security, but whom it resents for placing it in a position of dependency (baD).

The naming and classifying of the basic assumptions of the group rendered visible the tensions that existed between the individual and the group mentality, and the basic assumptions of the group in question. In experiencing itself in the group, in having its speech and conduct interpreted in terms of the basic assumptions, the group can become aware of the forces that prevent it from being a work group. Not that work groups are free of basic assumptions. Indeed, to become a work group, a group has to mobilize the emotions associated with one basic assumption in the attempt to cope with the emotions and phenomena associated with another – the more sophisticated a group becomes, the more it does so by suppressing one pattern of linked emotions by another. But, nonetheless, to become aware of these assumptions and the part they play is to go some way towards resisting them.

However, for Bion these initial formulations were unsatisfactory. They were to be reinterpreted in terms of features of the psychology of the individual – for the psychology of the individual is itself a kind of internal representation of relations amongst a number of entities, or, as Bion termed them, using Klein's vocabulary, part objects. The group evokes very primitive psychotic anxiety in its members. There is guilt that they are damaging the group, which is a very precious phenomenon closely associated with the mother's body. And there are fears that the group is devouring them.

These anxieties are forced out into the open in the group studying itself, whether the group is perceived as that which investigates the individual or that which is investigated by the individual. In such circumstances defences come into play: for example, the splitting of good and bad parts, and the projection of these respectively on to the analyst and the group. The ultimate sources of all group behaviour, concludes Bion, lie in the stresses that appertain to family patterns and, more especially, in the still more primitive anxieties of part object relationships. The basic assumptions were, essentially, secondary formations designed to hold at bay the anxieties which the group itself evoked.

Bion himself was soon to step aside from work with groups. But his conceptual and technical invention was to be developed and translated in a whole variety of ways. It could provide a clinical model for working with patient groups, one that emphasized the ways in which each individual member was caught up in, and responded to, the assumptions of the group: the total group dynamic could be used here in individual therapy in order to help individuals cope with their split-off relationships. But there were other kinds of group to which the expertise of group dynamics might be applied. First, there were work groups, that is to say, the groups that naturally emerged in particular situations of action such as the workplace. These have a defined direction of activity which is determined by the social system in which they are located. The task of those wishing to work with such a group was to pursue the issues of group dynamics that were pertinent to the extent that they were actually disturbing its performance. This was the direction in which Elliot Jaques would develop in his work with Glacier Metal, funded initially as part of the post-war governmental concern with productivity (Jaques 1951). It was through conceiving of work organization, at least in part, in terms of the psychodynamics of the group that one key line of Tavistock thought and intervention would develop in the post-war period (e.g. Jaques 1953; Menzies 1960; Rice 1951). But one could conceive of a different sort of group, an educational group: a group that has as its task neither the cure of individual pathology, nor the resolution of organizational pathology, but the *training* of participants in the very mechanisms and dynamics of the groups in which they participated. Such groups were to become the mechanisms *par excellence* for the transfiguration of professional personas.

Group Relations Training

Individuals, to state the obvious, tend to work in groups. And, often, groups do not work well: the members of the group fall out with one another, or bicker without clear reason; they are unable to define their purposes, or they are sidetracked from them; they fragment into warring factions and they make their members feel angry, distrustful, depressed, impotent. The dynamics of groups affect the ways in which individuals work in groups. Perhaps, then, if ordinary individuals in groups understood better the dynamics of groups, groups would work better.

Human relations training was first formalized in the United States, in the National Training Laboratory in Group Development (NTL). This was founded by Lee Bradford and his colleagues – one of the halves into which Kurt Lewin's MIT group split after his death in 1947. The training groups, or T groups, were associated with the Research Center for Group Dynamics at the University of Michigan, and from the late 1940s onward were run from Bethel in Maine. They grew out of the post-war conceptual and practical concern within American social psychology with the issue of 'prejudice'. Lewin had been asked, by the Connecticut State Interracial Commission, to use his skills to help train leaders in combating racial and religious prejudice. It soon appeared that if trained and impartial observers fed back information to participants in group discussions on the ways in which they had been behaving, they not only gained insight into group processes, but also gained a measure of objectivity and detachment in examining the ways in which they themselves related to others (see Morrow 1977; Lippitt, 1949). T groups set themselves the task of studying the group itself, with experts explaining personal experiences and behaviours while the group was in progress, though not in psychoanalytical terms. The task of the group, that is to say, was to study and learn from its own tensions.

The Tavi had a long-standing relation with Lewin and his co-workers: the journal *Human Relations* was initially conceived as a joint venture between the two groups and, in 1949, the International Conference for Group Dynamics was organized jointly between them. Nonetheless, the first ventures by the Tavi into group relations training took a rather different form. Soon after Bion began running his patient groups at the Tavi, he sought to demonstrate his interpretive methods in two training groups, one consisting of industrial managers, and one of educationalists. These groups did not fare well. It appeared that many of those who attended were 'patients in disguise' – and patients should admit that what they seek is not training but therapy, for attempts at 'training' with such persons produced wholly negative results. A similar salutary experience resulted from an exploratory residential conference held in Nottingham in 1946 under the auspices of the Industrial Welfare Society. One of the high-ranking managers who attended blamed his perforated ulcer on the experience and condemned the conference publicly. Thus when Eric Trist and Eleanore Herbert set up their working seminar on 'Human Relations in School' in the early 1950s, attended by a group of practising teachers, they had first to ask themselves what a training group should be. If, in such a group, you provide a lot of interpretation, you quickly end up with a patient group; if you restrict interpretation, you merely end up with a discussion of topics. The solution, it appeared, was to give the group a task to which it should address itself. The consultant could then interpret the ways in which the group sought to carry out its task, and help it to see the task in terms of its own behaviour. This was the germ of the technique that would become group relations training.

Meanwhile, in the United States, T groups were much in demand. By 1959, over 1,000 people had passed through the three-week summer sessions at Bethel, including executives from industry and government; members of the fighting services, the churches, trade unions and educational organizations; community leaders and research workers. Why should anyone attend events of this type, which so often seemed confusing for those taking part, lacked immediate pay-off in terms of qualifications or even clearly identifiable new skills, and sometimes ended in disturbance or distress for the participants? Of course, they might attend because they covertly sought psychotherapy – but this itself should have been sufficient to rule them out. Or they might want help with a specific task, in which case the experts should visit them and not the other way around. What did they want? Perhaps this has something to do with a certain 'crisis' in the justification of 'liberal' authority in the post-war period. The question for the liberal professions can be put as follows: how might one exercise one's authority over others in a way that was both effective in terms of the multitude of diverse and heterogeneous tasks that it often entailed, and legitimate in terms of the ways in which the inevitable differentials of power could be sanctioned (cf. Rose 1992a, 1996a)? It was to this set of problems that group relations training in particular seemed to provide a kind of answer.

It was not only individuals who discovered that they had a question to which training groups might offer an answer. The trigger, once more, was the problem of productivity, and hope was again to be invested in the economic potential of psychologically informed management of the enterprise. In 1956, the European Productivity Agency undertook a series of projects that sought to engender interest in Europe in improved methods of industrial training. As part of this programme, they invited four people to make trials of NTL procedures in European countries. Under the auspices of the British Institute of Management and the Industrial Welfare Society, and with the advice of a steering committee appointed by the Ministry of Labour and National Service, several seminars were held in London in 1955 and 1956, ranging in length from two days to a fortnight.

Lines of connection were beginning to form in which the Tavi was a key relay. On the Action Committee, formed after these sessions, were executives from the National Coal Board and Esso Petroleum; further requests to the Tavi came from the Council of Church Training Colleges and a social studies lecturer at Leicester University interested in promoting a residential course in group dynamics for social workers. A member of NTL, Hugh Coffey, arrived at the Institute to spend a sabbatical year in 1956/7, and worked with Trist and Bridger on the design of an English group relations training experience. With the support of the Head of the Department of Adult Education at Leicester, the first 'Leicester Conference' was born.

The event, held at Leicester University in September 1957, was a residential conference lasting two weeks (Trist and Sofer 1959; we have also drawn on the papers collected in Trist and Murray 1990). It attracted forty-five participants. They included the head of the Process Investigation Department at Glaxo, two production managers from the Mullard Radio Valve Company, personnel managers from a sausage manufacturer and a building contractor, a research officer from the Department of Scientific and Industrial Research, psychologists from the London County Council and the British Iron and Steel Federation, training officers from the Steel Company of Wales, a headmaster, a probation officer and a number of academics. All were nominated through their organizations, in order to provide some safeguards against their becoming covert patients. A staff group of fourteen was in attendance, headed by Eric Trist, chairman of the TIHR Management Committee, and including the deputy chairman Ken Rice, Jock Sutherland, medical director of the Tavistock Clinic, and Tavi members including Harold Bridger and Elizabeth Bott.

The focus in the first week was the small Study Group, in which between nine and twelve members would meet, together with a staff consultant and a staff observer, in twice-daily ninety-minute sessions. The small Study Group rapidly emerged as the central event of the Leicester experience. It was explicitly based on Bion's methods. The group met 'without an "external" task to be done, but with the specific task of examining the kinds of feelings and attitudes that arise spontaneously, these feelings and attitudes being those which each individual brings to any group situation, or which develop within it independently of whatever the external task may be' (Sutherland 1959: xx). The group struggled to find and explore appropriate topics, and through them its members came into contact with their own relationships; their unwitting resistance to certain types of understanding was analysed and interpreted by the consultant and the group. Most notably, these feelings concerned leadership: the group feels dependent and frustrated by the absence of the usual leadership behaviour; it feels angry and resentful at the consultant's obduracy; it engages in competition for alternative leaders; it takes flight from the absence of leaders; it breaks down into pairings. Through all this, the consultant remains objective, pointing out the group's struggles, expectations and assumptions, especially as they refer to the consultant, or leader.

'Any understanding that an individual acquires about his own behaviour should be a matter of his own choice' (Trist and Sofer 1959: 24). But what did individuals gain in understanding from such an event? In March 1958, twenty-six of the original forty-five members attended a follow-up conference. Members appeared to think they had gained something valuable from their experience, but they were less sure what that was, or how to communicate it to others. Of those who had tried applications of the approach, most had not found it easy. An attempt to apply it in order to resolve tensions in an industrial setting had failed. Put pessimistically, any insight gained appeared unusable in resolving organizational difficulties. But, more significantly, participants felt that they themselves had been improved. There had been gains in self-insight. Self-control and tolerance appeared to have been improved. This, it was thought, was not in basic contradiction with a gain for the organization – perhaps the reverse: the aim was, after all, not to provide 'prescriptions for "handling" others' but tolerance, understanding, a better appreciation of the nature of forces in groups, of the emotional aspects of groups and of one's own 'personal equation' – if this is achieved, individuals will be more likely to 'mobilize the positive forces which lie within them' (Sutherland 1959: 60).

The initial pessimism about the capacity of those who had undergone group relations training to apply its insights to their organization and its management did not last, though there were recurrent attempts to specify exactly what were the benefits of experiential learning in groups (Rice 1965; cf. E. J. Miller 1990). There were splits within the TIHR itself during the 1960s, with Harold Bridger seeking to develop forms of group training more directly focused on understanding the dynamics of groups in organizational life and effecting change in their own organizations (Bridger 1990). The development of a future for the original Leicester model that was both technically and financially viable was taken on by A. K. Rice and his fellow workers in the Centre for Applied Social Research (CASR) (E. J. Miller 1990; cf. Lawrence, 1979a, 1979b; Rice 1965). The theme of the single task, of the group studying its own processes in the here and now, was to provide the guiding principle of all the developments in conference technology which linked themselves to the CASR. The central question that emerged was one of authority: to assist one 'to struggle to exercise one's own authority, to manage oneself in role and to become less a captive of group and organizational processes' (E. J. Miller 1990: 169–70).

The conference technology proved transferable, reproducible and translatable into the projects of many professionals and others. Cyril Sofer, one of the authors of the study of the first Leicester Conference, was later to express his unease about the mass clienteles that these events attracted (Sofer 1972: xviii). But a national and international network of group relations training institutions was rapidly established, deploying what was termed 'the Tavistock Model'. Margaret Rioch of the Washington School of Psychiatry set up an American version of the Leicester Conference with Rice's assistance; after Rice's sudden death in 1969, she named it the A. K. Rice Institute. Within ten years, it had generated six other local nodes throughout the United States, including GREX in San Francisco and the Institute for Applied Study of Social Systems in New York. In Canada, similar conferences are organized by the Rosehill Institute of Human Relations; in Britain, analogous events were run by the Grubb Institute, the Chelmsford Cathedral Centre for Research and Training, the Centre for the Study of Group and Institutional Relations at Bath University and the Scottish Institute of Human Relations.

The construct of the group brought into existence a new domain of reality, a space for thought and intervention that was no longer confined to the consulting room. A new peripatetic laboratory for the study of human relations was opened up. It existed wherever humans were gathered together – in family, school, hospital, prison or factory. It was present whenever a meeting was convened to take a decision, whenever a seminar sought to discuss an argument, and whenever a case conference sought to agree a course of action. It could be re-created anywhere that one could find six people, a room and a consultant. And it could offer itself to a potentially limitless constituency: not to those who were sick and required psychotherapy, but to all those who had to operate in groups in order to pursue personal and professional projects – in other words, everyone.

The technology of the Tavistock Conference was transfigurative. It was 'designed to provide opportunities for members to internalize and make for themselves a "living methodology" for inspecting the conscious and unconscious realities of groups and institutions'. The method, that is to say, 'uses subjectivity': 'The individual is to "use" his subjectivity and sensibility to explore realities, forming working hypotheses about the realities as he construes them' (Lawrence 1979a: 4). What was offered to those who attended – what enrolled them into the therapeutic network – was a kind of fusion between a 'self' project and a 'professional' project: one could make oneself a better manager, teacher, prison officer, social worker, clergyman or nurse by making oneself, if not a better person, then, at least, a wiser one. This was a mutation in the very form of expert authority, in the relations between acts of government of others and ways of mastering the self.

The Relations of Marriage

If 'society' is remade by therapeutics, this is not so much at the global level of culture, but through a number of dispersed events in which the difficulties of daily life have become connected to the therapeutic machine. Similarly, if the mechanisms for resolving the problem of authority which were invented by the Tavi were widely applicable, they had, nonetheless, to be deployed in specific locales. Marriage was one of the most significant of such sites. It was to be intensively problematized in the aftermath of World War II. Divorce reached its peak in 1947. In that year, the Committee on Procedure in Matrimonial Causes, the Denning Committee, was established to advise on the problems caused by this increase in divorce (Home Office 1947). It recommended, amongst other things, the establishment of a 'Marriage Welfare Service, to afford help and guidance both in the preparation for marriage and also in difficulties after marriage'. This service was to occupy that ambiguous position – both inside and outside the field of politics – that characterized 'liberal' modes of welfare government: it 'should be sponsored by the State but should not be a State Institution'.

The Home Secretary set up the Harris Committee to investigate the practicalities of developing marriage guidance, and Tommy Wilson of the Tavi submitted a memorandum of 'Reflections and suggestions on the prevention and treatment of marital problems' (published in abridged form as Wilson 1949). Marital problems, he suggested, could not be seen in isolation from 'community factors and, particularly, the "atomisation" of society' (Wilson 1949: 234). The existing approaches to such problems were fragmented between doctors, psychiatrists, the probation services, friends and relatives, and traditional casework services were ill-equipped to deal with problems that did not spring from the lack of material resources. The specialist marital problem agencies that did exist were founded on a misleading 'commonsense', and amounted to little more than an erroneous admixture of ethical instruction derived from religious principles, and education on biological and physiological functioning. What was needed, argued Wilson, was a programme of preventive education during the marriage-planning period, one that would take place at antenatal clinics and other community centres, in health centres, in the schools, and through the mass media. But this programme required professionals trained to understand and help with the problems of family life.

The Harris Committee recommended that the Exchequer should fund marital welfare services, but that they should be run by voluntary organizations (the following account is indebted to Woodhouse 1990). The three organizations initially selected were the Marriage Guidance Council, the Catholic Marriage Advisory Council and the Family Welfare Association (FWA). During World War II, the FWA had run citizens' advice bureaux in London established as part of the wartime machinery for the government of citizens in conditions of total war. The formidable individual who was placed in charge of this work was Enid Eicholz.

Enid Eicholz had already confronted marital problems in her work with the citizens' advice bureaux: whilst individuals may have approached a bureau in connection with a housing problem, it was almost inevitable that the discussion would turn to marital difficulties. The Tavi became involved in discussions to work out the nature of a project that might lead to a marriage welfare service, initially sharing this role with representatives from the Peckham Pioneer Health Centre (Menzies 1949). Following these discussions, a pilot experiment was set up to run for a five-year period, funded partly by the Home Office through the FWA, partly by the London County Council, and partly from private sources. This project sought to link training and research with casework; to study marital problems at the necessary depth through therapeutic situations; to endorse the casework principle 'that nothing effective can be done to or for people, only with them' (Woodhouse 1990: 300).

Initially, the plan was to set up local offices to study marital problems, and to examine the effects of different types of therapy. Two offices were opened in contrasting areas of London, but their work remained at the stage of 'consumer research', holding discussions with some 450 people in fifty groups in community centres, infant welfare clinics, schools and ex-servicemen's clubs. A hidden continent of unhappiness and difficulty was revealed beneath the apparently calm and healthy surface of the normal marriage: the marriages that ended in divorce were only the tip of this iceberg within so-called 'normal' families.

Those facing such complex issues identified three key problems to be addressed. First, one needed more knowledge of patterns of living in ordinary families. A social anthropologist, Elizabeth Bott (later, as Elizabeth Bott-Spillius, to become a leading analyst), worked with a social psychologist and with therapists and caseworkers on the study that was to become a sociological classic as *Family and Social Network* (Bott, 1955, 1957). Second, one had to remove some of the stigma that prevented people in difficulty seeking help. The term 'family discussion' would replace that of 'welfare': the unit would be called the Family Discussion Bureau, or FDB. The notion of family discussion was neutral, it could apply to prevention as well as therapy, it suggested that what was involved was a joint endeavour of the caseworker and the family. Third, one had to confront the thorny issue of how one should work with marital cases. And there was no other way to do this but actually to work with cases.

There was a difficult problem here. On the one hand, it was rapidly agreed that work with families would be effective only if it was based on a psychoanalytical theory of personality, and used some of the methods of psychoanalysis to give effective help where problems stemmed from motives and unconscious forces of which the people involved were unaware. On the other hand, there could never be enough analysts, and certainly not enough medically trained analysts, to deal with these problems.

To resolve this dilemma, one needed to equip ordinary social workers with the requisite tools. They needed sufficient insight not only into analytical theory and methods that they might apply to others, but also into their own unconscious formations, if they were to work with the conflicting unconscious forces without being swept under by the pressures exerted upon them. A small number of workers were selected to undertake therapeutic work which would be carried out centrally and not at the local offices: they included a social worker, a sociologist, an educational psychologist and a priest.

But there remained the issue of how therapy was to proceed. It was to Michael Balint that Enid Eicholz turned for a solution – and she became Mrs Balint not long after. Michael Balint's response to the request to teach the FDB workers about the psychodynamics of the family was 'No teaching, but let us have some case conferences' (quoted in Bannister et al. 1955: 11). These case conferences were to become the key mechanism for forcing the new world of marriage dynamics into being, for developing a therapeutic technique in relation to it, and for training those who would engage therapeutically with the marital relation.

The Balint technique of the case conference would prove as transferable and reproducible as the Leicester Conference, and as powerful a method for enrolling and transfiguring professionals. The case conferences were held weekly (later twice weekly) and lasted for about two hours; they were attended by everyone who worked in the FDB. The group asked three questions about the people who had come to it for help: what were these two people like; what had drawn them together; what had gone wrong with the relationship? As they discussed their cases, and each worker presented their materials, each of those present gradually began to perceive what went on between worker and client, and what the worker had said and done, in a new way. Each participant has 'to learn to listen to things which her client has barely said, and in consequence will start listening to the same language in herself' (Balint 1954a, quoted in Bannister et al. 1955: 12). Gradually, there emerged a new attentiveness to what was being said and done underneath the surface of the words uttered.

Balint's case conferences acted as a kind of laboratory for studying and acting upon certain phenomena intrinsic to the marital relation. The isolating and intensifying of particular aspects of the marital relation, in a way analogous to the mechanisms of Bion's groups, were to force them for the first time into the field of vision. Although the FDB decided early on that it would, as far as possible, work exclusively with couples, it soon found that this caused complications, understood in terms of transference and counter-transference. A pragmatic decision was thus made that each partner should be worked with in a 'therapeutic pair', producing a 'four-person' therapeutic relationship. Caseworkers saw clients individually, not as husband and wife. Whilst caseworkers met after every session to discuss the marriage, the significant features of this dispensation of partners and therapists emerged in the case conferences.

Difficulties often seemed to arise between the caseworkers working with each partner in a marriage. At first this appeared to be because of the natural way in which each identified too closely with his or her own partner. But it gradually became clearer that the workers were actually acting out the marital problem of the couple. Instead of this being regarded as something to be avoided, it began to be seen as having a crucial therapeutic value, for the conference could actually try to understand it there and then. The case conference, that is to say, gave the workers experience of the same dynamic processes that they must use in their relationship with the client. Similarly, the role of the consultant also became that of exemplar, opening up possibilities for workers to discover for themselves a way of dealing with the client's problems, thereby demonstrating in the 'here and now' what he or she wanted to teach (for a summary of Balint's approach, see Bannister et al. 1955: 15).

The case conference method also resolved a very troubling issue for the Tavi in a way that could be generalized to any other group of professionals. For 'the basic task for anyone intending to deal with conflicts in human emotions is to understand himself sufficiently well to be able to keep free from the intense emotional pressures that are inevitably put upon the helper, and also to see the conflicting forces with sufficient detachment as to get a clear picture of them' (Sutherland 1955: x; see also Sutherland 1956). How could one allow caseworkers to use psychoanalytical techniques when they were not themselves analysts, and had not gone through those forms of training that analysts had designed to make the fledgeling analyst alive to the workings of his or her own unconscious and their possible consequences in therapy? The case conference, as devised by Michael Balint, provided the technology to enable the caseworker to undergo that 'limited, though considerable, change in [her] personality . . . necessary for her new skill' (Balint 1954b: 38).

By the early 1950s, Michael and Enid Balint were to transfer their case conference methods to the training of general practitioners. Whilst the early case conferences had operated in terms of relationships, transference and counter-transference, under their successors, the grammar of marital dynamics was now to be constructed in the language of object relations theory. This produced the profound 'simplification' of marital problems which was to prove so potent in enrolling so many professionals in the Tavistock network.

All happy families are alike, wrote Tolstoy at the opening of Anna Karenina, but an unhappy family is unhappy after its own fashion (Tolstoy 1954: 13). 'Social casework with marital problems' would show Tolstoy to be wrong (the account that follows is derived from Bannister et al. 1955). Despite appearances, despite the myriad apparent causes for marital trouble, despite the idiosyncratic narrative of each marriage and its tribulations, each unhappy family was unhappy in precisely the same way – or, at least, through the operation of the same processes with varying outcomes.

Marital problems were radically 'simplified' by locating them within a novel conceptual space in which traditional psychoanalytical conceptions of the unconscious and psychosexual development were combined with the dynamic and embattled universe of the inner world of images and objects pictured by Melanie Klein:

> The husband who storms and shouts if his dinner is not ready when he comes home, and whose contentment depends on his wife's immediate response to his sexual approach; the inordinately houseproud wife whose incessant scurry of polishing and tidying drives her husband out; the wife who judges her husband's love for her in terms of the flowers and sweets and dresses he buys her, and refuses him children with whom she would have to share his gifts, are all people whose relationships have remained partly at infantile or childhood levels, and who are continually playing out against their marital partners their phantasies of earlier situations. (Bannister et al. 1955: 32)

In the space of object relations, a world opened up within each individual, yet a world that was not bounded by the surfaces of the biological organism. Inner space, from the child's earliest years, was depicted as a complex universe of images, and each image was not a mere picture of a person or a situation in the outer world, but an object into which the most powerful and primitive emotions are invested. This inner world in which unconscious images moved had 'a compelling reality' (Bannister et al. 1955: 26). But the inner world does not remain within. This is because the unconscious internal world of images of 'people' structures the way each new relationship is experienced. New relationships can be made to fit an aspect of phantasy, thereby 'transferring' to the new relationship the responses corresponding to the earlier phantasy relationship. For instance, buried resentments associated with a parent may be expressed in the form of an unreasonable antagonism to a teacher (Bannister et al. 1955: 27). And where childhood has not given the individual the opportunities for psychic integration and development, for learning to confront phantasies with the realities of being loved and valued, and being able to love in return, the adult will remain subject to the compulsions and restrictions of an inner world which is only precariously organized, and dominated by the powerful phantasies that come between him or her and others.

No relationship is more haunted by these patterns than marriage. The kinds of emotional satisfaction that individuals seek in marriage through their choice of a marriage partner, the ways in which they seek approval from their spouse or demonstrate their affection, the things they find difficult or intolerable, all these will reflect the unconscious memories of the satisfactions and frustrations experienced in relation to those towards whom their love and hate were directed in their primitive intensity in childhood.

Marriage can help subdue these phantasies. But, regrettably often, marriage may arise from a neurotic collusion between the partners. The choice of a partner may be heavily weighted on the side of the unconscious. A marriage to an invalid husband may be used unconsciously as an opportunity for expressing the guilt and resentment previously felt towards an invalid father. The partner may seem to characterize a repressed or split-off part of the other's personality; often very dissimilar partners find in the other what they have most sternly repressed in themselves. For 'the unconscious wisdom' of the marital relation is that each partner projects into the other the unwanted parts of their own personality (Sutherland 1962, 1963). Even the most determined tirade against a partner who is presented as utterly intolerable may be a way of coping with the conflict between these 'bad' impulses towards the other and 'good' impulses, the longing to love and guard the other and make good the damage inflicted upon him or her. The simplification of marital problems is as unpretentious as it is profound: what raises anxieties in one partner about the other is actually a displaced, disowned and rejected part of themselves.

How, then, can one do therapy with such a complex realm of projections and projective identifications? By 1955, the technique could be laid out in more or less rationalized terms. Therapy may begin from the insight that this process of projective identification is not altogether malign: although painful, it can be seen as an attempt on the part of each partner to reintegrate the unwanted parts within themselves. But the caseworker is confronted with 'the unconscious collusion of both clients, and with a system of relationships in which each of them is living with the rejected, bad, part, projected onto the other. Each then punishes in the other that which they fear and reject in themselves and are stuck in that position' (Woodhouse n.d.: 82–3). The client coming to the caseworker may be seeking an unharmed 'good' person outside their marriage, and the caseworker will initially receive this 'transfer' of a client's positive feelings. If the caseworker can offer a safer relationship, one that accords with the client's unconscious hope to have found the 'good', unpunishing and undamaged 'parent' he or she really needs, some of the anxieties caused by internal chaos may be relieved. In the unreal world of the relation with the caseworker – unreal to the extent that the client knows nothing in reality of this partner – the caseworker will be invested with attributes that suit the other's inner needs and fit the other's phantasies. But it is also a 'real' experience, one in which the skilled worker will not play out either the phantasy of the disapproving or revengeful parent, or that of the over-indulgent person who can be manipulated. Instead, the caseworker will help the client become aware of how he or she is trying to use the relationship, hence allowing fears and expectations of others to be modified, and a more mature understanding to be reached of relationships past and present.

Whilst other marital guidance organizations spread by increasing the number of centres from which they worked, the FDB chose a different path: 'training the trainers'. Renamed as the Institute of Marital Studies (IMS), it would articulate its own vision of marital problems at the highest and most rigorous level. It would publicize its vision through articles and books. And it would spread it through the technologies of training. Intramural and extra-mural training provided much-needed financial support for the bureau. It enabled research to be localized within the centre rather than requiring the scattering of researchers to the diverse local sites of the phenomena they wished to investigate. The training events, and the groups within them, acted as laboratories which would concentrate and localize marital phenomena, laboratories in which concepts would be developed, and their applicability to an assortment of institutional, organizational and familial conditions tested out and refined. Training provided the much-needed 'multiplier effect' through which the bearers of the psychodynamic gaze would burgeon.

Over the course of the 1970s, the Tavi aspired to coordinate collaborative relations in the network of agencies and expertise in which marriage had become enmeshed. But the expansionist dreams of the professionals of welfare were brought up short by the financial and ideological changes of the 1980s. The strategies of organizations became increasingly defensive and reactive, boundaries between professional sectors were strengthened, assertions of independence became more aggressive. No longer was a pluralism of approaches to be defended as the form best suited to the pluralities of problems in the free field of marital difficulties; pluralism was rather an outcome of contestations between different approaches, each seeking to assert its own importance and potency. Nonetheless, the Tavi, through the FDB and the IMS, had played a key role in the invention and consolidation of the networks for the therapeutic government of marriage. It had helped forge alliances between the problems encountered by so many, and the languages and techniques elaborated by so few. Its modes of operation had transformed the previously theologically or commonsensically based interventions of organizations like the Marriage Guidance Council. Henceforth, those who were to provide authoritative treatment to those with marital problems would deploy a new ethics grounded in the dynamics of intrapersonal and interpersonal life. And henceforth, no professional would visualize marriage in other than psychodynamic terms. From Singapore to Malta, from Tel Aviv to New York, marriage would become one of the principal sites of the operation of therapeutics.

Conclusions

We have suggested that the rise of therapeutics be understood not so much in terms of the rise of an inward-turned culture of narcissism, nor in terms of the reflexive project of the self characteristic of late modernity, but through the formation of a complex and heterogeneous 'therapeutic machine' which has attached itself to diverse problems concerning the government of life conduct, and which has connected these up with certain types of thinking and ways of acting. This therapeutic machine has not colonized a pre-existing territory; indeed its potency has lain in its ability to spread a particular way of understanding, judging and intervening over a wide surface of practices and issues. Nor is therapeutics limited to speaking about and acting upon that which already exists. The expertises, technologies and representations that give a form to the therapeutic machine redefine the limits of vision, and create new ways of acting upon that which is brought into view.

Therapeutics, we have proposed, should be understood in part as the birth of a new species of authority, a new vocation for expertise. Indeed, if the spread of therapeutics has been conditional upon a 'crisis', this is less a crisis of identity amongst inhabitants of our present than a crisis of authority, the problem posed to and by those who claim authority over conduct as to the basis and justification for such authority and the ways in which it may legitimately and efficaciously be exercised. This reflexivity of authority, in which power subjects itself to scrutiny, is not new – indeed such self-scrutiny is a regulative ideal of all those forms of authority which call themselves liberal. But it achieved a peculiar salience in the period after World War II, with the proliferation of experts in the conduct of conduct, and the consequent demands for ways of deciding and acting that were grounded in a knowledge of the humans over whom authority was to be exercised, and for justifications for the authority with which those actions were to be imbued.

The birth of therapeutics occurs under what we term 'advanced liberalism' (Miller and Rose 1990; Rose and Miller 1992 [reproduced as chapters 2 and 3 of this volume, respectively]). To govern in an advanced liberal way is to presuppose the implantation of certain norms of self-promotion in these actors, and a willingness to turn to experts for advice in the decisions, both large and small, that are entailed in the conduct of the enterprise of one's life. Hence they also presuppose the existence of a multiplicity of agencies of advice and guidance, traversing contemporary experience with the languages, criteria and techniques by which we might act upon ourselves as subjects of freedom. It is here that the therapeutic vocation of authority comes into consonance with a whole new regime for the conduct of free individuals seeking to maximize their quality of life in a world of choice.

Therapeutics does not, of course, promise to institute personal happiness or interpersonal harmony, to realize those utopian dreams of undisturbed well-being which it, above all, knows to be fantasy. But it identifies a plethora of new points of friction, risk and danger in social encounters. It redistributes and intensifies the experience of distress, and locates it upon the territory of normality and pathology. It forms a new mode of attentiveness to conduct, a perceptual system which visualizes human encounters in terms of psychological relations within and between individuals. It inaugurates a new body of therapeutic expertise, equipped with novel ways of construing, evaluating and acting upon such relations and new sites for the practising of therapy, attaching themselves in new ways to the remit of other authorities. It entails new pedagogic practices, and new ways of learning how to be therapists that are intimately bound up with the creation of institutional sites which function simultaneously for research, for training and for the practice of therapy. It comprises a new set of relations between those authorities that act upon the conduct of conduct, relations that are intrinsically linked to the ethical relations that therapists have with themselves.

Through exploiting the transfigurative possibilities of the group, along a number of different dimensions, the Tavi was able to make itself the fulcrum of a proliferating complex of thought and action that would enmesh all those different varieties of professional expertise operating within the networks of welfare. The lure of these groups was not merely that they contributed to professional advancement. They provided a matrix within which all the mundane tasks engaged in by professionals of human conduct could be given a new simplicity, coherence and dignity. They made the exercise of power over others, the conduct of conduct, itself a therapeutic activity. And, in promising that 'considerable though limited' transfiguration of personality, they wove together the desire for professional development, the wish for an ethical justification for professional activity, and the desire of each professional of the soul to shape and cultivate his or her own self.

7

Production, Identity and Democracy

Debates in sociology about subjective identity in late- or post-modernity have accorded events in the sphere of production an ambiguous status. For some, economic transformations have been central to the claim that something fundamental has happened in our present and recent past: a shift from 'Fordism' to 'post-Fordism', from mass production to flexible specialization, and from mass consumption to individualized and diversified consumption regimes. Yet changing forms of identity are generally marginal to such concerns, or at best regarded as effects, rather than phenomena that may have a constitutive role in these events. Analysts of identity have tended to focus either on consumption (lifestyles, advertising, and shopping) or on the 'intimate' sphere of home, relationships, sexuality and family life. Arguments that contemporary 'self-identity' is characterized by enhanced reflexivity, autonomy or uncertainty have failed to recognize that the workplace is a principal site for the formation of identity (see, e.g., Beck 1992; Giddens 1991). Of course, there have been numerous sociological discussions of the effects of work on identity, and of attempts to reform and humanize work. But their perspective has largely been that of critique (see, e.g., Anthony 1977; Berg et al. 1979). Repetitively, sociologists of industry have recounted the tale of work as the site of degradation of subjectivity, and have grounded their accounts of resistance at work upon values of personal identity, agency and self-affirmation, which are seen as essential to the human subject (see, e.g., Braverman 1974; Lipietz 1992; Noble 1977, 1984). For such critiques, the vocabularies of participation, enrichment, quality of working life, empowerment, and the like, are little more than disingenuous devices for seeking to bind employees to managerial norms and ambitions, masking a fundamental contradiction between bosses and workers. According to this perspective, it is only through a fundamental transformation of macro-social, economic and political conditions of production that work can be truly liberated.

We differ from such approaches in that we view the workplace as a pre-eminent site for contestations about the nature of human identity, and for attempts to shape and reshape the identity of individuals (for similar arguments see Donzelot 1991a; du Gay 1993; Hirst and Zeitlin 1989, 1991; Knights and Willmott 1989). We argue that attempts since the beginning of the twentieth century to transform production relations, in particular those that have been animated by the imperatives of democracy, have depended on specific and changing conceptions of the person (cf. Hacking 1986; Meyer 1986c). These interventions upon work form the focus of this chapter. We address the ways in which particular conceptions of human identity, subjectivity and personhood have been intrinsic to attempts to govern the world of work in a manner deemed legitimate in democratic societies.

Transformations in identity, we suggest, should not be studied at the level of culture, or solely in terms of the history of ideas about the self. A genealogy of identity must address the practices that act upon human beings and human conduct in specific domains of existence, and the systems of thought that underpin these practices and are embodied within them. For at least the last century, ways of thinking about and acting on work have been fully engaged with the philosophical question of what kinds of persons human beings are. Work has been a key site for the formation of persons. Individuals have been encouraged to discover who they are not only in the domains of sexuality and the family, but on the shop floor, at the work bench, on the production line, in a manufacturing cell and in other analogous domains. And these concerns with the identity of the person at work have intersected with a range of different ways of problematizing the nature of work, democratic ideals and productivity.

It is not only in our own 'humane' times that the subjectivity of the person at work has been discovered, nor is a concern with the damaging effects of work on the person of the worker the prerogative of radical critics of capitalism. The identity of the economic actor – as worker and as manager – has been the object of analysis and intervention for at least a century. Theorists of management and organizations, as well as a multitude of other commentators and self-proclaimed experts, have sought to understand persons at work better, in order to govern them more effectively. On the one hand, all sorts of problems of work – turnover, unrest, accidents, inefficiency, boredom, and much more – have been problematized in psychological terms, and attempts have been made to ameliorate these problems by acting upon the psychological dimensions of the workplace – at the level of the individual and the group. On the other hand, the organization of the workplace has been problematized in relation to a much wider set of socio-political concerns – democracy, managerial authority, the legitimacy of the large corporation, the rights of citizens, and so forth – and again reform of the workplace on the basis of a knowledge of the subjectivity of the worker has been advocated in answer to such criticisms. These events have been bound up with the emergence of a new breed of experts of subjectivity, whose territory is the workplace and whose power in shaping the nature and politics of work is significant. These transformations have important implications for the emergence of new regimes of subjectivity and new ethics of personal existence.

It is from the perspective of 'government' that the full significance of this intersection of production, identity and democracy can be appreciated. A concern with government directs our attention to the intrinsic links between strategies for the regulation of the population as a whole, and strategies for knowing and regulating the nature of human individuals in their depths and details. In the context of this chapter, it points us to an investigation of the ways in which the personhood of the worker has been 'problematized' at the intersection of economic matters (such as the productivity of the enterprise) and political matters (such as the democratic legitimacy of economic power). By 'problematization' we mean the way in which experience comes to be organized so as to render something as a 'problem' to be addressed and rectified: interpretive schemes for codifying experience, ways of evaluating it in relation to particular norms, and ways of linking it up to wider social and economic concerns and objectives. We suggest that programmes and strategies for the reorganization of work have come to be posed in ways that incorporate wider concerns about productivity and democracy, and that these are related in turn to prevailing conceptions of the nature, rights and obligations of persons.

We argue that the government of the personal and emotional economy of the enterprise has been intrinsically related to the elaboration of a range of positive knowledges of this space of work, an expertise of the personal dimension of work. This knowledge of the world of work has been more than a speculative matter, more than a question of the rhetorical structure of discourses on work and economic life. Knowledges of productive life have opened up a space within which calculation, judgement and intervention can operate. Conceptions of the appropriate way to organize work have been linked to bodies of knowledge, as well as to blunt demands to increase output, speed up or transform production flows, increase efficiency, reduce wastage, improve competitiveness, and much else besides. The success or failure of particular technical arrangements of production has come to be seen as dependent upon what the worker is, what makes workers work or not work, what leads them to be absent or to leave, what reduces or increases workers' involvement in their work, and so forth. Programmes for the organization and reorganization of work have incorporated such conceptions of the worker within the design and management of the production process. The worker has come to be understood and targeted as an active participant in the activity of work, not merely as an instrument of production but as a person: a human being realizing his or her self through work, or as a democratic citizen with certain capacities and rights.

We exemplify these relations among production, identity and democracy by way of three historical examples: firstly, we consider the distinct concerns of the mental hygiene and the human relations movements in the early decades of the twentieth century; secondly, we consider the 'quality of working life' movement, and allied dreams of humane work that flourished in the 1970s; thirdly, we address the image of the enterprising subject that infused debates concerning the nature of work in the 1980s. We argue that these diverse ways of representing and seeking to act upon the world of work demonstrate both the political and the ethical significance of these modes of governing work.

From the Human Factor at Work to the Humanization of Work

Across the first half of the twentieth century, the identity of the worker emerges as a problem for the government of the workplace, and one can see a range of attempts to reconcile different understandings of the worker with different views on what gave work its political legitimacy. A brief overview of some of these early, and much analysed, interventions illustrates this.

Psychological interventions on the identity of the worker in the early decades of the twentieth century, in continental Europe, the United Kingdom and the United States, tended to see the human being as a productive force that should be utilized efficiently in the light of knowledge of its modes of activity, its capacities and its aptitudes. Psychotechnics, as this way of thinking was termed, presupposed and acted upon workers as if they were persons of a certain sort. This took two basic forms, each of which sought to optimize the utility of the worker as a psycho-physiological entity. The first was a design of the work process – place, lighting, height of equipment, and the like – in order to maximize efficient working and minimize the likelihood of accident. The second was a judicious process of selection and allocation of workers to different tasks in terms of a matching of their capacities to the demands of the activity.

This psychotechnical project is often seen as the psychological concomitant of 'Taylorist' programmes to establish managerial control over the whole process of production through systematic knowledge. It is true that, in psychotechnics, an expertise of work became, for perhaps the first time, dependent upon an expertise of the worker. The worker, like all other factors of production, was to become the object of a scientific knowledge and subordinated to a logic of efficiency. But the quest for efficiency that underpinned both this project and the endeavours of F. W. Taylor was a common element in a range of political programmes that sought to advance national efficiency through the application of science and rational technique. The perspective of efficiency was to be extended to the worker, who was to be accorded a new visibility in relation to norms of production, calibrated by tests and assessments in relation to such norms, and enmeshed within an array of calculative practices.

The corollary of this science of the worker was that management and other forms of expert administration of conduct were to be accorded a new form of authority. No longer was managerial power merely the blind, arbitrary or wilful exercise of authority; it could be depicted as scientifically grounded and rationally, objectively judged. The workplace could be managed according to a body of expertise that sought to set itself above and beyond the fray of politics. The government of the workplace could be made consonant with the political values of a democratic society, and grounded in knowledge of work and the worker which would legitimate the exercise of managerial authority over individuals.

Taylorism is no doubt the best-known, and the most vilified, attempt to govern the workplace systematically. But it was also one strand in a wider array of programmes in which the identity of the person was problematized in relation to political ideals, economic problems and the powers and legitimacy of authority. On the one hand, the workplace was one of a number of sites – including schools, asylums, courtrooms and military organizations – in which the person was to become a 'calculable individual' whose individuality could be assessed, and who was to be classified and acted upon in the light of this. On the other hand, as Miller and O'Leary (1987) have argued, scientific management was more than a 'technical' reorganization of the space of work undertaken in order to maximize profit and docility. Taylorism did not only appeal to the interests of big business and its political advocates. It also elaborated a set of principles and practices for administering the large corporation that offered Progressives in the United States a way of resolving many of the issues that had troubled them about the large corporation. In particular, Taylor's inventions addressed their concern that the unchecked concentration of power in the hands of the executive heads of large corporations posed a danger to the public interest, bringing the prospect of class cleavage, encouraging dubious relations between economic and political powers, reducing the dynamic for change and innovation that was provided by smaller entrepreneurs, and tending to remove individual accountability. By supplementing arbitrary authority with managerial expertise, Taylorism offered a 'democratic' solution to such problems, since it made available to managers an image of how they could manage legitimately, and it also made available a range of justifiable technologies for governing the enterprise, and thus avoided the need for the direct intervention of the state (Miller and O'Leary 1989a).

Nonetheless, these programmes maintained a distinction between the government of the individual within work and the government of the individual outside work (Donzelot 1991a). Within the workplace, the worker was 'individualized' and subjected to a form of government that sought to intensify labour in the service of enhanced productivity. Yet, in the early decades of the twentieth century, a 'social' terrain was taking shape, in which the individual was located in a web of collective bonds of obligation, dependency and solidarity: the struggles for the increase of workers' rights, for social security, social insurance and state regulation of the contract of employment were fought in terms of such a social image of the worker. The economic and the social seem opposed, with struggles in the latter undertaken either in the name of the defence of workers against the tyranny of the economic, or in the name of the security of society against the frustrations that the economic can engender. And with this opposition was a conflict, sometimes open and sometimes implicit, between two distinct models of the human being: as essentially distinct and individuated, with all the selfish interests that flow from this, or as essentially collective and social, and hence divided and damaged by current forms of industrial organization.

From the 1930s onwards, attempts to govern work sought to transcend this opposition between the individualized identity of the worker at work and the socialized conception of the individual as citizen, without violating the private character of the workplace and the individual character of the employment contract. To do this, it was necessary to abandon the Taylorist attempt to link the design of work and the engineering of the capacities of the worker within a single programme. The workplace became a social domain, but only to the extent that its sociality was understood as a field of psychological relations amongst individuals that were largely indifferent to the technical features of the production process.

This concern with the positive mental health of the worker was first articulated within the mental hygiene movement. In Britain, in France and in the United States, polemical campaigns for mental hygiene connected industrial problems and the identity of the worker through the notion of 'maladjustment'. The worker, they argued, was a person with a psychology, with wants, needs and instincts shaped in the family. The worker was an individual who sought gratification, in work as in the rest of life, of the instinctual wishes and desires that made up his or her character or temperament. For the mental hygienists, this meant that one should fit the person to the job, by careful assessment of character and intellect. One should also provide the correct mental atmosphere in the enterprise, through leadership and management, an atmosphere conducive to the satisfaction of the workers' instincts which went far beyond the desire for payment. Further, one should identify those individuals, whether workers or managers, who were 'maladjusted'. For not only could maladjustment, largely caused by problems in child rearing, lead to personal pathologies such as crime, delinquency and even full-blown insanity, but it also was at the basis of countless industrial problems, including petty jealousy, lack of cooperation, poor performance at work, apparently physical illness and incapacity, neuroses, accidents and even agitation. In the United States, it was estimated that half the annual cost of turnover was due to emotional maladjustment, and that this factor impaired the effectiveness of half of the labour force (see Fisher and Hanna 1932; Myers 1927; Viteles 1932).

Mental hygienism helped transform ways of governing the identity of the worker. The concern to identify, and then to treat or exclude, the industrial misfit, and to understand the problems of the normal worker in relation to the atmosphere of the factory, blurred the distinction between a psychology of adaptation and a psychiatry of pathology: the mental health of the worker was to be a positive objective to be achieved by judicious management. Further, through the grammar of mental hygiene, the government of the workplace was again linked into a wider complex of programmes of social government of the family, the schoolroom, the delinquent, and the like. Each had as its rationale the aspiration to transform these institutional sites into machines for constructing social hygiene, by generalized inspection, early intervention and prompt treatment. Each factory could become the locus of a technology that would promote general and beneficial social effects by a preventative and prophylactic reformation operating on the identity of the individual and the relations among individuals. Work was no longer accorded merely an economic value; it was to be governed in the light of a knowledge and ethics of the normal and the pathological person, and it was to be regarded as a vital site for production of the adjusted citizen.

By problematizing industrial efficiency in terms of the psychology of the individual worker, the mental hygienists provided a novel programme for governing the enterprise. They also helped establish a division of labour between those concerned with the 'technical' matter of the design of production arrangements, and those concerned with the personal problems of the employee. This division was maintained in the 'human relations' movement now indelibly associated with the name of Elton Mayo (Mayo 1933; Roethlisberger and Dickson 1939). The interpretation that Mayo placed on the investigations of the Hawthorne Works of the Western Electric Company is well known. Nonetheless, its contribution to the emergence of new modes of governing the workplace is worth noting.

Human relations did not, as some imply, merely legitimate existing powers in the workplace; it brought something new into existence. By opening up to intervention the intersubjective space of the factory, by redefining the identity of the worker, human relations helped create a mode of government of the workplace that could be deemed legitimate in the changed political culture of the 1930s. The government of the social relations between people as workers was one of a number of programmes that sought to develop psychologically informed techniques for acting upon the relations between human beings in the name of efficiency, harmony and contentment. This was not simply a matter of abstract theory, a question of conceptualizing the workplace as a domain of human relations. The theory was put to work, built into various instruments for interfering in the lives and activities of workers on the shop floor. The human relations of the workplace were to be charted by means of new devices such as the attitude or morale survey. Correlatively, they were to be managed through psychological techniques of leadership and communication. The plant was now understood as pervaded by an attitudinal and communicative atmosphere, a socio-psychological overlay to the actual organization of the productive process itself. Nonetheless, for human relations interventions on work, the technical organization of work, by and large, was not a matter for the social psychologist. There emerged a split between what one might term the relational engineering of the workplace, on the one hand, and the psychological engineering of the production process, on the other. This latter would be psychologized in a distinct way – it would become a matter for the physiological psychologist and the ergonomist.

Human relations established an exemplary linkage between the government of production and the government of the social field. Mayo was atypical in his use of a Durkheimian vocabulary to characterize the relations between the socializing effect of the factory on individuals and the threats of social disintegration and anomie. But the theme that work is important as much for its moral effect on the worker as for its economic effect runs through discourses on employment and employment to the present day (Miller 1986b). Production is problematized at the junction of a concern with the regulation of 'the social' and a concern with the government of 'the self'. On the one hand, work is connected to the territory upon which all manner of 'social' troubles are located and managed – crime, delinquency, indigence, drunkenness, prostitution, and the like – construed as threats to good order and social tranquillity. And, on the other hand, work is given a crucial role in the formation and maintenance of the forms of responsible selfhood upon which a free society is held to depend – regularity of habits, cleanliness, punctuality, diligence, persistence, responsibility to kin, and the like. No doubt this dual linkage may be traced back to discourses on work since the eighteenth century (Dean 1991; Procacci 1991). But, from the 1930s onwards, these themes became the object of a welter of empirical investigations conducted by sociologists, psychologists and psychiatrists that scrutinized the forms of life and personal feelings of the unemployed, charted their patterns of demoralization and de-socialization, and invented devices to ameliorate them – especially in the young, where their effects could be permanent – by instruction centres, job clubs, training and re-training schemes, and the like (Miller 1986b).

Human relations exemplified a new alliance between political thought and the government of the workplace, between attempts to transform production relations and attempts to create particular democratic forms. The link depended on a particular conception of the person as worker and citizen. From Roosevelt to Berle and Means, critics of the corporation in the United States of the 1930s argued that the concentration of resources within a few giant corporations had delivered the control of industrial life into the hands of a few unaccountable corporations (Berle and Means 1932; Roosevelt 1941). Yet, on the one hand, they had not delivered a system of production and distribution that would ensure national prosperity – as the Depression indicated so clearly. And, on the other hand, the growing autocracy of economic life was not compatible with the values of democracy. The large corporation was rendered deeply problematic, as were the forms of authority exercised within it. The writings of Mayo, together with those of others such as Barnard, helped transform the meanings of managerial authority and the modern corporation. The modern corporation could be reconciled with democratic ideals through the recognition that the individual was the fundamental unit on which all legitimate cooperative organization must be founded (Miller and O'Leary 1989a). The contractual principle linking citizens together in the polity was thus to be taken as the model for the bond between the individual and the enterprise. Through respect for the values of the individual, the corporation, together with the managerial authority it necessitated, could be represented as the perfect embodiment of democratic ideals.

In the period following World War II, the political problematization of work and the workplace, and the concern with the identity of the worker, took a rather different form, one that was, nonetheless, amenable to the application of human relations expertise. The British case exemplifies this well. On the one hand, politicians and others were concerned about the proper role of the worker as a citizen of a democracy who had gone to war to defend democratic values. On the other hand, there was the increasing problematization of economic activity in terms of 'productivity', coupled with the view, held by many, that war had demonstrated that central government could and should assume some responsibility for increasing industrial productivity (Tomlinson 1994). In the United Kingdom, the war had seen the growth of procedures that sought to involve unions and management in joint consultation procedures at plant, regional and national levels, quasi-corporatist arrangements forging direct alliances among government, employers and unions in the national partnership for directing economic affairs. However, in the post-war period in the United Kingdom, each of the sides to such tripartite arrangements began to voice suspicion. Whilst in other European countries and especially Scandinavia, collaborative arrangements among government, employers and trade unions at national and local level were to be developed, in the United Kingdom – as in the United States – such formal mechanisms of industrial democracy made little headway (see Bullock 1977 on the British experience).

British social psychologists of industry saw another way of linking democracy and productivity, which they believed was not just an alternative to formal mechanisms of representation, but a more adequate means of recognizing the democratic citizenship of the individual worker. J. A. C. Brown, G. R. Taylor and many others began to argue that the organization of the workplace should also respect the need for partnership and should embody recognition of the worker as a citizen of a democracy. They elaborated an idea of social dynamics based upon the American social psychology of Gordon Allport, Kurt Lewin, J. L. Moreno, Muzafer Sherif, and others, and the sociology of the Chicago School. Fusing this image of the dynamics of group relations with Mayoist human-relations arguments, they painted a picture of the worker as a human being, as one who searched for meaning in experience – and hence as someone who should be engaged in adequate structures of communication. Further, they argued, psychological experimentation had demonstrated that persons worked best when led democratically, not autocratically. This led them to advocate tactics for the government of the workplace that would not only produce human contentment, but also result in high productivity (Taylor 1950). This rationale underpinned a series of academic texts and government reports in the United Kingdom in the early 1950s which argued for increasing democracy at work in the name of enhancing both contentment and productivity. The management of the enterprise could, it was argued, be aligned with those images of enlightened government for which war had been fought, and that had underpinned victory – namely freedom, citizenship and respect for the individual. Democracy could walk hand in hand with industrial productivity and human contentment: a democratic identity for the individual as a citizen could be aligned with the role of the worker within industry.

As is well known, by the late 1950s these optimistic political aspirations for the democratic reform of work through the management of human relations fell into disrepute amongst both academics and politicians. Evaluation studies suggested that any improvements wrought by human-relations innovations were short-lived. Theorists and researchers on work drew attention to the technical features of industrial organization, and accorded them a pre-eminence over and above human factors. Sociologists discovered that the worker had a life outside work, one that had more influence upon attitudes and values in the workplace than any rejigging of 'atmosphere'. The identity of the worker was now reconceptualized – the worker was a rational economic actor, not looking for pleasure or social values in work, but merely seeking to maximize the financial returns provided by employment in order to satisfy desires located in the world of leisure, family and home. Radicals pointed to the inherent conflicts of interest between workers and management, which could not be conjured away by human-relations manipulation, and drew attention to the anti-trade-union ambitions of 'human relations' both in theory and in practice. Political problematizations of work, notably in the United Kingdom, came to focus upon the development of formal mechanisms to limit or rationalize conflicts between unions and management over pay, hours, and the like, conditions of work now figuring as merely one item amongst many over which bargaining between competing interests was to take place.

These changing presuppositions concerning the identity of the worker, and their correlations with changing modes of governing the workplace across the first half of the twentieth century, illustrate a general feature of programmes: their congenitally failing nature. The workplace is the site of heterogeneous and rivalrous programmes; the solutions put forward by one group are often viewed as problems by others; the aligning of problems and solutions can be only a temporary stabilizing of relations between multiple agents and arguments. But failure is not destructive but productive, for the 'failings' of one programme are the impetus for future programmes. The ability of human relations to align the government of the workplace, the political problems of democracy and the ethics of identity may have been temporary and short-lived. But in the 1960s, a new identity for the worker, a new programmatic agenda and a new way of intervening in the workplace were to be elaborated by experts of work, and these could be allied with a distinctive political rationality and a distinctive body of expertise. It is to this new agenda, which had as its objective improving 'the quality of working life', that we now turn.

The Quality of Working Life

Work must be humanized; work can be humanized. Such was the message of an international conference held in Toronto in 1981. Some two thousand people from East and West Europe, Scandinavia, the United States and Canada – managers, trade unionists, government officials, efficiency consultants, academics and others – were gathered together to review prospects for work reform in the 1980s. Those who attended were part of an international and self-consciously progressive politics of the workplace. The names given to these various projects for work reform were '*arbetsmiljö*', '*Humanisierung des Arbeitslebens*', '*amélioration des conditions de travail*', 'humanization of work' or, more generally, 'improving the quality of working life'. The local experiences they designated ranged from projects for industrial democracy in Norway to schemes of work redesign in the United States.

   These varied formulations shared one central goal: to improve the 'quality of working life'. This ideal was articulated in the name of the mental health and personal fulfilment of the worker, the ability and morality of the manager, the quality of the product, the efficiency and competitiveness of the enterprise, and the political legitimacy of the corporation. No longer, so they declared, was work to be a denial of the humanity of the worker. No longer was corporate power to be an anomalous domain of despotism in a political context imbued with the ethos of democracy. Through participative design, worker representation, flexible hours, job enrichment, job enlargement, self-managed work teams, continual retraining, and much else, work should, it was argued, become democratic, creative, innovative and productive. At issue here was a new mode of governing work, one that would be compatible with a more expanded and optimistic conception of the democratic government of the nation. A particular conception of the identity of the worker as citizen was to be aligned with the reorganization of work on the shop floor. A way of making this reorganization of work intelligible in psycho-social terms had to be provided if the aspirations to improve the quality of working life were to be provided with moral authority. The workplace had to be turned into a kind of laboratory, a site in which ideas, inscriptions and instruments would seek to transform the world of work (Miller 1991b).

The elements of this programme had first been brought together in Norway in the mid-1960s. Norway's experiment with industrial democracy occurred at a time when it was concerned about its economic position *vis-à-vis* the Common Market, and when a United Nations study appeared to show that all their resources were being utilized fully – with the exception of their human resources. The Norwegian project took this definition of the problem and sought to address it by linking the problem of productivity to the question of democracy, under the name of 'industrial democracy'. Under the banner of democracy, alliances were formed among the Norwegian government, the Norwegian Confederation of Trade Unions and the Confederation of Employers, linked together via a programme of research carried out jointly by the Norwegian Work Research Institute and the Tavistock Institute of Human Relations. And the 'socio-technical' strategy for work reform that had been developed by the Tavistock Institute was able to reformulate itself as, above all, a programme for real democracy.

The Norwegian project took as its starting point a decisive rejection of the notion that industrial problems may be overcome and productivity enhanced by public-opinion management in the enterprise, by improved communications, or, more generally, by acting managerially upon the atmosphere within which the social relations of production are conducted. It commenced with a study that drew essentially negative conclusions from an examination of attempts not only in Norway, but also in Britain, Poland, Yugoslavia and East Germany, to install democracy by the mechanism of worker representation on company boards. It appeared that representative structures in and of themselves would neither improve working life nor bring about a real democratization of the workplace. Fundamental to the development of an alternative programme of work reform was the argument that the technical conditions of work themselves must be analysed, calculated and reorganized in the name of a psychological conception of the identity of the worker that would simultaneously answer to the values of industrial efficacy and political morality.

The notion of 'socio-technical systems', as formulated in the work of the Tavistock Institute of Human Relations in the 1950s and 1960s, underpinned this attempt to incorporate the technical dimensions of work in a democratizing project guided by socio-psychological expertise. The intellectual and practical programme of socio-technical systems problematized the *technical organization* from the perspective of the *human relations* of the work process. In the studies of the industrial and productivity troubles engendered by the mechanization of coal mining, the workers themselves in certain pits had managed to find a congenial form of organization, in small groups whose members inter-changed tasks and exercised a degree of internal control over their work. An interesting phenomenon, no doubt, but hardly in itself particularly significant. However, when viewed through the perspective of Bion's analyses of leaderless groups (see chapter 6), the Tavistock's wartime discovery of therapeutic communities and Kurt Lewin's work on group dynamics, this appeared as not merely a managerially useful solution to a troubling set of difficulties, but also a powerful and versatile new way in which the 'human machine' might be allied with the 'productive machine' by expertise. It was powerful and versatile because humanizing work was no longer merely a matter of adjusting the subjective realm of work to its technical requirements by leadership and opinion management. Rather, human requirements were to be internalized within a technical reconfiguration of the work process itself. The worker was no longer to be understood merely as a logical apparatus, or a more or less adjusted psyche, or even as a creature seeking comfort, reassurance and satisfaction through the solidarities of the workplace. The worker was to be given a new identity – as an active and motivated individual, seeking autonomy, control, variety and a sense of worth, and finding this in the carrying out of meaningful tasks within a dynamic system of small-group relations. And this new identity for the worker was to be embedded in a novel design of the physical and spatial aspects of the production process.

The socio-technical programme invented a radically new mode of attention to the detailed organization of the plant – be it machine shop, calico mill, retail outlet or coal mine – thereby providing managers with a new way of thinking about and acting upon their domain (Emery and Trist 1960; Jaques 1951; Rice 1958; Trist and Bamforth 1951). It provided a profound 'simplification' of the diverse troubles that faced those who had to administer the working environment, based upon a social-psychological vocabulary that could make sense of such apparently distinct and mundane matters as the number of looms for which each weaver, battery filler or bobbin carrier ought to be responsible. In defining the enterprise as an 'open system', the socio-technical perspective implied that it was not merely a unit of administrative convenience, but a set of relations with theoretical salience, with its own self-regulating properties, linked to a changing social and economic environment. The physical and subjective organization of work was reconfigured at a level that made sense within the matrix of production – that of the group. Additionally, this provided a space for re-analysing the pathologies of individuals – absenteeism, defensiveness, hostility to innovation and change, and the like – in terms not of intractable problems of the individual psyche, but of the psychological consequences of particular group dynamics (Emery 1959). It promised a 'joint optimization' of the social and the technical. And it did so through one particular socio-technical device – that of the 'autonomous group', in which individuals in a group were given responsibility for a major section of a work task, setting their own targets and managing their own relationships with one another. By such means, or so it was hoped, motivation, satisfaction, efficiency and productivity would be correlatively increased.

The Norwegian case provided the first locale where the elements could be brought together to set this programme to work on a large scale: the democratic corporatist political rationality then prevalent provided the appropriate cultural ideals; the socio-technical expertise of the Tavistock Institute of Human Relations provided the requisite expertise; and a number of firms provided the vital laboratories. The research recommended nothing less than a fundamental redesign of work, a profound reorganization of the working environment along socio-technical lines. Drawing upon the experimental social psychology of Kurt Lewin, and Louis Davis's analysis of the practices of production engineers, experts sought to redesign jobs according to certain general principles: an optimum variety of tasks; a meaningful pattern of tasks to give each job a semblance of a single overall task; an optimum length for the work cycle; some scope for setting standards of quantity and quality of production and a suitable feedback of knowledge of results; the inclusion in the job of some of the auxiliary and preparatory tasks; the inclusion in the job of tasks involving some degree of care, skill, knowledge, or effort worthy of respect in the community; and the making of some perceivable contribution by the job to the utility of the product for the consumer (Davis 1957; Davis and Taylor 1972; Emery 1959; Emery and Thorsrud 1976; Lewin 1951). This redesign of work was more than a technical rearrangement of machines on the shop floor; it was to be the material basis for new relations among the demands of production, the personhood of the worker and the political ideals of democracy.

In the period that followed, the Tavistock Institute of Human Relations played a key role in linking together the diverse initiatives that began to proliferate on the basis of the Norwegian examples, and stabilizing them into a functioning assemblage of thought and action. A network of researchers and action research centres began to form in Holland, Sweden, Denmark, France and Ireland, as well as in the United States. By the early 1970s, the 'movement' was receiving enthusiastic support not only from researchers, consultants, employers and politicians, but also from such bodies as the International Labour Organization. The workers were enjoined to find dignity in work by identifying with the product, assuming responsibility for production, and finding their own worth embedded, reflected and enhanced in the quality of work as a product and an experience. The themes of job enrichment, job rotation, autonomous work groups, participation, self-management, design of work systems, and so forth, helped articulate a novel conception of the relations to be sought among the world of production, the identity of the worker and the meaning of work in a democracy. By 1972, when an international conference was held in New York, this network had formed itself into a self-conscious international movement that went under the banner of the Quality of Working Life: the task of 'humanizing work' was now a 'priority goal' of the 1970s (Herrick and Maccoby 1975; Rose 1983). An international council was also established to integrate the national 'nodes' of the movement into a supportive and expanding network that could put pressure on government and establish the necessary expertise.

The temporary potency of the movement for the quality of working life derived, in part, from its capacity to link together a wide variety of authorities on work into a loosely coupled alliance. This provided each with a shared rationality for their calculations and projects, and endowed their diverse ambitions, aspirations and activities with a renewed ethical basis. Managers, supervisors and trade unionists were concerned not merely with working conditions, but also with the content of jobs, the organization of work and the design of equipment. They were attracted by the possibility of redesigning production in a way that would not diminish, and might even enhance, efficiency, and yet would take into account also the increasing numbers of employees seeking greater opportunity to make fuller use of their capacities at work. Technologists and engineers concerned with automation found a language in which to promote their attempts to design new forms of production system, including the use of robots, that would modify and humanize tasks. Systems theorists found new conceptual and practical allies for their reconceptualization of organizations as 'open' socio-technical systems of a dynamic character, in which the production system had to be designed with recognition of its continuous transaction with a changing environment and the consequent need for flexibility. Accountants and economists discovered, in 'quality of working life', a further argument to support the introduction of new techniques such as social audit methods and human-resource accounting, which would align their expert role with contemporary values (Flamholtz 1979; Hopwood 1979). Doctors and others concerned with the safety and health of the worker in the workplace, and the consequences of work for physical and mental well-being, found a new impetus for their somewhat unfashionable concerns. And social researchers, industrial consultants and specialists in industrial relations found a new vocabulary for their activities and a new justification for their expertise that were simultaneously social, political, economic and ethical.

Despite this ardent enthusiasm and advocacy, this experiment with improving the quality of working life was to prove local and short-lived. Whilst the five experimental sites in which Emery and Thorsrud's Norwegian project had been installed achieved apparent success, the programme was not to diffuse across Norway as its originators had hoped. Instead, the technology of work reform was to jump national boundaries and to find, in the Swedish firms of Volvo and Saab Scania, its paradigmatic locus. Sweden was at the forefront of the articulation of democratic corporatism on a national scale, with representatives of government, employers and trade unions linked into an industrial democracy joint council, experimenting with ways of reforming work organizations, enhancing workers' power, promoting a new role for unions and establishing new methods of management in the interests of democracy, efficiency, productivity and equality. The experiments at Volvo's Kalmar car factory achieved a kind of mythical status. Introduced in an attempt to cure a growing problem of absenteeism and turnover, Volvo succeeded in cutting its absenteeism rate through a comprehensive system of job redesign. This involved splitting the assembly process into group working, allowing some rotation of jobs within groups, and providing some freedom for groups to change the layout of their working areas, to vary the pace of work, to alter the frequency of rest-periods, to regulate the speed of assembly machines, and the like (Elliott 1978; Gyllenhammar 1977).

Whilst some other European and North American motor manufacturers showed interest in a more limited 'humanization of work', the general take-up during the 1960s and 1970s was slow and unspectacular. In the United Kingdom, enthusiasm for this radical programme for improving the quality of working life by work redesign was largely confined to a few researchers and evangelists; its destiny was to be reabsorbed into a managerial technology for promoting worker commitment and contentment. And the alternative path that was followed for workers' representation on company boards was to prove a cul-de-sac (Elliott 1978).

Work redesign, in the sense of the fundamental reconfiguration of working arrangements on the shop floor, was thus intrinsically dependent upon the salience of its particular conceptions of the identity of the worker and upon more general political problematizations of the place of work in a democratic society. The sense of its relevance to the 'problems' of production depended on a complex set of alliances among political forces, employers, trade unionists, experts and workers. In the absence of such an alliance, its capacity to produce effects was greatly reduced. Further, the very comprehensiveness of the vision of work reform articulated in the 1970s, the total transformation of the technical organization of the workplace it envisaged, set limits to its penetrative capacity. Nonetheless, whatever the limits of its practical impact, the programme of humanizing work was to lose none of its seductiveness to work reformers in the following decade.

Indeed, throughout the 1970s, the notion of the humanization of work imbued a stream of politico-ethical problematizations of production from the perspective of identity and democracy. A plethora of books, articles, conferences and experiments on work reform took place in many different national contexts. In the United Kingdom, the Department of Employment published their report *On the Quality of Working Life* in 1973 (Wilson 1973). The publication of the report was marked by the announcement by the Conservative Secretary of State for Employment of the setting up of a tripartite steering group – significantly organized around the less contentious theme of 'job satisfaction' (Weir 1976). Papers and monographs began to appear reporting experiments and case studies in the humanization of work, in ICI, in Shell, in Phillips UK, in BOC, and elsewhere (Cotgrove and Vamplew 1971; Edward 1971; Hill 1971; Paul and Robertson 1970). Theories of job redesign and of the reform of the world of production were elaborated in the professional and academic literature (Cherns 1973; Cooper 1973; Davis and Taylor 1972; Little and Warr 1971) and a conference on work reform held in York, England, in 1974, and sponsored by the Scientific Affairs Division of NATO, drew eighteen participants from thirteen different countries (Warr 1976). No less economically determinist in their way than Marx, the work redesigners saw their role as both idealists and realists, as a new form of pragmatic activism in the struggle to reform social life through a reform of the sphere of production.

The international cast of the work-reform movement indicates something significant about the potency of the alliance that it promised between expertise and ethics, between identity and productivity, between practicable local organizational change and governmental objectives for national economic health. Thus, only one year after it was established by Willy Brandt in 1971, the *Kommission für wirtschaftlichen und sozialen Wandel* (Commission for Economic and Social Change) had commissioned Lisl Klein of the Tavistock Institute of Human Relations to review theories and methods in the field of work organization and to report on European developments in the design of jobs and the organization of work (Klein 1976). The International Labour Organization considered the development of new forms of work organization entirely in line with its interest, since its foundation in 1919, in making work more humane. It cooperated in a major study on the effects of group production methods on the humanization of work (Burbige 1976). It published a series of articles on the organization of work in *The International Labour Review* from 1975 onward, produced a *Bibliography on Major Aspects of the Humanisation of Work and the*

Quality of Working Life (Greve 1977), and included a systematic study of new forms of work organization in its programme for 1976–7, the first volume of studies on Denmark, Norway, Sweden, France, the Federal Republic of Germany, the United Kingdom and the United States appearing in 1979 (ILO 1979). Everywhere, it appeared industrialized countries were having to cope with the rapid pace of technical and social change; everywhere workers were becoming increasingly critical of conditions of work. New forms of work organization would provide some of the psychological incentives needed by all men and women as reasoning, social beings. And everywhere, such innovations would, it was argued, promote not only satisfaction, but also performance, democracy and adaptability to change.

The United States was a vital sector within the network for work reform. The humanization of work was to emerge there within a field of argument in which the traditional private corporation seemed to be proving itself inadequate to meet the imperatives of the new information technology, the pace of technological change, competition from the Third World and Japan, and the crucial importance of continual stimulation of consumption. These imperatives combined with a range of socio-political demands that production take as central the values of adaptability, innovation, flexibility, excellence, sensitivity to consumer pressures and the demands of the market. The work reformers argued that what was required was a mode of administering the corporation so that it could adjust itself dynamically to the changing demands of this economic environment. And whilst there were innumerable recipes for the revitalization of economic activity, the programmes of work reform could present their own schemes as being as well suited for the purpose as the old systems of organizational hierarchy were ill suited (Emery and Trist 1965).

Further, there were specific changes in the perception of the system of collective bargaining and industrial relations in America (Kochan et al. 1986). The American labour movement was widely thought to have reached a crisis after more than twenty years of decline – reducing in size and influence, unable to cope with new technological and social demands, outflanked by a range of popularly publicized agreements struck in non-unionized collective bargaining settings over issues that departed from the traditional agenda of improved wages, job security and fringe benefits. The unions were faced with the question of whether they could find a role for themselves within this new environment of labour relations, one in which their membership now came predominantly from the public sector, whose workers were attached to the values of individual quality of life. Additionally, demands and programmes for the reform of work linked up with another set of concerns: political problematizations of the corporation that focused upon its lack of social responsibility, its democratic deficit. The repeated attempts in the United States to confer political legitimacy upon the corporation had not succeeded in reconciling the concentration of economic power in private hands with democratic ideals: as Kristol put it, 'No other institution in American history – not even slavery – has ever been so consistently unpopular as has the large corporation with the American public. It was controversial from the outset, and it has remained so today' (Kristol 1975: 126). And Mintzberg argued that, if such significant sections of the population have come to feel swamped by corporate actions and corporate values – in their roles as workers, managers, consumers, citizens concerned about the natural and social environment, and about the human costs of unplanned technology – the obvious question becomes, 'Who is wielding all of that power? Who controls the corporation, decides what it does . . . ? *The giant corporation is typically controlled by its own administrators, despite the absence of a fundamentally legitimate basis for their power*' (Mintzberg 1973: 525). Of course, the responses to this democratic deficit were varied, but work reform could begin to stake out a powerful space within the field of programmes for government regulation, worker representation, increased powers for consumers and lobbyists, and the like. In this context, the redesign of jobs held the promise 'to decrease mental and physical health costs, increase productivity, and improve the quality of life for millions of Americans at all occupational levels' (Work in America 1973: xv). The reform of the world of production, that is to say, was to be an element in a pedagogic programme for the re-education of the disaffected in the values of democracy.

In the space opened by the intersection of these diverse concerns, a range of national organizations was established. There was the National Center for Productivity and Quality of Working Life, established by executive order in 1970 and given statutory authority by Congress in 1971 – it explicitly linked the problem of improving the rate of productivity with that of improving the quality of working life. There was the National Quality of Work Center, founded in 1974 in affiliation with the Institute of Social Research of the University of Michigan – it helped set up and evaluate demonstration projects ranging from those involving the Tennessee Valley Authority to those involving the United Mine Workers of America and the Mining Company. There was the Center for the Quality of Working Life, formed in 1975 in affiliation with the Institute of Industrial Relations of the University of California at Los Angeles – it sought to formulate and publicize approaches that would enhance the quality of life in the workplace. There was the Work in America Institute, formed in 1985 – it aimed to improve the nature and organization of work, and to increase productivity and enhance the quality of life. And there were innumerable similar bodies at the state and local level (Davis 1977).

Despite its explicit emphasis on union participation and its espousal of emancipatory values, the same criticisms that had been levelled at human-relations doctrines were redirected at the Quality of Working Life (Rose 1983). No doubt they contain more than a germ of truth. But the significance of the notion of Quality of Working Life was not merely its capacity to disarm, disguise and legitimate. These dreams of humane work were more than mere ideology, managerial apologetics, self-interested professional entrepreneurship or palliatives for industrial discontent. They articulated a new image of work and a new way of making this image practicable, one that could be aligned with the aspirations and objectives of so many groups: not only workers, unions, managers and bosses, but also politicians trying to programme a reorganization of work to cope with the 'turbulent environment' brought about by technological change, international competition and the new aspirations of citizens. The apparent power of Quality of Working Life lay in its capacity to establish a kind of mutual translatability of economic, industrial, social, political and ethical concerns into practicable programmes for the reform of the technical and organizational dimensions of work in line with a new image of the identity of the citizen in advanced liberal democracies.

But the technical forms of production organization that could make such programmes operable were only available in limited domains. Attempts to realize the programme in anything like its full form were limited to a few hundred organizations in the United States, and even fewer elsewhere. When this technical transformation was more widely available – in the form of cellular manufacturing, Just-In-Time production systems, zero inventory levels, computer-integrated manufacturing, and so forth – it was linked up to a new and distinctive set of ideals concerning production and the identity of the worker, one that was apparently better able to align ideals of individualism with those of group solidarity. The central term of these new programmes was enterprise.

The Enterprising Subject

During the 1980s, especially in Britain and the United States, a new set of political ideals were to be articulated. The new right was most vocal in problematizing national life in terms of its neglect of the values of autonomy, entrepreneurship and individual self-motivation. But these programmes shared something with the otherwise very different arguments of civil libertarians, traditional liberals and left-wing radicals: all were sceptical about the powers that had been acquired by regulatory states, and that had formed around the corporatist relations among business, unions and government, and all based their criticisms on the wish to restore control to the citizen as a free individual. These political arguments took shape in a context in which a rather different set of concerns were being articulated about products and production in the formerly pre-eminent manufacturing nations of the West. The sphere of production was being problematized here in a new way: in terms of lack of international competitiveness, poor quality and neglect of the supreme importance of the customer. Such problematizations took one country as their supreme point of reference: Japan. The threat of Japan in the struggle for markets was linked to many things – price, quality, innovation, and much more – but it was Japanese working practices that were believed to be at the root of each of these. And one myth of the Japanese worker – as valuing group harmony over individuality, company loyalty over self-advancement, conformity over innovation – was laid aside in favour of another. It was now argued that what made Japanese companies successful, competitive, innovative, efficient and market-responsive, what gave them their deadly combination of high quality and high productivity, was the way in which they made use of the capacities and commitment of their employees (Alston 1985; Pascale and Athos 1981). Whatever the validity of these pictures of Japanese work practices, this new way of problematizing production in Europe and the United States tied programmes of work reform to a new image of the worker that had been taking shape in industrial psychology and management theory during the 1980s: the worker was an individual seeking to fulfil him- or herself through work, and work was an essential element in the path to self-fulfilment.

The notion that the manager should seek to instrumentalize the self-actualizing impulses of the worker was not invented in the 1980s. But it was in that decade that an entrepreneurial identity for the individual became central to a new political problematization of work, and simultaneously to a new set of ethical norms for the citizen in a democracy. The political vocabulary of enterprise, as it took shape in this period, established a versatile set of relations among a critique of contemporary institutional forms, a programme for the revitalization of economic life and national power, and an ethics of the self.

From the mid-1970s on, American theorists from Maslow to Berg, from Vroom to Peters and Waterman, painted a new picture of the worker as an entrepreneurial individual seeking to actualize and fulfil him- or herself in work as in all aspects of life (see Rose 1989a). Doctrines of management constructed within this problem space sought to overcome organizational problems, and to ensure dynamism, excellence and innovation by activating and engaging the self-fulfilling aspirations of the individuals who make up the workforce. Work, they argued, must no longer be viewed as the imposition of constraint, order and routine upon the individual, whose individuality and personal goals were at best an obstacle to company objectives. The worker was depicted as an enterprising individual in search of meaning, responsibility and a sense of personal achievement in life, and hence in work.

For management doctrines articulated in these terms, the new political salience accorded to an entrepreneurial identity for the individual opened a fertile territory for the development of a variety of programmes for reinvigorating personal and economic existence. The 'enterprising' activities of businesses, organizations and individuals, rather than planning and state intervention, would reconcile what was known of 'human nature' with the economic imperatives of production and the democratic imperatives of politics. Enterprise here meant not simply an organizational form – that of separate units in competition – but an image of a certain mode of activity that could be applied equally to organizations such as hospitals or universities, to individuals within such organizations whether these be managers or workers, and, more generally, to persons in their everyday existence. The 'enterprising self' was a new identity for the employee, one that blurred, or even obliterated, the distinction between worker and manager. The 'enterprising self' *was* the active citizen of democracy at work, whether in charge of a particular product division, a large corporation or a particular set of activities on the shop floor. Whilst much was made, in political programmes over this period, of the need to reduce government intervention wherever it was found, the notions of enterprise and the 'enterprising self' were not linked to an abolition of expert intervention in work, but gave rise to new strategies for seeking to govern the workplace. Individuals had to be governed in light of the imperative that they each conduct their lives as a kind of enterprise of the self, striving to improve the 'quality of life' for themselves and their families through the choices that they took within the marketplace of life (Gordon 1991). The task for management was to ensure that the maximum benefit to the firm was obtained through the interplay of these autonomous entities, each seeking to maximize its own advantage in a competitive market, taking risks, striving to do better, calculating what would best advance its own interests.

The emergence of concepts and practices of enterprise as central to the mentalities of politics was more than a matter of reference to certain texts of neo-liberal political philosophy. It entailed the elaboration of a new territory for political debate and contestation, running across the political spectrum, in which the self-actualizing individual was to provide the basis and presupposition for the formulation and evaluation of political strategies and the transformation of social and economic life. Once more, governmental reason was to found itself upon a certain conception of the subjective identity of the person, once more an ethic of personal identity was to underpin and inspire intervention in a range of specific sites, and once more changing regimes of production could be seen as a central site for the genealogy of identity. It was in these terms that new relations were to be established among production, identity and democracy.

Conclusion

In this chapter, we have proposed an analysis of work reform from the perspective of government. We have argued for a positive analysis of all those dreams and schemes for the calculated administration of life that seek to make operable a particular identity for the worker, and at the same time to embody principles compatible with a particular understanding of democracy. And we have suggested that psycho-social expertise has acquired a vital place in the diverse attempts to link individuals subjectively and emotionally to their productive activity. For in the attempts of work reformers of varying kinds to accord meaning to work, a space has been opened up for the elaboration of a body of knowledges of work and of the worker. Programmes of work reform are, we argue, intrinsically 'performative'. They provide ways of imagining the nature of work that are reciprocally related to conceptions of the nature of the individual who is to carry it out. Alignments among production, identity and democracy are forged in large part by those expertises that claim a knowledge of both the technical nature of work and the psycho-social nature of the worker.

To locate work reform on the register of government is to address indirectly the issue of authority in liberal democratic societies. For a claim to expertise based in knowledge is an ethical condition for the exercise of authority in so many domains of such societies. The authority of authorities to act upon the actions of others is established to the extent that such actions can be seen to be secured on the basis of a 'true' understanding of the nature of the entity to be governed. Before employers can be persuaded to engage in costly and risky experiments with their production processes, those who promise efficiency gains to management as well as personal fulfilment to workers and unions have to establish a set of legitimated claims to competence. And, insofar as the programmes of work reform that we have analysed here appeal to democratic principles, the knowledge of the worker and of work has itself to be congruent with prevailing conceptions of the rights and responsibilities of citizens in a democracy.

Perhaps a word on the notions of 'success' and 'failure' is in order here. For it is not our concern to assess the extent to which such dreams have been implemented, to measure the discrepancy between ideal and reality. Indeed we suggest that 'failure' is intrinsic to such programmes. Whilst attempts to reform work are eternally optimistic, they are also eternally judged to have failed, and the reasons for this failure are utilized as the basis for further attempts to reform work. The question of success and failure is further complicated because programmes of work reform are not coherent and seamless realizations of any one theory or politics: as we have demonstrated, they are alliances between multiple and heterogeneous components, and what appears as a 'solution' within one programme may well appear to be the 'problem' for another. But insofar as attempts to govern the world of work are made up of elements ranging from ethical ideals and principles to devices for designing and acting upon the technical composition of the work process, there is an incessant process of seeking to align each with the other so that the technical redesign of the workplace can be conducted in a manner deemed appropriate to a democratic society.

To analyse such a process is not to arbitrate on whether it is essentially humanizing or dehumanizing, liberating or imprisoning. For to do so would be to presuppose that a particular device or argument is 'good' or 'bad' in and of itself. We suggest here instead the importance of analysing a shifting ensemble of norms and practices, a temporarily stabilized assemblage of ideas and devices, a complex of ways of thinking and intervening that seek to regulate and shape the world of work and the politics of work at any particular time. We have argued that ethical concerns about the nature of work are themselves shaped by the changing identity for the person – as psycho-physiological machine, as an adjusted or maladjusted individual, as a social being seeking solidarity, as a responsible and autonomous subject, as a creature striving for actualization, or as an 'enterprising self' – elaborated by psychological expertise. We have argued that they are shaped also by the various issues in relation to which work has been problematized – social unrest, maladjustment, industrial conflict, falling productivity, international competitiveness, innovation, flexibility and democratic deficit.

Analysing work from this perspective illustrates its crucial importance for a genealogy of identity. For it is in work, as much as in 'private life', that human beings have been required to civilize themselves and encouraged to discover themselves. It is around work, as much as around sexuality, that truths about the nature of humans as persons have been elaborated, and that norms and judgements about the conduct of individuals have crystallized. It is in relation to work, as much as in relation to intimacy, that authorities have gained a legitimated competence to pronounce truths about persons and about the ways in which our lives should be conducted. And it is in work, as much as in some realm outside the factory gates or outside the office complex, that we have been taught the techniques of life conduct, of fashioning and monitoring ourselves in order to become a labourer, a worker on the production line or within a manufacturing cell, a foreman, an administrator or a manager. A genealogy of subjectivity needs to address the intrinsic links among these attempts to create and re-create the identity of individuals in the sphere of production, and the broader issue of the government of individuals in a democracy.

8

Governing Advanced Liberal Democracies

When feminists began to campaign under the slogan 'the personal is the political', they drew attention to fundamental flaws in modern political reason. Politics had become identified, on the one hand, with the party and the programme and, on the other, with the question of who possesses power in 'the State', rather than the dynamics of power relations within the encounters that make up the everyday experience of individuals. One of the virtues of the approach to governmentality which we have described in this book has been further to problematize the forms of political reason that constituted this orthodoxy, to demonstrate the debility of the language that has captivated political philosophy and sociology for over a century, with its constitutive oppositions of state/civil society, domination/emancipation, public/private, and the like. In the name of public *and* private security, life has been accorded a 'social' dimension through a hybrid array of devices for the management of insecurity. In the name of national *and* individual prosperity, an 'economic machine' has taken shape, which may have as its object an economy made up of enterprises competing in a market, but structures that domain through implanting modes of economic calculation, setting fiscal regimes and mandating techniques of financial regulation and accounting. In the name of public citizenship *and* private welfare, the family has been configured as a matrix for organizing domestic, conjugal and child-rearing arrangements and instrumentalizing wage labour and consumption. In the name of social *and* personal well-being, a complex apparatus of health and therapeutics has been assembled, concerned with the management of the individual and social body as a vital national resource, and the management of 'problems of living', made up of techniques of advice and guidance, medics, clinics, guides and counsellors.

The strategies of regulation that have made up our modern experience of 'power' are thus assembled into complexes that connect up forces and institutions deemed 'political' with apparatuses that shape and manage individual and collective conduct in relation to norms and objectives but yet are constituted as 'non-political'. Each complex is an assemblage of diverse components, persons, forms of knowledge, technical procedure and modes of judgement and sanctions. Each is a machine for government only in the sense in which Foucault compared the French legal system to one of those machines constructed by Tinguely – more Heath Robinson than Audi (cited in Gordon 1980). Each assemblage is full of parts that come from elsewhere, strange couplings, chance relations, cogs and levers that do not work and yet which 'work' in the sense that they produce effects that have meaning and consequences for us. The lines between public and private, compulsory and voluntary, law and norm operate as internal elements within each of these assemblages, as each links the regulation of public conduct with the subjective emotional and intellectual capacities and techniques of individuals, and the ethical regimes through which they govern their lives

The term 'politics' can no longer be utilized as if its meaning was self-evident; it must itself be the object of analysis. Indeed, at stake within our own unsettled political reason is the very meaning, legitimacy and limit of politics itself. The idea of 'the State' was, and is, certainly one of the most powerful ways of seeking to codify, manage and articulate, or alternatively contest, overturn and rearticulate the proliferation of practices of authoritative rule throughout our 'modern' experience. But the dream or nightmare of a society programmed, colonized or dominated by 'the cold monster' of the state is profoundly limiting as a way of rendering intelligible the way we are governed today. One needs to ask how, and in what ways, and to what extent have the rationales, devices and authorities for the government of conduct in the multitude of bedrooms, factories, shopping malls, children's homes, kitchens, cinemas, operating theatres, classrooms, and so forth, become linked up to a 'political' apparatus? How did the obligations of political authorities come to extend to the health, happiness and well-being of the population and those families and individuals who comprised it? How did different political forces seek to programme these new domains? To what extent were they successful in establishing centres of calculation and action such that events in distant places – hospitals, social security offices, workplaces, homes, schools – could be known and regulated by political decisions? What new authorities in the conduct of conduct – notably bureaucrats, managers and experts – were born or transformed in the process? And what, if anything, has been specific about attempts to govern in ways that term themselves liberal and democratic?

Three Propositions on Liberal Rule

What is liberalism if we consider it neither as a political philosophy nor as a type of society but from the perspective of governmentality? On the basis of the studies presented earlier, we can put forward three hypotheses.

1. Nineteenth-century liberalism, if it is considered as a rationality of rule and not simply as a set of philosophical and normative reflections upon rule, produced a series of 'problems' about the governability of individuals, families, markets and populations. These arose out of the insistence upon the necessary limits of political authority, notably in relation to economic and industrial life, public freedoms of debate and the expression of thought, religious practice and familial authority. Authority arising out of a claim to knowledge, to neutrality and to efficacy came to provide a number of solutions to this apparent opposition between the need to govern in the interests of morality and order, and the need to restrict government in the interests of liberty and economy. Liberal rule was thus rendered operable, not merely by the politico-philosophical pronouncement of the sanctity of the opposition of public and private, politics and market, state and civil society, but through the capacity of various knowledgeable persons to render this formula operable. The philanthropist may be seen as one of the first of these personae, exercising a new form of moral and technical authority. But over the second half of the nineteenth century philanthropy was supplemented and displaced by the truths produced and disseminated by the positive sciences of economics, statistics, sociology, medicine, biology, psychiatry and psychology. One sees also the rise of the expert figures of the scientist, the engineer, the civil servant and the bureaucrat: new techniques for the ethical formation and capacitation of persons who would exercise authority, and the deployment of a range of scientific and technical knowledges that allowed the possibility of exercising rule over time and space (Barry 1996; Barry et al. 1996; Osborne 1994).

2. Over the late nineteenth and early twentieth centuries, this formula of government was perceived, from a variety of political, moral and philosophical perspectives, as failing to produce the necessary economic, social and ethical consequences. One sees the rise of a new formula for the exercise of rule, which one can call 'social'. The authority of expertise becomes inextricably linked to the formal political apparatus of rule, as rulers are urged to accept the obligation to tame and govern the undesirable consequences of industrial life, wage labour and urban existence in the name of society: social solidarity, social security, social peace, social prosperity. The theories, explanations, modalities of information and specialist

techniques offered by experts were, through different struggles and strategies, connected into complex devices of rule that sought to re-establish the integration of individuals in a social form. This was not so much a process in which a central state extended its tentacles throughout society, but the invention of various 'rules for rule' that sought to transform the state into a centre that could programme, shape, guide, channel, direct, control events and persons distant from it. Persons and activities were to be governed through society, that is to say, through acting upon them in relation to a social norm, and constituting their experiences and evaluations in a social form. In the face of the threat of a socialism conceived as the swallowing up of society by the state, these formulae for a state of welfare sought to maintain a certain extra-political sphere at the same time as developing a proliferating set of techniques for acting upon it. The truth claims of expertise were highly significant here. Through the powers of truth, distant events and persons could be governed 'at arm's length': political rule would not itself set out the norms of individual conduct, but would install and empower a variety of 'professionals', investing them with authority to act as experts in the devices of social rule. And the subject of rule was reconceptualized: whereas the subject invented in the nineteenth century was subjected by means of a kind of individualizing moral normativity, the subject of welfare was a subject of needs, attitudes and relationships, to be embraced within, and governed through, a nexus of collective solidarities and dependencies.

3. The strategies of rule generated under this formula of 'the state of welfare' have changed fundamentally since the last half of the twentieth century. These changes have arisen, on the one hand, through an array of different critiques that problematized welfare from the point of view of its alleged failings and its deleterious consequences for public finances, individual rights and private morals. On the other hand, strategic mutations have been made possible through the proliferation of new devices for governing conduct that have their roots, in part at least, in the 'success' of welfare in authorizing expertise in relation to a range of social objectives, and in implanting in citizens the aspiration to pursue their own civility, well-being and advancement. In the multiple encounters between these two lines of force, a new formula of rule took, shape, one that we have termed 'advanced liberal'.

Liberalism

Eighteenth-century European science of police dreamed of a time in which a territory and its inhabitants would be transparent to knowledge: all was to be known, noted, enumerated and documented (Foucault 1989, 1991; cf. Pasquino 1991). The conduct of persons in all domains of life was to be specified and scrutinized in minute particulars, through detailed regulations of habitation, dress, manners, and the like – warding off disorder through a fixed ordering of persons and activities (cf. Oestreich 1982). Liberalism, as a mentality of rule, abandons this megalomaniac and obsessive fantasy of a totally administered society. Government now confronts itself with realities – market, civil society, citizens – who have their own internal logics and densities, their own intrinsic mechanisms of self-regulation. As Graham Burchell has pointed out, liberalism thus repudiates *raison d'état* as a rationality of rule in which a sovereign exercises his totalizing will across a national space (Burchell 1991, and cf. Burchell 1996). Rulers are confronted, on the one hand, with subjects equipped with rights and interests that *should not* be interdicted by politics. On the other hand, rulers are faced with a realm of processes that they *cannot* govern by the exercise of sovereign will, because they lack the requisite knowledge and capacities. The objects, instruments and tasks of rule must be reformulated with reference to these domains of market, civil society and citizenship, with the aim of ensuring that they function to the benefit of the nation as a whole.

The two, apparently illiberal, poles of 'power over life' that Foucault identifies – the disciplines of the body and the biopolitics of the population – thus find their place within liberal mentalities of rule; as rule becomes dependent upon ways of rendering intelligible and practicable these vital conditions for the production and government of a polity of free citizens (Foucault 1977, 1979). Those mechanisms and devices operating according to a disciplinary logic, from the school to the prison, seek to produce the subjective conditions, the forms of self-mastery, self-regulation and self-control, necessary to govern a nation now made up of free and 'civilized' citizens. At the same time, biopolitical strategies, statistical inquiries, censuses, programmes for enhancement or curtailment of rates of reproduction or the minimization of illness and the promotion of health seek to render intelligible the domains whose laws liberal government must know and respect: legitimate government will not be arbitrary government, but will be based upon intelligence concerning those whose well-being it is mandated to enhance (Foucault 1980a). From this moment onwards, rule must be exercised in the light of a knowledge of that which is to be ruled: a child, a family, an economy, a community – a knowledge of its general laws of functioning (supply and demand, social solidarity), of its particular state at any one time (rate of productivity, rate of suicide), and of the ways in which it can be shaped and guided in order to produce desirable objectives while at the same time respecting its autonomy.

We can draw out four significant features of liberalism from the perspective of government.

1. A new relation between government and knowledge. Although all formulae of government are dependent upon a knowledge of that which is to be governed, and indeed themselves constitute a certain form of knowledge of the arts of government, liberal strategies tie government to the positive knowledges of human conduct developed within the social and human sciences. The activity of government becomes connected up to all manner of facts (the avalanche of printed numbers and other information examined by Ian Hacking [1991]), theories (philosophies of progress, conceptualizations of epidemic disease . . .), diagrams (sanitary reform, child guidance . . .), techniques (double-entry book-keeping, compulsory medical inspection of school children . . .), knowledgeable persons who can speak 'in the name of society' (sociologists, statisticians, epidemiologists, social workers . . .). Knowledge here flows around a diversity of apparatuses for the production, circulation, accumulation, authorization and realization of truth: in the academy, in government bureaux, in reports of commissions, public inquiries and pressure groups. It is the 'know-how' that promises to render docile the unruly domains over which government is to be exercised, to make government possible and to make government better.

2. *A novel specification of the subjects of rule as active in their own government.* Liberal mentalities of rule are characterized by the hopes that they invest in the subjects of government. The claim, in politics, law, morality, and so forth, that subjects are individuals whose freedom, liberty and rights are to be respected by drawing certain limits to the legitimate scope of political or legal regulation goes hand in hand with the emergence of a range of novel practices which seek to shape and regulate individuality in particular ways. Liberal strategies of government thus become dependent upon devices (schooling, the domesticated family, the lunatic asylum, the reformatory prison) that promise to create individuals who do not need to be governed by others, but will govern themselves, master themselves, care for themselves. And although the abstract subject of rights may be specified in universalistic form, novel technologies of rule throughout the nineteenth century produce new demands and possibilities for positive knowledges of particular subjects. This is the moment of the disciplines, which simultaneously specify subjects in terms of certain norms of civilization, and effect a division between the civilized member of society and those lacking the capacities to exercise their citizenship responsibly: the infanticidal woman or the monomaniacal regicide in the court of law, the delinquent boys and girls to be reformed in industrial or reformatory

establishments, the prostitute or fallen woman, the men and women thought mad. One sees the beginning of a painful and resisted migration of rights to truth over humans from theology or jurisprudence to the disciplines that owe their very conditions of disciplinization to these new technologies of government.

From this time forth, liberal governmentalities will dream that the national objective for the good subject of rule will fuse with the voluntarily assumed obligations of free individuals to make the most of their own existence by conducting their life responsibly. At the same time, subjects themselves will have to make their decisions about their self-conduct surrounded by a web of vocabularies, injunctions, promises, dire warnings and threats of intervention, organized increasingly around a proliferation of norms and normativities.

3. An intrinsic relation to the authority of expertise. Liberal arts of rule from the middle of the nineteenth century sought to modulate events, decisions and actions in the economy, the family, the private firm, and to re-shape the conduct of the individual person, while in each case maintaining and promoting autonomy and self-responsibility. These modes of intervention did not answer to a single logic or form part of a coherent programme of 'state intervention' (cf. Foucault 1980a). Rather, largely through the proselytizing of independent reformers, a number of frictions and disturbances – epidemics and disease, theft and criminality, pauperism and indigence, insanity and imbecility, the breakdown of marital relations – were recoded as 'social' problems that had consequences for national well-being and thus called for new forms of remedial authoritative attention. The relations that were brought into being between political authorities, legal measures and independent authorities differed according to whether one was seeking, for example, to regulate economic exchanges through contract, to mitigate the effects of factory labour upon health, to reduce the social dangers of epidemics through sanitary reform, or to moralize the children of the labouring classes through industrial schools. In each case, experts, in demanding that economic, familial and social arrangements are governed according to their own programmes, attempt to mobilize political resources such as legislation, funding or organizational capacity for their own ends. Political forces seek to give effect to their strategies, not only through the utilization of laws, bureaucracies, funding regimes and authoritative State agencies and agents, but also through utilizing and instrumentalizing forms of authority other than those of 'the State' in order to govern – spatially and constitutionally – 'at a distance'. Authority is accorded to formally autonomous expert authorities, and simultaneously the exercise of that autonomy is shaped through various forms of licensure, through professionalization and through bureaucratization. From this time forth, the domain of 'politics' will be distinguished from other spheres of authoritative rule, yet inextricably bound to the authority of expertise.

4. A continual questioning of the activity of rule. Sociologies of our postmodern condition have stressed the 'reflexivity' that they consider to be characteristic of our age (Giddens 1990; Lash and Urry 1994). But the 'reflexivity' that imbues all attempts to exercise rule in our present is not distinctive to some terminal stage of modernity; it characterized liberal political rationalities from their inception. Liberalism confronts *itself* with the question 'Why rule?' – a question that leads to the demand that a constant critical scrutiny be exercised over the activities of those who rule, by others, and by authorities themselves. For if the objects of rule are governed by their own laws, 'the laws of the natural', under what conditions can one legitimately subject them to 'the laws of the political'? Further, liberalism confronts itself with the question 'Who can rule?' Under what conditions is it possible for one to exercise authority over another, what founds the legitimacy of authority? This question of the authority of authority must be answered, not transcendentally or in relation to the charismatic persona of the leader, but through various technical means – of which democracy and expertise prove to be two rather durable solutions. Liberalism inaugurates a continual dissatisfaction with government, a perpetual questioning of whether the desired effects are being produced, of the mistakes of thought or policy that hamper the efficacy of government, a recurrent diagnosis of failure coupled with a recurrent demand to govern better.

Governing the State of Welfare

The real history of liberalism, over the late nineteenth and twentieth centuries, is bound up with a series of transformations in the problematics of rule. What Foucault refers to as the governmentalization of the state is here bound up with the emergence of a problem in which the governability of democracy – to use Jacques Donzelot's term – seems to raise a number of difficulties to which the 'socialization of society' seemed to be the solution (Donzelot 1991b; see also Ewald 1991; Rabinow 1989: chs 4–6). From a variety of perspectives it was argued that the projects of nineteenth-century liberalism had failed, and the philanthropic and disciplinary projects for avoiding demoralization and maintaining moral order in urban labouring classes were proving powerless in the face of the forces of social fragmentation and individualization of modern society, evidenced by rates of suicide, crime and social disaffection. Further, economic affairs, in particular the uncertainties of employment and the harsh conditions of factory work, had profound social consequences that had not been alleviated by the vestigial constraint of factory legislation and the like. They damaged health, produced danger through the irregularity of employment and encouraged the growth of militant labour. 'Welfare' was one formula for recoding, along a number of different dimensions, the relations between the political field and the management of economic and social affairs, in which the authority of experts – as those who can speak and enact truth about human beings in their individual and collective lives – was to be accorded a new role. Within this new formula of welfare, political authorities, through their utilization of the financial, technical and juridical possibilities of the state, were to become the guarantor of both the freedom of the individual and the freedom of the capitalist enterprise. The state was to take responsibility for generating an array of technologies of government that would 'socialize' both individual citizenship and economic life in the name of collective security. This was a formula of rule somewhere between classical liberalism and nascent socialism. Perhaps its most contested plane of action was the economic domain itself, where interventions would weaken the privacy of the market and the enterprise while retaining their formal autonomy. But the security of economy was also to be assured by acting upon the social milieux within which production and exchange occurred: by governing society itself (cf. Procacci 1989).

Social insurance and social work can exemplify two axes of this new formula of government: one inclusive and solidaristic, one individualizing and responsibilizing. Social insurance is an inclusive technology of government (O'Malley 1992, 1996; Rose 1993c). It incarnates social solidarity in collectivizing the management of the individual and collective dangers posed by the economic riskiness of a capricious system of wage labour, and by the corporeal riskiness of a body subject to sickness and injury, under the stewardship of a 'social' state. And it enjoins solidarity in that the security of the individual across the vicissitudes of a life history is guaranteed by a mechanism that operates on the basis of what individuals and their families are thought to share by virtue of their common sociality. Social insurance thus establishes new connections and association between 'public' norms and procedures and the fate of individuals in their 'private' economic and personal conduct. It was only one of an assortment of ways in which, at the start of the twentieth century, the 'privacy' of the private spheres of family and factory was attenuated. Together with other regulatory devices, such as public housing schemes, health and safety legislation and laws on child-care, the autonomy of both economic and familial spaces was weakened, and new vectors of responsibility and obligation took shape between State and parent, child or employee.

Social work, correlatively, operates within a strategy in which security is to be secured by enjoining the responsibilities of citizenship upon individuals who are incapable or aberrant members of society (Donzelot 1979b; Parton 1991; Rose 1985). It acts on specific problematic cases, radiating out to them from locales of individualized judgement on particular conducts judged as pathological in relation to social norms. The juvenile court, the school, the child guidance clinic, operate as centres of adjudication and coordination of these strategies, targeted not so much at the isolated individual citizen, but at individuals connected within the matrix of the family. The everyday activities of living, the hygienic care of household members, the previously trivial features of interactions between adults and children, were to be anatomized by experts, rendered calculable in terms of norms and deviations, judged in terms of their social costs and consequences and subject to regimes of education or reformation. The family, then, was to be instrumentalized as a social machine – both made social and utilized to create sociality – implanting the techniques of responsible citizenship under the tutelage of experts and in relation to a variety of sanctions and rewards. Complex assemblages would constitute the possibility of state departments, government offices, and so forth, acting as centres, by enabling their deliberations to be relayed into a whole variety of micro-locales within which the conduct of the citizen could be problematized and acted upon by means of norms that calibrated personal normality in a way that was inextricably linked to its social consequences. The individual and the family were to be 'simultaneously assigned their social duties, accorded their rights, assured of their natural capacities, and educated in the fact that they need to be educated by experts in order to responsibly assume their freedom' (Rose 1993c: 13).

The political subject was thus to be reconceptualized as a citizen, with rights to social protection and social education in return for duties of social obligation and social responsibility, both re-figuring and retaining the liberal character of 'freedom' and 'privacy' (Rose 1987). Security would be combined with responsibility in a way that was conducive both to democracy and to liberty. When counterposed to the moralistic, philanthropic and disciplinary projects of nineteenth-century liberalism, social government extends the boundaries of the sphere of politics via proliferating networks through which the state could seek to extend its rule over distant events, places and persons. Expertise acquires powerful capacities, not only in linking deliberations in one place with actions in another, but also in promising to align the self-governing capacities of subjects with the objectives of political authorities by means of persuasion, education and seduction rather than coercion. These new technologies of expert social government appear to depoliticize and technicize a whole swathe of questions by promising that technical calculations will overrule existing logics of contestation between opposing interests. Judgements and deliberations of experts as to rates of benefit or patterns of child-care are accorded capacities for action that were previously unthinkable. But in becoming so integral to the exercise of political authority, experts gain the capacity to generate 'enclosures', relatively bounded locales or fields of judgement within which their authority is concentrated, intensified and rendered difficult to countermand.

Advanced Liberalism

The conditions that stripped the self-evidence away from social government were heterogeneous. In the immediate aftermath of World War II, at the very same time as some were learning the lesson that it was feasible for the whole of the productive and social organization of a nation to be governed, in some way or other, by a central state, a number of European intellectuals drew exactly the opposite conclusion. Most notable, perhaps, was Friedrich von Hayek's suggestion that the logics of the interventionist State, as they had been manifested in the wartime organization of social and economic life, were not only inefficient and self-defeating, but also set nations on the very path towards the total state that had been manifested in Nazi Germany and could be seen in Stalin's Soviet Union – they were subversive of the very freedoms, democracies and liberties they sought to enhance (Hayek 1944; cf. Gordon 1987, 1991; the following discussion draws on Rose 1993a). The arguments Hayek set out in *The Road to Serfdom* (Hayek 1944) were to be elaborated in a series of subsequent texts: the principle of individual freedom was both the origin of our progress and the guarantor of future growth of civilization; although we must shed the hubristic illusion that we can, by decisions and calculations of authority, deliberately create 'the future of mankind', we must also recognize that freedom itself is an artefact of civilization, for 'the discipline of civilization . . . is at the same time the discipline of freedom' (Hayek 1960: 163).

It was some three decades later that such critiques of the social state were assembled into a politically salient assault on the rationalities, programmes and technologies of welfare in Britain and the United States, and somewhat later, and less dramatically, in some other European countries. An economic thesis articulated in different forms by left and right had a particular significance here – the argument that the increasing levels of taxation and public expenditure required to sustain social, health and welfare services, education, and the like, were damaging to the health of capitalism as they required penal rates of tax on private profit. This contradiction was formulated from the left in terms of the 'fiscal crisis of the State' and from the right in terms of the contradiction between the growth of an 'unproductive' welfare sector that created no wealth at the expense of the 'productive' private sector in which all national wealth was actually produced (Bacon and Eltis 1976; O'Connor 1972). The very socialization of capitalist private enterprise and market relations that had been seen as its salvation in the face of the twin threats of socialism and moral and social disintegration now appeared to be antithetical to the survival of a society based upon a capitalist economy.

This economic argument chimed with a range of other criticisms of social government: of the arrogance of government overreach; of the dangers of imminent government overload; the absurdity of politicians trying to second-guess the market by picking winners; claims that Keynesian demand management stimulated inflationary expectations and led to the debasement of the currency. Others claimed that measures intended to decrease poverty had actually increased inequality; that attempts to assist the disadvantaged had actually worsened their disadvantage; that controls on minimum wages hurt the worst-paid because they destroy jobs. Further, welfare bureaucracies themselves, together with their associated specialisms of welfare and social expertise, came under attack from all parts of the political spectrum – from classical liberals and libertarians; from left-wing critics of the social control of deviance; from social democratic activists concerned about the lack of effectiveness of social government in alleviating inequality and disadvantage. It appeared that behind the welfare sector's impassioned demands for more funding for their services lay a covert strategy of empire building and the advancement of sectional interests; that it was actually the middle classes, rather than the poor, who benefited both from the employment opportunities and from the services of the welfare state; and that welfare services actually destroyed other forms of social support such as church, community and family; that they did not produce social responsibility and citizenship but dependency and a client mentality (Adler & Asquith 1981; Friedman and Friedman 1982; Murray 1980; cf. for an earlier version Reich 1964, and for a discussion of all these 'rhetorics of reaction', see Hirschman 1991).

Simultaneously, the empire of social expertise was itself fracturing into rivalry between different specialisms: experts on the child, the elderly, the disabled, the alcoholic, the drug abuser, the single mother, as well as psychiatric nurses, community workers, occupational therapists and many more. Each of these specialisms sought to organize on professional lines, to demand its own rights and field of discretion: the world of welfare fragmented through an ever-finer division of labour and through divergent conceptual and practical allegiances. Equally, clients of expertise came to understand and relate to themselves and their 'welfare' in new ways. In a whole range of sectors, individuals came to reconceptualize themselves in terms of their own will to be healthy, to enjoy a maximized normality. Surrounded by images of health and happiness in the mass media and in the marketing strategies deployed in commodity advertising and consumption regimes, narrativizing their dissatisfactions in the potent language of rights, they organized themselves into their own associations, contesting the powers of expertise, protesting against relations that now appeared patronizing and demeaning of their autonomy, demanding increased resources for their particular conditions and claiming a say in the decisions that affected their lives. In the face of the simultaneous proliferation, fragmentation, contestation and de-legitimization of the place of experts in the devices of social government, a new formula for the relation between government, expertise and subjectivity would take shape.

It would be misleading to suggest that the neo-conservative political regimes that were elected in Britain and the United States from the late 1970s through the 1980s were underpinned by a coherent and elaborated political rationality that they then sought to implement, still less one that identified bureaucratic and professional power as a key problem. Initially, no doubt, these regimes merely sought to engage with a multitude of different problems of welfare, to reduce cost, to undercut the power of professional lobbies, etc. But gradually, these diverse skirmishes were rationalized within a relatively coherent mentality of government that came to be termed neo-liberalism. Neo-liberalism managed to reactivate the sceptical vigilance over political government basic to classical liberalism, by linking different elements of the 'rhetoric of reaction' with a series of techniques – none of them in itself particularly new or remarkable – that could render these criticisms governmental. Indeed one thing that is perhaps paradoxical about neo-liberalism is that, despite posing itself as a critique of political government, it retains the programmatic *a priori*, the presupposition that the real is programmable by authorities: the objects of government are rendered thinkable in such a way that their difficulties appear amenable to diagnosis, prescription and cure (cf. Rose and Miller 1992: 183 [reproduced as chapter 3 of the present volume, see p. 63]). Neo-liberalism does not abandon the 'will to govern': it maintains the view that failure of government to achieve its objectives is to be overcome by inventing new strategies of government that will succeed.

What is it 'to govern in an advanced liberal way'? Over the closing decades of the twentieth century, 'advanced liberal' strategies could be observed in national contexts from Finland to Australia, advocated by political regimes from left and right, and in relation to problem domains from crime control to health. They sought to develop techniques of government that created a distance between the decisions of formal political institutions and other social actors, conceived of these actors in new ways as subjects of responsibility, autonomy and choice, and hoped to act upon them through shaping and utilizing their freedom. We can identify three characteristic shifts.

1. A new relation between expertise and politics. Welfare might be considered a 'substantive' rationality of rule: expert conceptions of health, income levels, types of economic activity, and the like, were to be more or less directly transcribed into the machinery and objectives of political government. Simultaneously, the very powers that the technologies of welfare accorded to experts enabled them to establish enclosures within which their authority could not be challenged, effectively insulating experts from external political attempts to govern them and their decisions and actions. In contrast, advanced liberal modes of rule have a certain 'formal' character. The powers once accorded to positive knowledges of human conduct are to be transferred to the calculative regimes of accounting and financial management. And the enclosures of expertise are to be penetrated through a range of new techniques for exercising critical scrutiny over authority: budget disciplines, accountancy and audit being three of the most salient. These certainly rely upon a claim to truth, but it is one that has a different character from that of the social and human sciences: these 'grey sciences', these know-hows of enumeration, calculation, monitoring, evaluation, manage to be simultaneously modest and omniscient, limited yet apparently limitless in their application to problems as diverse as the appropriateness of a medical procedure and the viability of a university department.

2. A new pluralization of 'social' technologies. Strategies of pluralization and autonomization, which characterized many programmes for reconfiguring social technologies that took shape over this period, embodied a wish for a kind of 'degovernmentalization of the State' and a 'de-statization of government' – a phenomenon that is linked to a mutation in the notion of 'the social', that invention of the late nineteenth century that both sociology and welfare government constituted as their object and target. The relation between the responsible individual and their self-governing community came to substitute for that between the social citizen and their common society (cf. Rose 1996b). In the course of this mutation, one sees a partial detaching of the centre from the various regulatory technologies that, over the twentieth century, it sought to assemble into a single functioning network, and the adoption instead of a form of government through shaping the powers and wills of autonomous entities: enterprises, organizations, communities, professionals, individuals. This has entailed the implantation of certain modes of calculation into agents, and the supplanting of particular norms, such as service and dedication, by others, such as competition, quality and customer demand. It has entailed the establishment of different networks of accountability and reconfigured flows of accountability and responsibility in fundamental ways.

Perhaps most significant has been the disassembling of a variety of governmental activities previously assembled within the political apparatus: the phenomenon referred to, in Britain, as the 'quango-ization' of the state. Quasi-autonomous non-governmental organizations have proliferated, taking on regulatory functions – such as the regulation of securities and investments in the financial sector – planning functions – as in the rise of new entities for the government and regeneration of urban locales – educative functions – as in the rise of organizations responsible for the provision of training to school leavers – and responsibilities for the provision of previously 'public' utilities such as water, gas, electricity, and the 'privatization' of the civil service, prisons and police. This has been linked to the invention and deployment of a raft of other measures for the government of these entities, measures whose emphasis upon the apparent objectivity and neutrality of numbers underpins a claim that they now operate according to an apolitical agenda (cf. Hood 1991). Contracts, targets, indicators, performance measures, monitoring and evaluation are used to govern their conduct while according them a certain autonomy of decisional power and responsibility for their actions. One sees the displacement of electoral mechanisms as the way of ensuring democratic control via the intermediary of local councils by novel techniques of accountability, such as representation of 'partners' from different 'communities' – business, local residents, voluntary organizations, local councils – on the boards. The reconfiguration of political power involved here cannot usefully be understood in terms of the opposition of State and market: shaped and programmed by political authorities, new mechanisms are utilized to link the calculations and actions of a heterogeneous array of organizations into political objectives, governing them 'at a distance' through the instrumentalization of a regulated autonomy.

3. A new specification of the subject of government. The enhancement of the powers of the client as customer – consumer of health services, of education, of training, of transport – specifies the subjects of rule in a new way: as active individuals seeking to 'enterprise themselves', to maximize their quality of life through acts of choice, according their life a meaning and value to the extent that it can be rationalized as the outcome of choices made or choices to be made (Rose 1992b, 1996a). Political reason must now justify and organize itself by arguing over the arrangements that are adequate to the existence of persons as, in their essence, creatures of freedom, liberty and autonomy. Within this new regime of the actively responsible self, individuals are to fulfil their national obligations not through their relations of dependency and obligation to one another, but through seeking to fulfil themselves within a variety of micro-moral domains or 'communities' – families, workplaces, schools, leisure associations, neighbourhoods. Hence the problem is to find means by which individuals may be made responsible through their individual choices for themselves and those to whom they owe allegiance, through the shaping of a lifestyle according to grammars of living that are widely disseminated, yet do not depend upon political calculations and strategies for their rationales or for their techniques (Rose 1996b).

It has become possible to actualize this notion of the actively responsible individual because of the development of new apparatuses that integrate subjects into a moral nexus of identifications and allegiances in the very processes in which they appear to act out their most personal choices. Contemporary political rationalities rely upon and utilize a range of technologies that install and support the civilizing project by shaping and governing the capacities, competencies and wills of subjects, yet are outside the formal control of the 'public powers'. To such basic nation-forming devices as a common language, skills of literacy and transportation networks, the twentieth century has added the mass media of communication, with their pedagogies through documentary and soap opera; opinion polls and other devices that provide reciprocal links between authorities and subjects; the regulation of lifestyles through advertising, marketing and the world of goods; and the experts of subjectivity (Rose 1989a). These technologies do not have their origin or principle of intelligibility in 'the State', but nonetheless they have made it possible to govern in an 'advanced liberal' way. They have provided a plethora of indirect mechanisms that can translate the goals of political, social and economic authorities into the choices and commitments of individuals, locating them within actual or virtual networks of identification through which they may be governed.

Each of the two dimensions of social government discussed earlier undergoes a mutation. Thus social insurance, as a principle of social solidarity, gives way to a kind of privatization of risk management. In this new prudentialism, insurance against the future possibilities of unemployment, ill health, old age, and the like, becomes a private obligation. Not merely in relation to previously socialized forms of risk management, but also in a whole range of other decisions, the citizen is enjoined to bring the future into the present, and is educated in the ways of calculating the future consequences of actions as diverse as those of diet and home security. The active citizen thus is to add to his or her obligations the need to adopt a calculative prudent personal relation to fate, now conceived in terms of calculable dangers and avertable risks (O'Malley 1992, 1996). And social work, as a means of civilization under tutelage, gives way to the private counsellor, the self-help manual and the telephone helpline, as practices whereby each individual binds themselves to expert advice as a matter of their own freedom (Rose 1989a). The regulation of conduct becomes a matter of each individual's desire to govern their own conduct freely in the service of the maximization of a version of their happiness and fulfilment that they take to be their own, but such lifestyle maximization entails a relation to authority in the very moment that it pronounces itself the outcome of free choice.

Here we can witness the 'reversibility' of relations of authority: what starts off as a norm to be implanted into citizens can be repossessed as a demand which citizens can make of authorities. Individuals are to become 'experts of themselves', to adopt an educated and knowledgeable relation of self-care in respect of their bodies, their minds, their forms of conduct and that of the members of their own families. Of course, this new configuration has its own complexities, its own logics of incorporation and exclusion. However, the 'power effects' certainly do not answer to a simple logic of domination, and nor are they amenable to a 'zero sum' conception of power.

This is not to suggest that the 'making up' of the modern citizen as an active agent in his or her government is in some ways an 'invention' of recent political regimes: the conditions for this shift in our 'relation to ourselves' are complex, and have no single origin or cause (Rose 1995a, 1995b; cf. Hacking 1986). Nonetheless, the ethical *a priori* of active citizenship in an active society is perhaps the most fundamental, and most generalizable, characteristic of these new rationalities of government, and one that justifies the assertion that what we are seeing here is not merely the vicissitudes of a single political ideology – that of neo-liberal conservatism – but something with a more general salience, which underpins mentalities of government from all parts of the political spectrum, and which justifies the designation of all these new attempts to 'reinvent government' as 'advanced liberal'.

Conclusions

Strategies of welfare sought to govern through society. Advanced liberal strategies of rule ask whether it is possible to govern without governing *society,* that is to say, to govern through the regulated and accountable choices of autonomous agents – citizens, consumers, parents, employees, managers, investors – and to govern through intensifying and acting upon their allegiance to particular 'communities'. As an autonomizing and pluralizing formula of rule, it has been dependent upon the proliferation of little regulatory instances across a territory and their multiplication, at a 'molecular' level, through the interstices of our present experience. It has also been dependent upon a particular relation between political subjects and expertise, in which the injunctions of the experts merge with our own projects for self-mastery and the enhancement of our lives.

The 'freedom' programmed by these reconfigurations of power and expertise was certainly no simple liberation of subjects from their dreary confinement by the shackles of political power into the sunny uplands of liberty and community. But neither was it merely an ideological fiction or a rhetorical flourish. The freedom upon which liberal strategies of government depend, and which they instrumentalize in so many diverse ways, is no 'natural' property of political subjects, awaiting only the removal of constraints for it to flower forth in forms that will ensure the maximization of economic and social well-being. The practices of modern freedom have been constructed out of an arduous, haphazard and contingent concatenation of problematizations, strategies of government and techniques of regulation. This is not to say that our freedom is a sham. It is to say that the agonistic relation between liberty and government is an intrinsic part of what we have come to know as freedom.

As the twenty-first century reaches the end of its first decade, these practices of freedom, and the political rationalities that have depended upon them, have come under strain as never before. A multiplicity of distinct, yet overlapping, sometimes reinforcing, and sometimes divergent forces are testing the limits, questioning the rationalities and troubling the technologies of advanced liberal rule.

The desire to bring the future into the present, so as to manage it better, has now assumed a new scale both geographically and temporally, as attempts to manage the planet and its sustainability into the distant future are coming at last to be taken seriously, albeit reluctantly. Meanwhile, in a somewhat ironic reversal of the trajectories that we have been mapping out in this volume, projects of risk regulation – particularly as pertaining to large corporations and other large organizations – come to be increasingly detailed and meticulous in what they expect, irrespective of the likelihood of it being successful in producing 'good management'. While the rationalities of prevention, precaution and preparedness may have acquired a novel intensity, the dream of governing in depth and detail is as strong as ever: no doubt this dream will persist along with what we have called here in this volume the perpetually and intrinsically failing nature of such strategies for governing each and all.

The activation of subjectivity, so central to advanced forms of liberalism, creates its own challenges. In many counties across the globe, individuals are indeed becoming more active, their capacities to know and to question enhanced by trans-national media, the internet and many other communicative technologies whose power, form and penetration were difficult to imagine even a decade ago. Expert knowledge escapes the enclosures of professional control, and formally accredited experts are called increasingly to account. New collectivities are forming, some of which are surprisingly and resolutely local, while others have no regard at all for national boundaries. These include local ecological campaigns and activist groups of those diagnosed with genetic diseases, but they also include criminal networks involved in the trading of persons, organs and commodities, and, of course, terrorist organizations. These new collectivizations, often termed 'trans-national', particularly when they are more formalized and linked to regulatory aspirations, problematize many technologies for regulation and control that were historically territorialized on national political spaces.

As the term 'globalization' becomes the common way of coding these trans-national problems of governing, this vocabulary of globalization simultaneously highlights a range of seemingly intractable difficulties in transferring the techniques that were developed, over a century and a half, for managing the inequities of industrialized, urbanized and democratizing liberal polities to a planetary territory. The very communication technologies that transgress national boundaries draw attention, in the starkest possible terms, to inequities in forms of life and capacities for selfhood that seem to call for action by those who would govern legitimately, at the same time as they elude the solutions they seem able to invent. The new problematizations of migration, the cluster of ways of trying to manage the geographical mobility of human beings, perhaps illustrate these challenges most clearly. We can see the invention or redeployment of a whole variety of technological solutions to this novel problematization, from development aid that seeks to remove the incentive to migrate, through border controls using advanced biometric technologies, securitization of national territories, and the control of the reciprocal growth of people trading. These developments demonstrate the limits of the advanced liberal pacts of citizenship that we have examined in this volume.

Can the authority of those who would govern still claim that governing is legitimate because it is grounded in a knowledge of the nature of those persons and things over which it is to be exercised? Can expertise still successfully transform so many political problems of inequity and disparities of power into technical questions concerning the best way of organizing and managing regimes of security, enterprises and persons? Can the pluralization of governing technologies and the dispersal of powers that we have documented here and elsewhere be reconciled with growing demands for national systems of surveillance and management of populations in the face of perceived threats to security from malign forces engaged in a fundamental struggle with liberalism and its values? What will be the future for those forms of advanced liberal citizenship that we have analysed, with their obligations of responsible self-government for the majority, and the expert management or frank control of those marginalized anti-citizens unwilling or unable to accept these burdens? New global securitization strategies are set in place, and a new archipelago of institutions of supervision and confinement is emerging, at the same time as the language of freedom is imbuing political discourse in many states that have never experienced a liberal moment. So, to what extent will the twenty-first century still be a century of government through freedom? These are just some of the questions which confront those who would analyse contemporary governmentalities; we hope that some of the conceptual tools and methodological approaches that we have set out in this volume can contribute to the analytical inventiveness necessary to address them.

Bibliography

Adlam, D. and Rose, N. (1981). 'The Politics of Psychiatry', in D. Adlam, L. Culley, B. Hindess, et al., *Politics and Power 4: Law, Politics and Justice*, London, Routledge and Kegan Paul.

Adler, M. and Asquith, S., eds (1981) *Discretion and Welfare*, London: Heinemann.

Ahrenfeldt, R. H. (1958) *Psychiatry in the British Army in the Second World War*, London: Routledge and Kegan Paul.

Allport, F. H. (1924) *Social Psychology*, Boston, MA: Houghton Mifflin.

Allport, G. (1935) 'Attitudes', in C. A. Murchison, ed., *Handbook of Social Psychology*, Worcester, MA: Clark University Press.

Alston, P. J. (1985) *The American Samurai: Blending Japanese and American Management Practices*, New York: De Gruyter.

Anderson, B. (1991) *Imagined Communities*, London: Verso.

Anthony, P. (1977) *The Ideology of Work*, London: Tavistock.

Ashford, D. (1981) *Policy and Politics in Britain*, Oxford: Blackwell.

Ashmore, M., Mulkay, M. J. and Pinch, T. J. (1989) *Health and Efficiency: A Sociology of Health Economics*, Milton Keynes: Open University Press.

Atkinson, D. (1994) *The Common Sense of Community*, London: Demos.

Bacon, R. and Eltis, S. (1976) *Britain's Economic Problems: Too Few Producers?* London: Macmillan.

Baechler, J., Hall, J. A. and Mann, M., eds (1988) *Europe and the Rise of Capitalism,* Oxford: Blackwell.

Baistow, K. (1995) 'Liberation and regulation? Some paradoxes of empowerment', *Critical Social Policy* 42: 34–46.

Balint, M. (1954a) 'Training general practitioners in psychotherapy', *British Medical Journal*, 16 Jan.: 115–20.

Balint, M. (1954b) 'Training general practitioners in psychotherapy', *British Journal of Medical Psychology* 27: 37–42.

Ballard, J. (1992) 'Sexuality and the state in time of epidemic', in R. W. Connell and G. W. Dowsett, eds, *Rethinking Sex: Social Power and Sexuality*, Melbourne: Melbourne University Press.

Bannister, K. A., Lyons, A., Pincus, L., Robb, J., Shooter, A. and Stephens, J. (1955) *Social Casework in Marital Problems*, London: Tavistock Publications.

Barron, A. (1995) 'The enactment of freedom: empowering parents and governing schools', working paper given at London History of the Present Seminar, March.

Barry, A. (1996) 'Lines of communication and spaces of rule', in A. Barry, T. Osborne and N. Rose, eds, *Foucault and Political Reason: Liberalism, Neo-Liberalism and Governmentality*, London: UCL Press.

Barry, A., Osborne, T. and Rose, N., eds (1996) *Foucault and Political Reason: Liberalism, Neo-Liberalism and Governmentality*, London: UCL Press.

Bartos, M. (1994) 'Community vs. population: the case of men who have sex with men', in P. Aggleton, P. Davies and G. Hart, eds, *AIDS: Foundations for the Future*, London: Taylor and Francis.

Baudrillard, J. (1983) *In the Shadow of the Silent Majorities or 'The Death of the Social'*, New York: Semiotext(e).

Beck, U. (1992) *Risk Society: Towards a New Modernity*, London: Sage.

Bell, V. (1993) 'Governing childhood', *Economy and Society* 22 (3): 390–405.

Berg, I., Freedman, M. and Freedman, M. (1979) *Managers and Work Reform: A Limited Engagement*, New York: Free Press.

Berle, A. A. and Means, G. C. (1932) *The Modern Corporation and Private Property*, New York: Macmillan.

Beveridge, W. (1942) *Social Insurance and Allied Services (Cmd. 6404)*, London: HMSO.

Bion, W. R. (1946) 'The leaderless group project', *Bulletin of the Menninger Clinic* 10: 77–81.

Bion, W. R. (1948–51) 'Experiences in Groups I–VII', *Human Relations* I–IV.

Bion, W. R. (1961) *Experiences in Groups*, London: Tavistock Publications.

Bion, W. R. and Rickman, J. (1943) 'Intra-group tensions in therapy: their study as a task of the group', *The Lancet*, 27 Nov.: 678–81.

Bocock, R. (1993) *Consumption*, London: Routledge.

Bott, E. (1955) 'Conjugal roles and social networks', *Human Relations* 8: 345–84, reprinted in a shortened version in E. Trist and H. Murray, eds (1990), *The Social Engagement of Social Science, Volume 1*, London: Free Association Books.

Bott, E. (1957) *Family and Social Network*, London: Tavistock Publications.

Braverman, H. (1974) *Labor and Monopoly Capital: The Degradation of Work in the Twentieth Century*, New York: Monthly Review Press.

Bridger, H. (1970) 'Companionship with humans', paper presented at the Health Congress of the Royal Society of Health at Eastbourne, East Sussex, April.

Bridger, H. (1990) 'The discovery of the therapeutic community: the Northfield experiments', in E. L. Trist and H. Murray, eds, *The Social Engagement of Social Science, Volume 1*, London: Free Association Books.

Brown, E. R. (1979) *Rockefeller Medicine Men: Medicine and Capitalism in America*, Berkeley: University of California Press.

Brown, J. A. C. (1954) *Social Psychology of Industry*, Harmondsworth: Penguin.

Brown, J. A. C. (1963) *Techniques of Persuasion: From Propaganda to Brainwashing*, Harmondsworth: Penguin.

Brown, W. and Jacques, E. (1965) *Glacier Project Papers*, London: Heinemann Educational Books.

Bullock, A. (1977) *Report of the Committee of Enquiry on Industrial Democracy*, London: HMSO.

Bulpitt, J. (1986) 'The discipline of the new democracy: Mrs Thatcher's domestic statecraft', *Political Studies* 34: 24.

Burbige, J. L. (1976) *Final Report on a Study of the Effects of Group Production Methods on the Humanization of Work, Prepared at the Completion of a Study Executed under Contract to the International Labour Office by the International Centre for Advanced Technical and Vocational Training*, Turin: ILO.

Burchell, D. (1995) 'The attributes of citizens: virtue, manners and the modern activity of citizenship', *Economy and Society* 24 (4): 540–58.

Burchell, G. (1991) 'Peculiar interests: governing "the system of natural liberty"', in G. Burchell, C. Gordon and P. Miller, eds, *The Foucault Effect: Studies in Governmentality*, Hemel Hempstead: Harvester Wheatsheaf.

Burchell, G. (1996) 'Liberal government and techniques of the self', in A. Barry, T. Osborne and N. Rose, eds, *Foucault and Political Reason*, London: UCL Press.

Burchell, G., Gordon, C. and Miller, P., eds (1991) *The Foucault Effect: Studies in Governmentality*, Hemel Hempstead: Harvester Wheatsheaf.

Burchell, S., Clubb, C., Hopwood, A. G., Hughes, J. and Nahapiet, J. (1980) 'The roles of accounting in organization and society', *Accounting, Organizations and Society* 5: 5–27.

Burchell, S., Clubb, C. and Hopwood, A. G. (1985) 'Accounting in its social context: towards a history of value added in the United Kingdom', *Accounting, Organizations and Society* 10: 381–413.

Cairncross, S. E. and Sjostrom, L. B. (1950) 'Flavour profiles – a new approach to flavour problems', *Food Technology* 4: 308–11.

Callon, M. (1986) 'Some elements of a sociology of translation', in J. Law, ed., *Power, Action and Belief*, London: Routledge and Kegan Paul.

Callon, M. and Latour, B. (1981) 'Unscrewing the Big Leviathan: how actors macro-structure reality and how sociologists help them to do so', in A. Cicourel and K. Knorr-Cetina, eds, *Advances in Social Theory*, London: Routledge.

Callon, M. J., Law, J. and Rip, A. (1986) *Mapping the Dynamics of Science and Technology*, London: Macmillan.

Castel, F., Castel, R. and Lovell, A. (1982) *The Psychiatric Society*, New York: Columbia University Press.

Castel, R. (1976) *L'Ordre psychiatrique*, Paris: Éditions de Minuit.

Castel, R. (1988) *The Regulation of Madness*, Cambridge: Polity.

Castel, R. (1991) 'From dangerousness to risk', in G. Burchell, C. Gordon and P. Miller, eds, *The Foucault Effect: Studies in Governmentality*, Hemel Hempstead: Harvester Wheatsheaf.

Chancellor of the Exchequer (1961) *Control of Public Expenditure (Cmnd. 1432)*, London: HMSO.

Cherns, A. (1973) 'Better working lives – a social scientist's view', *Occupational Psychology* 47 (1/2): 23–8.

Clarke, P. (1979) *Liberals and Social Democrats*, Cambridge: Cambridge University Press.

Collini, S. (1979) *Liberalism and Sociology*, Cambridge: Cambridge University Press.

Commission on Social Justice (1994) *Social Justice: Strategies for National Renewal*, London: Vintage.

Committee of the Civil Service (1968) *Report (Cmnd. 3638)*, London, HMSO.

Connelly, W. (1987) 'Appearance and reality in politics', in M. T. Gibbons, ed., *Interpreting Politics,* Oxford: Basil Blackwell.

Cotgrove, S. and Vamplew, C. (1971) *The Nylon Spinners*, London: George Allen and Unwin.

Craig, F. W. S. (1975) *British General Election Manifestos 1900–1974*, London, Macmillan.

Cruikshank, B. (1994) 'The will to empower: technologies of citizenship and the war on poverty', *Socialist Review* 23 (4): 29–55.

Curtis, B. (1995) 'Taking the state back out: Rose and Miller on political power', *British Journal of Sociology* 46 (4): 575–89.

Cutler, A., Hindess, B., Hirst, P. Q. and Hussein, A. (1977) *Marx's 'Capital' and Capitalism Today, Vol. 1*, London: Routledge and Kegan Paul.

Cutler, A., Hindess, B., Hirst, P. Q. and Hussein, A. (1978) *Marx's 'Capital' and Capitalism Today, Vol. 2*, London: Routledge and Kegan Paul.

Davis, L. E. (1957) 'Towards a theory of job design', *Industrial Engineering* 8: 305–9.

Davis, L. E. (1977) 'Enhancing the quality of working life: developments in the United States', *International Labour Review* (July–Aug.): 53–65.

Davis, L. E. and Taylor, J. C., eds (1972) *Design of Jobs*, London: Penguin.

Dean, M. (1991) *The Constitution of Poverty*, London: Routledge.

Dean, M. (1995) 'Governing the unemployed self in an active society', *Economy and Society* 24 (4): 559–83.

Defert, D. (1991) 'Popular life and insurance technology', in G. Burchell, C. Gordon and P. Miller, eds, *The Foucault Effect: Studies in Governmentality*, Hemel Hempstead: Harvester Wheatsheaf.

Deleuze, G. (1979) 'Introduction', to J. Donzelot, *The Policing of Families: Welfare versus the State*, London: Hutchinson.

Deleuze, G. (1988). *Foucault*, Minneapolis, University of Minnesota Press.

Deleuze, G. (1989) 'Qu'est-ce qu'un dispositif?', in *Michel Foucault, philosophe*, Paris: Éditions du Seuil.

Deleuze, G. (1995) 'Postscript on control societies', in *Negotiations*, New York: Columbia University Press.

Deleuze, G. and Guattari, F. (1980) *Mille plateaux: Capitalisme et schizophrénie*, Paris: Éditions de Minuit.

Deleuze, G. and Parnet, C. (1987) *Dialogues*, London: Athlone.

Dicks, H. (1970) *Fifty Years of the Tavistock Clinic*, London: Routledge and Kegan Paul.

Dillon, M. (1989) 'Modernity, discourse and deterrence', *Current Research on Peace and Violence* 2: 90–104.

Donzelot, J. (1979a) 'The poverty of political culture', *Ideology and Consciousness* 5: 73–86.

Donzelot, J. (1979b) *The Policing of Families: Welfare versus the State*, London, Hutchinson.

Donzelot, J. (1984) *L'invention du social*, Paris: Vrin.

Donzelot, J. (1991a) 'Pleasure in work', in G. Burchell, C. Gordon, and P. Miller, eds, *The Foucault Effect: Studies in Governmentality*, Hemel Hempstead: Harvester Wheatsheaf.

Donzelot, J. (1991b) 'The mobilization of society', in G. Burchell, C. Gordon and P. Miller, eds, *The Foucault Effect*, Hemel Hempstead: Harvester Wheatsheaf.

du Gay, P. (1993) 'Enterprise culture and the ideology of excellence', *New Formations* 13: 45–61.

Edward, G. (1971) *Readings in Group Technology*, London: Machinery Publishing.

Elliot, B. (1962) *A History of English Advertising*, London: Business Publications.

Elliot, J. (1978) *Conflict or Cooperation: The Growth of Industrial Democracy*, London: Kogan Page.

Emery, F. E. (1959) *Characteristics of Socio-Technical Systems*, Human Resources Centre, Tavistock Institute of Human Relations, Doc. 527.

Emery, F. and Thorsrud, E. (1969) *Form and Content in Industrial Democracy*, London: Tavistock Publications.

Emery, F. E. and Thorsrud, E. (1976) *Democracy at Work*, Leiden: Nijhof.

Emery, F. E. and Trist, E. L. (1960) *Socio-Technical Systems*, Oxford: Pergamon Press.

Emery, F. E. and Trist, E. L. (1965) 'The causal texture of organizational environments', *Human Relations* 18: 21–32.

Etzioni, A. (1993) *The Spirit of Community*, New York: Crown.

European Commission (1994) *European Social Policy: A Way Forward for the Union: A White Paper*, Luxembourg: Office for Official Publications of the European Communities.

Evans, P. J., Rueschemeyer, D. and Skocpol, R. (1985) *Bringing the State Back In*, Cambridge: Cambridge University Press.

Ewald, F. (1986) *L'État providence*, Paris: Grasset.

Ewald, F. (1991) 'Insurance and risk', in G. Burchell, C. Gordon and P. Miller, eds, *The Foucault Effect: Studies in Governmentality*, Hemel Hempstead: Harvester Wheatsheaf.

Ewen, S. (1976) *Captains of Consciousness: Advertising and the Social Roots of Consumer Culture*, New York: McGraw-Hill.

Featherstone, M. (1991) *Consumer Culture and Postmodernism*, London: Sage.

Fisher, D. (1993) *Fundamental Development of the Social Sciences: Rockefeller Philanthropy and the United States Social Science Research Council*, Ann Arbor: University of Michigan Press.

Fisher, V. E. and Hanna, J. V. (1932) *The Dissatisfied Worker*, New York: Macmillan.

Flamholtz, E. G. (1979) *Human Asset Accounting*, Encino, CA: Dickenson Publishing.

Foucault, M. (1967) *Madness and Civilization: A History of Insanity in the Age of Reason*. London: Tavistock.

Foucault, M. (1973) *The Birth of the Clinic: An Archaeology of Medical Perception*, London: Tavistock.

Foucault, M. (1977) *Discipline and Punish: The Birth of the Prison*, London: Penguin.

Foucault, M. (1978) *The History of Sexuality, Vol. I: An Introduction*, London: Allen Lane.

Foucault, M. (1979) 'On governmentality', *I&C* 6: 5–22.

Foucault, M. (1980a) 'The politics of health in the eighteenth century', in C. Gordon, ed., *Michel Foucault: Power/Knowledge: Selected Interviews and Other Writings 1972–1977*, Brighton: Harvester.

Foucault, M. (1980b) 'Two lectures', in C. Gordon, ed., *Michel Foucault: Power/Knowledge: Selected Interviews and Other Writings 1972–1977*, Brighton: Harvester.

Foucault, M. (1982) 'The subject and power', in H. L. Dreyfus and P. Rabinow, eds, *Michel Foucault: Beyond Structuralism and Hermeneutics*, Brighton: Harvester.

Foucault, M. (1986) 'Space, knowledge and power', in P. Rabinow (ed.), *The Foucault Reader*, Harmondsworth: Penguin.

Foucault, M. (1988) 'Technologies of the self', in L. H. Martin, H. Gutman and P. H. Hutton, eds, *Technologies of the Self*, London: Tavistock Publications.

Foucault, M. (1989) *Résumé des cours (1970–1982)*, Paris: Éditions Julliard.

Foucault, M. (1991) 'On governmentality', in G. Burchell, C. Gordon and P. Miller, eds, *The Foucault Effect: Studies in Governmental Rationality*, Hemel Hempstead, Harvester Wheatsheaf.

Foucault, M. (1996) 'The impossible prison', in S. Lotringer, ed., *Foucault Live: Interviews 1961–1984*, New York: Semiotext(e).

Foucault, M. (2007) *Security, Territory, Population: Lectures at the Collège de France*, London: Palgrave Macmillan.

Fourquet, F. (1980) *Les comptes de la puissance*, Paris: Encres.

Freud, S. (1955) 'Group psychology and the analysis of the ego', in *Standard Edition of the Collected Works of Sigmund Freud, Vol. XVIII*, ed. J. Strachey, London: Hogarth.

Friedman, M. (1962) *Capitalism and Freedom*, Chicago: University of Chicago Press.

Friedman, M. and Friedman, R. (1982) *Free to Choose*, London: Secker and Warburg.

Giddens, A. (1985) *The Nation State and Violence,* Cambridge: Polity.

Giddens, A. (1990) *Consequences of Modernity,* Cambridge: Polity.

Giddens, A. (1991) *Modernity and Self-Identity,* Cambridge: Polity.

Gigerenzer, G., Swijtink, Z., Porter, T., Daston, L., Beatty, J. and Kruger, L. (1989) *The Empire of Chance: How Probability Changed Science and Everyday Life,* Cambridge: Cambridge University Press.

Gilbert, B. (1966) *The Evolution of National Insurance in Great Britain,* London: Michael Joseph.

Gordon, C. (1980) 'Afterword', in C. Gordon, ed., *Michel Foucault: Power/ Knowledge: Selected Interviews and Other Writings 1972–1977,* Brighton, Harvester.

Gordon, C. (1986) 'Question, ethos, event: Foucault on Kant and Enlightenment', *Economy and Society* 15 (1): 71–87.

Gordon, C. (1987) 'The soul of the citizen: Max Weber and Michel Foucault on rationality and government', in S. Lash and S. Whimster, eds, *Max Weber, Rationality and Modernity,* London: Allen and Unwin.

Gordon, C. (1991) 'Governmental rationality: an introduction', in G. Burchell, C. Gordon, and P. Miller, eds, *The Foucault Effect: Studies in Governmental Rationality,* Hemel Hempstead: Harvester Wheatsheaf.

Greco, M. (1993) 'Psychosomatic subjects and "the duty to be well"', *Economy and Society* 22 (3): 357–72.

Greve, R. M. (1977) *Bibliography on Major Aspects of the Humanisation of Work and the Quality of Working Life,* Geneva: International Labour Office.

Grey, J. (1996) *After Social Democracy,* London: Demos.

Gyllenhammar, P. G. (1977) *People at Work,* London: Wesley.

Hacking, I. (1982) 'Biopower and the avalanche of printed numbers', *Humanities in Society* 5: 279–95.

Hacking, I. (1983) *Representing and Intervening,* London: Cambridge University Press.

Hacking, I. (1986) 'Making up people', in T. C. M. Sosna and D. E. Wellbery, eds, *Reconstructing Individualism: Autonomy, Individuality and the Self in Western Thought,* Stanford: Stanford University Press.

Hacking, I. (1990) *The Taming of Chance,* Cambridge: Cambridge University Press.

Hacking, I. (1991) 'How should we do the history of statistics?', in G. Burchell, C. Gordon and P. Miller, eds, *The Foucault Effect: Studies in Governmental Rationality,* Hemel Hempstead: Harvester Wheatsheaf.

Hall, J. A. ed. (1986) *States in History,* Oxford: Blackwell.

Hall, J. A. and Ikenberry, G. J. (1989) *The State,* Milton Keynes: Open University Press.

Haraway, D. (1989) *Primate Visions: Gender, Race and Nature in the World of Modern Science,* London: Routledge.

Harden, I. and Lewis, N. (1986) *The Noble Lie: The British Constitution and the Rule of Law,* London: Hutchinson

Hayek, F. A. (1944) *The Road to Serfdom,* London: Routledge and Kegan Paul.

Hayek, F. A. (1960) *The Constitution of Liberty*, London: Routledge and Kegan Paul.

Henry, B. ed. (1986) *British Television Advertising: The First Thirty Years*, London: Century.

Herrick, N. Q. and Maccoby, M. (1975) 'Humanizing work: a priority goal of the 1970s', in L. E. Davis and A. C. Cherns, *The Quality of Working Life, Vol. 1: Problems, Prospects and the State of the Art*, New York: Free Press.

Hill, P. (1971) *Towards a New Philosophy of Management*, London: Gower.

Hindess, B. (1993) 'Liberalism, socialism and democracy', *Economy and Society* 22 (3): 300–13.

Hindess, B. (1994a) 'Politics without politics: anti-political motifs in Western political discourse', paper delivered to Vienna Dialogue on Democracy, July.

Hindess, B. (1994b) 'Governing what economy?', paper delivered to Governing Australia conference, Sydney, November.

Hindess, B. (1996) *Discourses of Power: From Hobbes to Foucault*, Oxford: Blackwell.

Hirschman, A. O. (1977) *The Passions and the Interests*, Princeton, NJ: Princeton University Press.

Hirschman, A. O. (1991) *The Rhetoric of Reaction*, Cambridge, MA: Belknap Harvard.

Hirst, P. and Thompson, G. (1992) 'The problem of "globalization": international economic relations, national economic management and the formation of trading blocs', *Economy and Society* 21 (4): 357–96.

Hirst, P. and Thompson, G. (1996) *Globalization in Question*, Cambridge: Polity.

Hirst, P. and Zeitlin, J., eds (1989) *Reversing Industrial Decline? Industrial Structure and Policy in Britain and Her Competitors*, Oxford: Berg.

Hirst, P. and Zeitlin, J. (1991) 'Flexible specialization versus post-Fordism: theory, evidence and policy implications', *Economy and Society* 20 (1): 1–56.

Home Office (1947) *Report of the Committee on Procedure in Matrimonial Causes (Cmd. 7024)*, London: HMSO.

Hood, C. (1991) 'A public management for all seasons', *Public Administration* 69 (1): 3–19.

Hopwood, A. G. (1979) 'Economic costs and benefits of new forms of work organisation', in *New Forms of Work Organisation, Vol. 2*, Geneva: International Labour Office.

Hopwood, A. G. (1984) 'Accounting and the pursuit of efficiency', in A. G. Hopwood and C. Tomkins, eds, *Issues in Public Sector Accounting*, Oxford: Philip Allan.

Hopwood, A. G. (1985) 'Accounting and the domain of the public: some observations on current developments', The Price Waterhouse Public Lecture on Accounting, University of Leeds, reprinted in A. G. Hopwood (1988), *Accounting from the Outside: The Collected Papers of Anthony G. Hopwood*, New York and London: Garland.

Hopwood, A. G. (1986) 'Management accounting and organizational action: an introduction', in M. Bromwich and A. G. Hopwood, eds, *Research and Current Issues in Management Accounting*, London: Pitman.

Hopwood, A. G. (1987) 'The archaeology of accounting systems', *Accounting, Organizations and Society* 12: 207–34.

Hopwood, A. G. and Miller, P., eds (1994) *Accounting as Social and Institutional Practice*, Cambridge: Cambridge University Press.

Hoskin, K. and Macve, R. (1988) 'The genesis of accountability: the West Point connections', *Accounting, Organizations and Society* 13: 37–73.

Hunter, I. (1988) *Culture and Government: The Emergence of Literary Eeducation*, London: Macmillan.

Hunter, I. (1994) *Rethinking the School*, St Leonards, NSW: Allen and Unwin.

Hutton, W. (1995) *The State We're In*, London: Cape.

ILO (1979) *New Forms of Work Organisation, Vol. 1*, Geneva: International Labour Office.

Jaques, E. (1951) *The Changing Culture of a Factory*, London: Tavistock.

Jaques, E. (1953) 'On the dynamics of social structure', *Human Relations* 6 (3): 3–24.

Jessop, B. (1990) *State Theory*, Cambridge: Polity.

Joseph Rowntree Foundation (1995) *Enquiry into Income and Wealth*, 2 vols, York: Joseph Rowntree Foundation.

Joyce, P. (1994) 'The end of social history', *Social History* 20 (1): 73–91.

Katona, G. (1951) *Psychological Analysis of Economic Behavior*, New York: McGraw-Hill.

Katz, M. B. (1993) *The 'Underclass' Debate: Views from History*, Princeton, NJ: Princeton University Press.

Keane, J. (1984) *Public Life and Late Capitalism*, Cambridge: Cambridge University Press.

Keane, J. (1988a) *Democracy and Civil Society*, London: Verso.

Keane, J. (1988b) 'Despotism and democracy', in J. Keane (ed.), *Civil Society and the State*, London: Verso.

Klein, L. (1976) *New Forms of Work Organization*, Cambridge: Cambridge University Press.

Klein, R. (1983) *The Politics of the National Health Service*, London: Longman.

Knights, D. and Willmott, H. (1989) 'Power and subjectivity at work: from degradation to subjugation in social relations', *Sociology* 23 (4): 535–58.

Kochan, T. A., Katz, H. C. and McKersie, R. B. (1986) *The Transformation of American Industrial Relations*, New York: Basic Books.

Kraupl Taylor, F. (1958) 'A history of group and administrative therapy in Great Britain', *British Journal of Medical Psychology* 31: 153–73.

Kristol, I. (1975) 'On corporate capitalism in America', *The Public Interest*, Fall: 124–41.

Langman, L. (1992) 'Neon cages: shopping for subjectivity', in R. Shields (ed.), *Life-Style Shopping: The Subject of Consumption*, London: Routledge.

Lasch, C. (1980) *The Culture of Narcissism*, London: Abacus.

Lasch, C. (1984) *The Minimal Self: Psychic Survival in Troubled Times*, New York: Norton.

Lash, S. and Friedman, J. eds (1992) *Modernity and Identity*, Oxford: Blackwell.

Lash, S. and Urry, J. (1994) *Economies of Signs and Spaces*, Cambridge: Polity.

Latour, B. (1986) 'The powers of association', in J. Law (ed.), *Power, Action and Belief*, London: Routledge and Kegan Paul.

Latour, B. (1987a) 'Visualization and cognition: thinking with eyes and hands', *Knowledge and Society: Studies in the Sociology of Culture, Past and Present* 6: 1–40.

Latour, B. (1987b). *Science in Action*, Milton Keynes: Open University Press.

Lawrence, W. G. (1979a) 'Introductory essay: exploring boundaries' in W. G. Lawrence, ed., *Exploring Individual and Organizational Boundaries*, London: Wiley.

Lawrence, W. G. (1979b) 'A concept for today: managing oneself in role', in W. G. Lawrence, ed., *Exploring Individual and Organizational Boundaries*, London: Wiley.

Le Bon, G. (1895) *The Crowd: A Study of the Popular Mind*, London: Fisher Unwin.

Leiss, W., Kline, S. and Jhally, S. (1986) *Social Communication in Advertising Persons, Products and Images of Well-Being*, London: Methuen.

Leruez, J. (1975) *Economic Planning and Politics in Britain*, London: Martin Robertson.

Levitas, R. (1996) 'The concept of social exclusion and the new Durkheimian hegemony', *Critical Social Policy* 16 (1): 5–20.

Lewin, K. (1946) *Resolving Social Conflicts: Selected Papers on Group Dynamics*, ed. G. W. Lewin, New York: Harper and Row.

Lewin, K. (1951) *Field Theory in Social Science: Selected Theoretical Papers*, ed. D. Cartwright. New York: Harper.

Lipietz, A. (1992) *Towards a New Economic Order: Postfordism, Ecology and Democracy*, Cambridge: Polity.

Lippitt, R. (1949) *Training in Community Relations*, New York: Harper and Row.

Little, A. and Warr, P. (1971) 'Who's afraid of job enrichment?', *Personnel Management* 3 (2): 34–7.

Loft, A. (1986) 'Towards a critical understanding of accounting: the case of cost accounting in the U.K.', *Accounting, Organizations and Society* 11: 137–69.

McCloskey, D. N. (1985) *The Rhetoric of Economics*, Madison: University of Wisconsin Press.

McDougall, W. (1920) *The Group Mind*, Cambridge: Cambridge University Press.

MacIntyre, A. (1981) *After Virtue: A Study in Moral Theory*, London: Duckworth.

Main, T. (1946) 'The hospital as a therapeutic institution', *Bulletin of the Menninger Clinic* 10: 66–70.

Main, T. (1989) *The Ailment and Other Psychoanalytic Essays*, London: Free Association Books.

Mann, M. (1986) *The Sources of Social Power, Vol. 1*, Cambridge: Cambridge University Press.

Mann, M. (1988) *States, War and Capitalism*, Oxford: Blackwell.

Marcuse, Herbert (1968) *One-Dimensional Man*, London: Sphere.

Marshall, T. H. (1975) *Social Policy*, London: Hutchinson.

Mayo, E. (1933) *The Human Problems of an Industrial Civilization*, New York: Macmillan.

Menzies, I. (1949) 'Factors affecting family breakdown in urban communities', *Human Relations* 2: 363–73; reprinted in I. Menzies Lyth, *The Dynamics of the Social: Selected Essays, Vol. II*, London: Free Association Books, 1989.

Menzies, I. (1960) 'Social systems as a defence against anxiety', *Human Relations* 13: 95–121.

Menzies Lyth, I. (1989) 'The development of ice cream as a food', a revised version of a paper written with Eric Trist and originally entitled 'Changing the perspective on the psychological position of ice cream in society', in I. Menzies Lyth, *The Dynamics of the Social: Selected Essays, Vol. II*, London: Free Association Books.

Meuret, D. (1981) 'Political economy and the legitimation of the state', *I&C* 9: 29–38.

Meyer, J. W. (1986a) 'Social environments and organizational accounting', *Accounting, Organizations and Society* 11: 345–56.

Meyer, J. W. (1986b) 'The self and the life course: institutionalization and its effects', in A. Sorensen, F. Weinert and L. Sherrod, eds, *Human Development and the Life Course*, Hillsdale, NJ: L. Erlbaum.

Meyer, J. W. (1986c) 'Myths of socialization and of personality', in T. C. Heller, M. Sosna and D. E. Wellbery, eds, *Reconstructing Individualism*, Stanford: Stanford University Press.

Meyer, J. W. (1986d) 'Social environments and organizational accounting', *Accounting, Organizations and Society* 11: 345–56.

Miller, E. J. (1990) 'Experiential learning in groups I: the development of the Leicester model', in E. Trist and H. Murray, eds, *The Social Engagement of Social Science, Vol. 1*, London: Free Association Books.

Miller, P. (1980) 'The territory of the psychiatrist: a review of Robert Castel's *L'Ordre psychiatrique*', *I&C* 7: 63–106.

Miller, P. (1981) 'Psychiatry – the regulation of a territory: a review of F. Castel et al. *La Société Psychiatrique Avancée*', *I&C* 8: 97–122.

Miller, P. (1986a) 'Accounting for progress – national accounting and planning in France – a review essay', *Accounting, Organizations and Society* 11 (1): 83–104.

Miller, P. (1986b) 'Psychotherapy of work and unemployment', in P. Miller and N. Rose, eds, *The Power of Psychiatry*, Cambridge: Polity.

Miller, P. (1987) *Domination and Power*, London: Routledge and Kegan Paul.

Miller, P. (1989) 'Managing economic growth through knowledge: the promotion of discounted cash flow techniques', Working Paper.

Miller, P. (1990) 'On the interrelations between accounting and the state', *Accounting, Organizations and Society* 15 (3): 15–38.

Miller, P. (1991a) 'Accounting innovation beyond the enterprise: problematizing investment decisions and programming economic growth in the UK in the 1960s', *Accounting, Organizations and Society* 16: 733–62.

Miller, P. (1991b) 'Accounting and objectivity: the invention of calculating selves and calculable spaces', *Annals of Scholarship* 8 (3/4): 61–86.

Miller, P. and O'Leary, T. (1987) 'Accounting and the construction of the governable person', *Accounting, Organizations and Society* 12: 235–65.

Miller, P. and O'Leary, T. (1989a) 'Hierarchies and American ideals 1900–1940', *Academy of Management Review* 14 (2): 250–65.

Miller, P. and O'Leary, T. (1989b) 'Accounting expertise and the entrepreneurial society: new rationalities of calculation', paper presented at Conference on Accounting and the Humanities, University of Iowa, September.

Miller, P. and O'Leary, T. (1990) 'Making accountancy practical', *Accounting, Organizations and Society* 15 (5): 479–98.

Miller, P. and Rose, N. eds (1986) *The Power of Psychiatry*, Cambridge: Polity.

Miller, P. and Rose, N. (1988) 'The Tavistock programme: the government of subjectivity and social life', *Sociology* 22: 171–92.

Miller, P. and Rose, N. (1989) 'Political rationalities and technologies of government', in S. Hanninen and K. Palonen, eds, *Texts, Contexts, Concepts*, Helsinki: Finnish Political Science Association.

Miller, P. and Rose, N. (1990) 'Governing economic life', *Economy and Society* 19 (1): 1–31.

Miller, P. and Rose, N. (1991) 'Programming the poor: poverty, calculation and expertise', in J. Lehto, ed., *Deprivation, Social Welfare and Expertise*, Helsinki: National Agency for Welfare and Health.

Miller, P. and Rose, N. (1994) 'On therapeutic authority: psychoanalytical expertise under advanced liberalism', *History of the Human Sciences* 7: 29–64.

Miller, P. and Rose, N. (1995a) 'Production, identity and democracy', *Theory and Society* 24: 427–67.

Miller, P. and Rose, N. (1995b) Political thought and the limits of orthodoxy: a response to Curtis. *British Journal of Sociology* 46 (4): 590–7.

Mills, C. W. (1956) *The Power Elite*, New York: Oxford University Press.

Mintzberg, H. (1973) *Power in and around Organizations*, Englewood Cliffs, NJ: Prentice Hall.

Mirowski, P. (1989) *More Heat than Light: Economics as Social Physics; Physics as Nature's Economics*, New York: Cambridge University Press.

Moreno, J. L. (1934) *Who Shall Survive? A New Approach to the Problem of Human Interrelations*, Washington, DC: Nervous and Mental Diseases Publishing Co.

Morgan, K. O. (1984) *Labour in Power*, Oxford: Oxford University Press.

Morrow, A. J. (1977) *The Practical Theorist: The Life and Work of Kurt Lewin*, New York: Basic Books.

Mort, F. (1988) ' "Boy's Own?": Masculinity, Style and Popular Culture', in R. Chapman and J. Rutherford, eds, *Male Order*. London: Lawrence and Wishart.

Mort, F. (1996) *Cultures of Consumption: Masculinities and Social Space in Late Twentieth-Century Britain*, London: Routledge.

Moscovici, S. (1988) *The Age of the Crowd: An Historical Treatise on Mass Psychology*, Cambridge: Cambridge University Press.

Murray, C. (1980) *Losing Ground: American Social Policy 1950–1980*, New York: Basic Books.

Myers, C. S. (1927) *Industrial Psychology in Great Britain*, London: Cape.

NEDC (1965) *Investment Appraisal*, London: HMSO.

Nelson, J. S., Megill, A. and McCloskey, D. N., eds (1987) *The Rhetoric of the Human Sciences: Language and Argument in Scholarship and Public Affairs*, Madison: University of Wisconsin Press.

Nevett, T. (1982) *Advertising in Britain: A History*, London: Heinemann.

Nietzsche, F. W. (1969) *Thus Spoke Zarathustra*, London: Penguin.

Noble, D. F. (1977) *America by Design: Science, Technology and the Rise of Corporate Capitalism*, Oxford: Oxford University Press.

Noble, D. F. (1984) *Forces of Production: A Social History of Industrial Automation*, New York: Oxford University Press.

O'Connor J. (1972) *The Fiscal Crisis of the State*, New York: St Martin's Press.

Oestreich, G. (1982) *Neostoicism and the Early Modern State*, Cambridge: Cambridge University Press.

Office of Health Economics (1967) *Efficiency in the Hospital Service*, London: Office of Health Economics.

O'Malley, P. (1992) 'Risk, power and crime prevention', *Economy and Society* 21 (3): 252–75.

O'Malley, P. (1995) 'The prudential man cometh: life insurance, liberalism and the government of thrift', paper presented to the Annual Meeting of the Law and Society Association, Toronto, June.

O'Malley, P. (1996) 'Risk and responsibility', in A. Barry, T. Osborne and N. Rose, eds, *Foucault and Political Reason*, London: UCL Press.

Osborne, T. (1993) 'Liberalism, neo-liberalism and the liberal profession of medicine', *Economy and Society* 22 (3): 345–56.

Osborne, T. (1994) 'Bureaucracy as a vocation: governmentality and administration in nineteenth-century Britain', *Journal of Historical Sociology* 7 (3): 289–313.

Packard, V. (1960) *The Hidden Persuaders*, 2nd edition, Harmondsworth: Penguin.

Parton, N. (1991) *Governing the Family: Child Care, Child Protection and the State*, London: Macmillan.

Pascale, T. R. and Athos, A. G. (1981) *The Art of Japanese Management*, New York: Simon and Schuster.

Pasquino, P. (1991) '"Theatrum politicum": the genealogy of capital – police and the state of prosperity', in G. Burchell, C. Gordon, and P. Miller, eds, *The Foucault Effect: Studies in Governmental Rationality*, Hemel Hempstead: Harvester Wheatsheaf.

Paul, W. J. and Robertson, K. (1970) *Job Enrichment and Employee Motivation*, London: Gower.

Pearson, J. and Turner, G. (1965) *The Persuasion Industry*, London: Eyre and Spottiswoode.

Perkin, H. (1989) *The Rise of Professional Society: England since 1880*, London: Routledge.

Perrot, M., ed. (1980a) *L'Impossible prison*, Paris: Éditions du Seuil.

Perrot, M. (1980b) 'Questions of method', *I&C* 8 (6): 3–14.

Peters, T. J. and Waterman, R. H. (1982) *In Search of Excellence: Lessons from America's Best-Run Companies*, New York: Harper and Row.

Pickering, A., ed. (1992) *Science as Practice and Culture*, Chicago: University of Chicago Press.

Poggi, G. (1978) *The Development of the Modern State*, London: Hutchinson.

Polanyi, K. (1944) *The Great Transformation: The Political and Economic Origins of Our Time*, Boston: Beacon Press.

Pollitt, C. (1984) 'The state and health care', in G. McLennan, D. Held and S. Hall, eds, *State and Society in Contemporary Britain*, Cambridge: Polity,

Porter, T. (1986) *The Rise of Statistical Thinking, 1820–1900*, Princeton, NJ: Princeton University Press.

Porter, T. (1995) *Trust in Numbers: The Invention of Objectivity*, Princeton, NJ: Princeton University Press.

Power, M. (1994) *The Audit Explosion*, London: Demos.

Procacci, G. (1989) 'Sociology and its poor', *Politics and Society* 17: 163–87.

Procacci, G. (1991) 'Social economy and the government of poverty', in G. Burchell, C. Gordon and P. Miller, eds, *The Foucault Effect: Studies in Governmental Rationality*, Hemel Hempstead: Harvester Wheatsheaf.

Procacci, G. (1993) *Gouverner la misère: la question sociale en France, 1789–1848*, Paris: Éditions du Seuil.

Public Records Office (1950) CAB 134/518. Cabinet Committee on the National Health Service: Enquiry into the Financial Workings of the Service – Report by Sir Cyril Jones.

Qualter, T. (1991) *Advertising and Democracy in the Mass Age*, New York: St Martin's Press.

Rabinow, P. (1989) *French Modern: Norms and Forms of the Social Environment*, Cambridge, MA: MIT Press.

Rees, J. R. (1945) *The Shaping of Psychiatry by War*, London: Chapman Hall.

Reich, C. (1964) 'Individual rights and social welfare', *Yale Law Journal* 74: 1245.

Reich, R. (1992) *The Work of Nations: Preparing Ourselves for 21st Century Capitalism*, New York: Vintage.

Rice, A. K. (1951) 'The use of unrecognized cultural mechanisms in an expanding machine shop', *Human Relations* 4: 143–60.

Rice, A. K. (1958) *Productivity and Social Organization: The Ahmedabad Experiment*, London: Tavistock.

Rice, A. K. (1965) *Learning for Leadership: Interpersonal and Intergroup Relations*, London: Tavistock Publications.

Rieff, P. (1966) *The Triumph of the Therapeutic: Uses of Faith after Freud*, Chicago: University of Chicago Press.

Roethlisberger, F. W. and Dickson, W. J. (1939) *Management and the Worker*, Cambridge, MA: Harvard University Press.

Roosevelt, F. D. (1941) *Collected Papers, 1938*, New York: Macmillan.

Rose, M. (1983) *Reworking the Work Ethic*, London: Batsford.

Rose, N. (1980) 'Socialism and social policy: the problems of inequality', *Politics and Power* 2: 11–36.

Rose, N. (1985) *The Psychological Complex: Psychology, Politics and Society 1869–1939*, London: Routledge and Kegan Paul.

Rose, N. (1986) 'Psychiatry: the discipline of mental health', in P. Miller and N. Rose, eds, *The Power of Psychiatry*, Cambridge: Polity.

Rose, N. (1987) 'Beyond the public/private division – law, power and the family', *Journal of Law and Society* 14 (1): 61–76.

Rose, N. (1988) 'Calculable minds and manageable individuals', *History of the Human Sciences* 1: 179–200.

Rose, N. (1989a) *Governing the Soul: The Shaping of the Private Self*, London: Routledge.

Rose, N. (1989b) 'Individualizing psychology', in J. Shotter and K. J. Gergen, *Texts of Identity*, London: Sage.

Rose, N. (1991) 'Governing by numbers: figuring out democracy', *Accounting, Organizations and Society* 16 (7): 673–92.

Rose, N. (1992a) 'Engineering the human soul: analysing psychological expertise', *Science in Context* 5 (2): 351–69.

Rose, N. (1992b) 'Governing the enterprising self', in P. Heelas and P. Morris, eds, *The Values of the Enterprise Culture: The Moral Debate*, London: Routledge.

Rose, N. (1993a) 'Eriarvoisuus ja valta hyvinvointivaltion jalkeen' (Finnish translation of 'Disadvantage and power "after the welfare state"'), *Janus* (Journal of the Finnish Society for Social Policy) 1: 44–68.

Rose, N. (1993b) 'Government, authority and expertise in advanced liberalism', *Economy and Society* 22 (3): 283–99.

Rose, N. (1993c) *Towards a Critical Sociology of Freedom*, Inaugural Lecture delivered on 5 May 1992 at Goldsmiths' College, University of London, Goldsmiths' College Occasional Paper, London: Goldsmiths' College (excerpted in P. Joyce, ed., *Class: A Reader*, Oxford: Oxford University Press, 1995).

Rose, N. (1994) 'Expertise and the government of conduct', *Studies in Law, Politics and Society* 14: 359–97.

Rose, N. (1995a) 'Authority and the genealogy of subjectivity', in P. Heelas, P. Morris and S. Lash, eds, *De-Traditionalization: Authority and Self in an Age of Cultural Uncertainty*, Oxford: Blackwell.

Rose, N. (1995b) 'Identity genealogy, history', in S. Hall and P. du Gay, eds, *Questions of Cultural Identity*, London: Sage.

Rose, N. (1996a) 'Social psychology as a science of democracy', in *Inventing Ourselves*, New York: Cambridge University Press.

Rose, N. (1996b) *Inventing Ourselves: Psychology, Power and Personhood*, Cambridge: Cambridge University Press.

Rose, N. (1996c) 'The death of the social? Refiguring the territory of government', *Economy and Society* 25 (3): 327–56.

Rose, N. and Miller, P. (1989) 'Rethinking the state: governing economic, social and personal life', Working Paper.

Rose, N. and Miller, P. (1992) 'Political power beyond the state: problematics of government', *British Journal of Sociology* 43 (2): 173–205.

Schmitter, P. C. (1974) 'Still the century of corporatism', *Review of Politics* 36: 85–131.

Schmitter, P. C. and Lehmbruch, C., eds (1979) *Trends toward Corporatist Intermediation*, London: Sage.

Schudson, M. (1984) *Advertising: The Uneasy Persuasion*, New York: Basic Books.

Schumpeter, J. A. (1950) *Capitalism, Socialism and Democracy*, 3rd edition, New York: Harper and Row.

Schumpeter, J. A. (1954) *History of Economic Analysis*, ed. E. Boody Schumpeter, London: Allen and Unwin.

Sennett, R. (1976) *The Fall of Public Man*, New York: Knopf.

Shapin, S. and Schaffer, S. (1985) *Leviathan and the Air Pump*, Princeton, NJ: Princeton University Press.

Shapiro, M., ed. (1984) *Language and Politics*, Oxford: Basil Blackwell.

Shearing, C. (1995) 'Reinventing policing: police as governance', in O. Marenin, ed., *Policing Change: Changing Police*, New York: Garland Press.

Shields, R., ed. (1992a) *Lifestyle Shopping: The Subject of Consumption*, London: Routledge.

Shields, R. (1992b) 'Spaces for the subject of consumption', in R. Shields, ed., *Lifestyle Shopping: The Subject of Consumption*, London: Routledge.

Sklar, H., ed. (1980) *Trilateralism: The Trilateral Commission and Elite Planning for World Management*, Montreal: Black Rose Books.

Sofer, S. (1972) *Organizations in Theory and Practice*, London: Heinemann.

Starr, P. and Immergut, E. (1987) 'Health care and the boundaries of politics', in C. S. Maier (ed.), *Changing Boundaries of the Political*, Cambridge: Cambridge University Press.

Stenson, K. (1993) 'Community policing as a governmental technology', *Economy and Society* 22 (3): 373–89.

Sutherland, J. D. (1955) 'Introduction', in K. A. Bannister, A. Lyons, L. Pincus, J. Robb, A. Shooter and J. Stephens, *Social Casework in Marital Problems*, London: Tavistock Publications.

Sutherland, J. D. (1956) 'Psychotherapy and social casework: I', in E. M. Goldberg, E. E. Irvine, A. B. Lloyd Davies and K. F. McDougall, eds, *The Boundaries of Casework*, London: Association of Psychiatric Social Workers.

Sutherland, J. D. (1959) 'The study group method of training', in E. L. Trist and C. Sofer, eds, *Explorations in Group Relations*, Leicester: Leicester University Press.

Sutherland, J. D. (1962) 'Introduction', in *The Marital Relation as a Focus for Casework*, London: Institute of Marital Studies.

Sutherland, J. D. (1963) 'Object relations theory and the conceptual model of psychoanalysis', *British Journal of Medical Psychology* 36: 109–20.

Taylor, C. (1987) 'Language and human nature', in M. T. Gibbons, ed., *Interpreting Politics*, Oxford: Basil Blackwell.

Taylor, G. R. (1950) *Are Workers Human?*, London: Falcon Press.

Thevenot, L. (1984) 'Rules and implements: investment in forms', *Social Science Information* 23 (1): 1–45.

Thompson, G. (1982) 'The firm as a "dispersed" social agency', *Economy and Society* 11: 233–50.

Thompson, G. (1987) 'The American industrial policy debate: any lessons for the U.K.?', *Economy and Society* 16: 1–74.

TIHR (1950) 'Changes in habits concerning the development of ice cream as a food', Document No. 248 (September), Tavistock Institute of Human Relations.

TIHR (1951) 'An appraisal of the attitudes of women towards their hair', Document No. 270 (January), Tavistock Institute of Human Relations.

TIHR (1956a) 'Some psychological and sociological aspects of toilet tissues – Yorkshire Area', Document No. 408a (June), Tavistock Institute of Human Relations.

TIHR (1956b) 'Some psychological and sociological aspects of toilet tissues – final report', Document No. 419 (July), Tavistock Institute of Human Relations.

TIHR (1959a) I. Menzies, 'Report on a study of the social and psychological aspects of the purchase and consumption of Toblerone and other Tobler products', Document No. 539 (July), Tavistock Institute of Human Relations.

TIHR (1959b) F. E. Emery, 'Social and psychological functions of alcohol drinking: a critical review of studies', Document No. 548 (November), Tavistock Institute of Human Relations.

TIHR (1959c) 'Sociological and psychological aspects of the purchase of petrol and oil: interim report', Document No. 542 (September), Tavistock Institute of Human Relations.

TIHR (1959d) H. P. Hildebrand, 'Report of a preliminary investigation into housewives' attitudes to Birds Eye frozen fish shapes', Document No. 549 (November), Tavistock Institute of Human Relations.

TIHR (1960a) 'Clinic shampoo: notes on some psychological aspects of the use and choice of shampoos', Document No. 606 (October), Tavistock Institute of Human Relations.

TIHR (1960b) F. E. Emery, 'Characteristics of Guinness drinkers', Document No. 567 (February), Tavistock Institute of Human Relations.

TIHR (1960c) F. E. Emery, 'A study of some Guinness advertising symbols', Document No. 570 (April), Tavistock Institute of Human Relations.

TIHR (1960d) 'Liquid scourer – report on a brief survey of social and psychological factors involved in the use of scourers, with particular reference to the product trial of a liquid scourer', Document No. 579 (May), Tavistock Institute of Human Relations.

TIHR (1961) 'Some social and psychological aspects of shaving: preliminary report', Document No. 621 (April), Tavistock Institute of Human Relations.

TIHR (1962a) F. E. Emery and M. Foster, 'The making of gravy – a pilot study', Document No. 676 (May), Tavistock Institute of Human Relations.

TIHR (1962b) J. G. Field, 'Baby foods: a small psychological enquiry among mothers', Document No. T 16 (October), Tavistock Institute of Human Relations.

TIHR (1962c) F. E. Emery, 'In search of some principles of persuasion', Document No. T 10 (October), Tavistock Institute of Human Relations.

TIHR (1962d) F. E. Emery, 'Some psychological aspects of prices', Document No. 664 (March), Tavistock Institute of Human Relations.

TIHR (1963a) F. E. Emery, 'Flavour profiles of beers and stouts', Document No. T 78 (March), Tavistock Institute of Human Relations.

TIHR (1963b) M. Foster, 'An enquiry into the use of vitamin C drinks and of drinks for the 5–15 year-olds, with some views about three Delrosa commercials', Document No. T 165 (August), Tavistock Institute of Human Relations.

TIHR (1963c) M. Foster, 'The advertising of diamond engagement rings', Document No. 182 (September), Tavistock Institute of Human Relations.

TIHR (1963d) M. Foster, 'A general exploration of attitudes to Bovril and Marmite', Document No. T 216 (November), Tavistock Institute of Human Relations.

TIHR (1964) M. Foster, 'A study of hair care', Document No. T 344 (June), Tavistock Institute of Human Relations.

TIHR (1965a) H. Bridger, M. Foster and S. White, 'The nature of pet ownership – notes for discussion', Document T 501, Tavistock Institute of Human Relations.

TIHR (1965b) J. M. M. Hill, 'Shell-Mex and BPIDynamar: advertising research project – a first report on a consumer study', Document No. T 594 (July), Tavistock Institute of Human Relations.

TIHR (1965c) J. M. M. Hill, 'The holiday: a study of social and psychological aspects with specific reference to Ireland', Document No. T 678 (December), Tavistock Institute of Human Relations.

Tilly, C., ed. (1975) *The Formation of National States in Western Europe*, Princeton, NJ: Princeton University Press.

Tolstoy, L. (1954) *Anna Karenin*, Harmondsworth: Penguin.

Tomlinson, J. (1981a) *Problems of British Economic Policy 1870–1945*, London: Methuen.

Tomlinson, J. (1981b) 'Why was there never a "Keynesian Revolution" in economic policy?', *Economy and Society* 10: 73–87.

Tomlinson, J. (1983) 'Where do economic policy objectives come from? The case of full employment', *Economy and Society* 12: 48–65.

Tomlinson, J. (1994) 'The politics of economic measurement: the rise of the "productivity problem" in the 1940s', in A. G. Hopwood and P. Miller, eds, *Accounting as Social and Institutional Practice*, Cambridge: Cambridge University Press.

Tribe, K. (1978) *Land, Labour and Economic Discourse*, London: Routledge and Kegan Paul.

Trist, E. L. (1980) 'Interview with Marshall Sashkin', *Group and Organization Studies* 5 (2): 144–66.

Trist, E. L. and Bamforth, K. (1951) 'Some social and psychological consequences of the method of coal-getting', *Human Relations* 4: 3–38.

Trist, E. L. and Murray, H., eds (1990) *The Social Engagement of Social Science, Vol. 1*, London: Free Association Books.

Trist, E. L. and Murray, H., eds (1993) *The Social Engagement of Social Science, Vol. 2*, Philadelphia: University of Pennsylvania Press.

Trist, E. L. and Sofer, C., eds (1959) *Explorations in Group Relations*, Leicester: Leicester University Press.

Trist, E. L., Higgins, G. W., Murray, H. and Pollock, A. B. (1963) *Organizational Choice*, London: Tavistock.

Trotter, W. (1916) *Instincts of the Herd in Peace and War*, London: Fisher Unwin.

Tully, J. (1989) 'Governing conduct', in E. Leites, ed., *Conscience and Casuistry in Early Modern Europe*, Cambridge: Cambridge University Press.

Tully, J. (1995) *Strange Multiplicities: Constitutionalism in an Age of Diversity*, Cambridge: Cambridge University Press.

Van Ginneken, J. (1992) *Crowds, Psychology and Politics 1871–1899*, Cambridge: Cambridge University Press.

Veyne, P. (1978) 'Foucault révolutionne l'histoire', in *Comment on écrit l'histoire*, Paris: Éditions du Seuil.

Veyne, P. (1997) 'Foucault revolutionizes history', in A. I. Davison, ed., *Foucault and His Interlocutors*, Chicago: University of Chicago Press.

Viteles, M. S. (1932) *Industrial Psychology*, New York: Norton.

Wallerstein, I. (1984) *The Politics of the World Economy: The States, the Movements and the Civilization*, Cambridge: Cambridge University Press.

Walters, W. (1994) 'The discovery of "unemployment"', *Economy and Society* 23 (3): 265–90.

Warr, P., ed. (1976) *Personal Goals and Work Design*, London: Wiley.

Watts, P. (1994) 'Absolutely positive: AIDS, the self and the performance of community in the user discourses of the Body Positive organization', paper given to London History of the Present Research Network, June.

Weir, M., ed. (1976) *Job Satisfactions: Challenge and Response in Modern Britain*, London: Fontana.

Whitley, R. (1986) 'The transformation of business finance into financial economics: the roles of academic expansion and changes in U.S. capital markets', *Accounting, Organizations and Society* 11: 171–92.

Whyte, W. H. (1956) *The Organization Man*, New York: Simon and Schuster.

Williams, K., Haslam, C., Wardlow, A. and Williams, J. (1986) 'Accounting for failure in the nationalised enterprises: coal, steel and cars since 1970', *Economy and Society* 15: 167–219.

Williamson, J. (1978) *Decoding Advertisements: Ideology and Meaning in Advertising*, London: Marion Boyars.

Wilson, A. T. M. (1949) 'Some reflections and suggestions on the prevention and treatment of marital problems', *Human Relations* 2: 233–52.

Wilson, N. A. B. (1973) *On the Quality of Working Life,* Manpower Papers No. 7, London: HMSO.

Wise, N. (1989) 'Mediating Machines', *Science in Context* 2: 77–113.

Woodhouse, D. (1990) 'Non-medical marital therapy: the growth of the Institute of Marital Studies', in E. Trist and H. Murray, eds, *The Social Engagement of Social Science, Vol. 1,* London: Free Association Books.

Woodhouse, D. (n.d.) 'Short residential courses for post-graduate social workers', in R. Gosling, D. H. Miller, D. Woodhouse and P. M. Turquet, *The Use of Small Groups in Training,* n.p.: Codicote Press in conjunction with the Tavistock Institute of Medical Psychology.

Work in America (1973) *Work in America: Report of a Special Task Force to the Secretary of Health, Education and Welfare,* Cambridge, MA: MIT Press.

Zukin, S. (1991) *Landscapes of Power: From Detroit to Disney World,* Berkeley: University of California Press.

Index